PENGUIN  CLASSICS

THE SOULS OF BLACK FOLK

WILLIAM EDWARD BURGHARDT DU BOIS (1868–1963) was born in Great Barrington, Massachusetts. He attended public schools there prior to attending Fisk University, where he received his BA degree in 1888. Thereafter he received a second BA degree, and an MA and PhD from Harvard. He studied at the University of Berlin as well. He taught at Wilberforce University and the University of Pennsylvania before going to Atlanta University in 1897, where he taught for many years. A sociologist, historian, poet, and writer of several novels, Du Bois was one of the main founders of the National Association for the Advancement of Colored People. He was a lifelong critic of American society and an advocate of black people against racial injustice. He spent his last years in Ghana, where he died in exile at the age of ninety-five.

IBRAM X. KENDI is the author of the *New York Times* bestseller *Stamped from the Beginning: The Definitive History of Racist Ideas in America*, for which he became the youngest ever winner of the National Book Award for Nonfiction. He is also the author of the award-winning book *The Black Campus Movement: Black Students and the Racial Reconstruction of Higher Education, 1965–1972*. A professor of history and international relations and the founding director of the Antiracist Research and Policy Center at American University, he lives in Washington, DC.

W. E. B. DU BOIS

The Souls of Black Folk

WITH "THE TALENTED TENTH" AND
"THE SOULS OF WHITE FOLK"

Introduction by
IBRAM X. KENDI

Notes by
MONICA M. ELBERT

PENGUIN BOOKS

PENGUIN BOOKS

An imprint of Penguin Random House LLC
375 Hudson Street
New York, New York 10014
penguin.com

First published in the United States of America by A. C. McClurg & Company 1903
"The Souls of White Folk" originally published in 1920 by Harcourt, Brace and Company
"The Talented Tenth" originally published in 1903 by James Pott & Company
This edition with an introduction by Ibram X. Kendi published in Penguin Books 2018

LIBRARY OF CONGRESS CATALOGING-IN-PUBLICATION DATA
Names: Du Bois, W. E. B. (William Edward Burghardt), 1868–1963 author. | Du Bois, W. E. B.
(William Edward Burghardt), 1868–1963. Talented tenth. | Du Bois, W. E. B. (William Edward
Burghardt), 1868–1963. Souls of white folk.
Title: The souls of black folk : with "The talented tenth" and "The souls of white folk" /
W.E.B. Du Bois ; introduction by Ibram X. Kendi ; notes by Monica M. Elbert.
Other titles: Talented tenth | Souls of white folk
Description: New York, New York : Penguin Books, [2017] | "Originally published: The souls
of black folk. A. C. McClurg & Company, 1903." | Includes bibliographical references.
Identifiers: LCCN 2017041778 (print) LCCN 2017042067 (ebook) | ISBN 9781101078143
(ebook) | ISBN 9780140189988
Subjects: LCSH: African Americans.
Classification: LCC E185.6 (ebook) | LCC E185.6 .D797 2017 (print) | DDC 323.092—dc23
LC record available at https://lccn.loc.gov/2017041778

Printed in the United States of America
45 47 49 50 48 46 44

Set in Sabon LT Std Roman

Contents

Introduction

The Soul of W. E. B. Du Bois:
An Introduction to the Veil

The dispute lasted for more than a year between itinerant black farmer Sam Hose and his wealthy white employer, Alfred Cranford. Hose requesting his wages. Cranford refusing to pay up. The dispute grew like the crops on Cranford's farm outside of Atlanta, in Coweta County.

On April 12, 1899, Cranford aimed murderous threats and his loaded gun at Hose. Hose grabbed a nearby ax, threw it at Cranford, and ran into the Georgia wilderness.

Newspapers got wind of the incident and started blaring sensational details of the murderous Hose who raped Cranford's wife as Cranford lay dying.[1]

The murder-rape story was a lie, but Jim Crow had flown on the winds of lies for decades.[2] In the lead-up to North Carolina's election day in 1898, Josephus Daniels, editor of the Raleigh *News and Observer*, published a series of articles on the "unbridled lawlessness and rule of incompetent officials," the "worthless police force," and "incidents of housebreaking and robbery in broad daylight" in a Wilmington "under Negro domination."

In reality, Wilmington was one of the few places where black majorities ruled democratically in the post–Reconstruction South. A majority black city of 19,000 residents, it had been governed, since March 1898, by an alliance of black Republicans and antiracist white populists. All year long, elite white Democrats had been organizing for regime change. When Josephus Daniels's racist lies failed to manipulate Wilmington voters, violence followed. An army of 2,000 white Democrats invaded Wilmington two days after election day, on November

10, 1898, gun-battled it out with black residents, ejected the
mayor and aldermen, terminated all black city workers, ordered
thousands of blacks to vacate the town, burned the black community of "Brooklyn," and installed white Democrats in political posts and city jobs. As many as sixty black people died
in the first successful armed overthrow of a city government in
U.S. history.[3]

W. E. B. Du Bois did not have a juddering front-row seat at
the Wilmington massacre. But he was keenly aware of the racial
tensions in Georgia in 1899, tensions that boiled over in August,
when armed blacks drove back a lynch mob in McIntosh
County.[4] He knew as well as anyone how difficult it was to hold
off lynch mobs mobilized by lies.

No lie circulated as far and wide over space and time as the
original racist one that prefigured the Negro a beast. "No other
news goes out to the world save that which stamps us as a race of
cut-throats, robbers, and lustful wild beasts," Ida B. Wells wrote
in her 1892 antilynching manifesto, "Southern Horrors."[5]

Beasts, most agreed, did not have *souls*.

A beast could be traded and enslaved. A beast should be segregated and lynched. A beast cannot stop raping and killing. A
beast could be subdued by only a mob or a jail cell. A beast so
brutal even trained police officers fear for their lives. The Negro
a beast.

"They lived like beasts, without any custom of reasonable
beings," wrote Gomes Eanes de Zurara in his 1453 cradle of
racist ideas, defending Portugal's pioneering slave trading of
Africans.[6] A century later, pioneering British slave trader John
Lok described Africans as "people of beastly living."[7] In 1899,
the *Wilmington Messenger* reprinted an 1898 speech of Georgia's Rebecca Felton, who in 1922 would become the nation's
first female U.S. senator. If "it requires lynching to protect woman's dearest possession from ravening, drunken human beasts,"
she said, "then I say lynch a thousand a week."[8] In 1900, the
bestseller of segregationist demagogues was Mississippi professor Charles Carroll's *Mystery Solved: The Negro a Beast*.[9]
Thomas Dixon brought this thesis to life in his bestselling 1902
novel, *The Leopard's Spots: A Romance of the White Man's*

Burden, the first step in the march toward D. W. Griffith's fanciful film *The Birth of a Nation*.[10]

It is difficult to comprehend how daring it was for W. E. B. Du Bois to publish the most acclaimed book of his career in the face of this avalanche of beastly labels rushing down onto the Negro. Du Bois stared into the grisly faces of the racist past and present and decreed that blacks were not soulless beasts. "Ain't I a human?" he seemed to be asking, just as fifty years earlier the legendary black feminist Sojourner Truth famously asked, "Ain't I a woman?"

In publishing *The Souls of Black Folk*, on April 18, 1903, Du Bois argued, implicitly, that the world needs to know the humanity of black folk by listening carefully to the "strivings" in their souls. And we can hear in the book the strivings in the soul of Du Bois as much as we can hear the strivings in the souls of other black folk. We hear about Du Bois's racial worldview (essay one: "Of Our Spiritual Strivings"). We learn of his ideological problem with Booker T. Washington (essay three: "Of Booker T. Washington and Others"). We take in his college-age experiences as a schoolteacher in rural Tennessee (essay four: "Of the Meaning of Progress"). We come to understand his personal loathing of Atlanta's greed (essay five: "Of the Wings of Atalanta"). We hear his plan for the Talented Tenth (essay six: "Of the Training of Black Men"). We read about his perspective on the impact of slavery on morality (essay nine: "Of the Sons of Master and Man"). We cry with him as he buries his firstborn son (essay eleven: "Of the Passing of the First-Born"). We learn about one of his idols (essay twelve: "Of Alexander Crummell"). We cry again during his tragic short story about an educated black man demolished by racism (essay thirteen: "Of the Coming of John").

But Du Bois's soul reflected many souls. Many could personally relate to John in "Of the Coming of John." Many idolized Alexander Crummell, the founder of America's first black intellectual society. Many buried their firstborns in the cemetery of 1890s racism. Many believed slavery had destroyed morality. Many looked up to the Talented Tenth. Many loathed Atlanta's gold rush. Many knew about those rural schoolhouses. Many had problems with Booker T. Washington. These essays touched readers in 1903 and beyond, and harmonized with Du Bois's more scholarly but no less lyrical essays on the Freedmen's Bureau (essay two: "Of the Dawn of Freedom"), on "the massed millions of the black peasantry" (essays seven and eight: "Of the Black Belt" and "Of the Quest of the Golden Fleece"), on African American religion (essay ten: "Of the Faith of the Fathers"), and on African American spirituals (essay fourteen: "The Sorrow Songs").

Much as Du Bois's soul reflected those of others, though, it remained uniquely his. Like all souls, it is poetic, and *The Souls of Black Folk* speaks to humanity like one long poem. In order to understand this long poem and why Du Bois wrote it when he did, we must understand the major ideas, events, and forces that nurtured it, particularly the power of the Veil.

The Veil separated black folk from white folk. Within it, black folk endured racism, exploitation, and heartache that white people did not see, or did not want to see. The Veil doubled as both the oppression and the mirror of oppression. But the mirror—the Veil—could really be seen only by black people. Black folk could see the freedoms white people enjoyed outside of the Veil. White folk struggled to see the slaveries black folk recoiled from within the Veil.

Du Bois could not let the murder-rape lie about Sam Hose live another day. He knew Hose's life was at stake within the Veil. Sometime around April 23, 1899, he composed a restrained letter that laid out the facts of the case. He placed the letter in an envelope, picked up another envelope containing a letter of introduction he had written to the *Atlanta Constitution* editor Joel Chandler Harris, then dashed out of his hall on Atlanta University's campus and headed down Mitchell Street to the newspaper's office. His hope was for the letter about the case to be printed on the *Constitution*'s editorial page, and then for reason to take over.

But the red light of lynching news stopped Du Bois. He learned that Hose had been captured, on April 22. Two trainloads of Atlantans arrived in Newnan, Georgia, to join the two thousand white men, women, and children who cheered the mutilation of Hose's body. Hose's fingers, hands, ears, and genitals were sliced off. The flesh on his face was skinned off. Some people fought over his body parts; the rest watched his body hanging from a tree and being burned alive.

Hose's knuckles were on display at a store farther down Mitchell Street, if Du Bois cared to see. Instead he turned back to campus in disgust.[11]

After that public tragedy in April came a private one, in May. Du Bois's two-year-old firstborn son, Burghardt, contracted nasopharyngeal diphtheria. The infection became severe, and Du Bois searched in vain for medical care. He could not find the town's two or three black doctors, and Atlanta's white doctors refused to see black patients. Like Hose's, Burghardt's black life did not matter within the Veil. Within ten days Burghardt died, on May 24, 1899. Du Bois writes in *Souls* about his short life, filled with unspeakable joy, misery, and meaning, in "Of the Passing of the First-Born."[12]

At the beginning of his scholarly career, in 1894, Du Bois wrote: "The ultimate evil was stupidity" about black lives by "the majority of white Americans. . . . The cure for it was knowledge based on scientific investigation."[13] But after the public lynching of Sam Hose, after the private lynching of his firstborn son, after being surrounded by black Southern poverty, Du Bois realized he "could not be a calm, cool, and detached scientist while Negroes were lynched, murdered, and starved; and secondly, there was no such definitive demand" for his scholarly work: The world did not want to "learn the truth." In 1899, his "young man's idealism" had passed away like his young son.[14]

After laying his son to rest, Du Bois laid to rest his own detached scholarly identity and headed down a path that would lead to *The Souls of Black Folk*. It was a path paved with crisis—the crisis of American democracy. Du Bois believed that "the majority of Americans would rush to the defense of democracy . . . if they realized how race prejudice was threatening it."[15] It became his job to show how: He became a public intellectual.

Du Bois increased his literary output to the major publications of the day, like the *Atlantic Monthly, World's Work,* and

Dial. But he did not neglect sending essays to scholarly specialized publications, like *Annals of the American* of Political and Social Science and *New World*. In 19 cago's McClurg publishing company started asking about collecting some of his essays into a book. Du B tually agreed to put together "a number of my fugitiv But he resisted at first, "because books of essays almo fall so flat."[16]

With the publication in 1903 of *The Souls of B l* Du Bois had an unlikely bestseller. And in the past essay collections have returned to popularity. Witne cess of the anthology *The Fire This Time*, edited Ward, and of Chimamanda Ngozi Adichie's *We Sh* Feminists, Ta-Nehisi Coates's *Between the World a* Roxane Gay's *Bad Feminist*.[17] The year of the essay Literature declared 2014, ended with Roxane Ga an essay collection by Meghan Daum in the *New Y* In borrowing a lyric from rapper Kendrick Lama "how we might consider the essay—blood in the p sayist, inking the personal to bring about an en sponse,"[19] Gay could have been describing Du opening section of *The Souls of Black Folk* tha forethought, Du Bois expressed the hope that these be of "interest to you, Gentle Reader; for the pr Twentieth Century is the problem of the color-line" in the twenty-first century, when the essay is res are taking another hard look at the color line, it is moment for this new edition of *The Souls of Bl*

Nine of the fourteen essays in *The Souls of B l* first published between 1897 and 1902. Four o published in 1901, one of the most critical yea intellectual life, and in the racial life of the Uni

On January 29, 1901, North Carolina repres H. White gave his farewell address to Congress. last representative was leaving Washington, af bid for a third term, since black voter suppre made reelection impossible. "This, Mr. Chai the negroes' temporary farewell to the American Congress," White said, "but let me say, Phoenix-like he will rise up some-day and come again."[20] As all those white male Congressmen settled into Washington, they were able to ease any guilt by reading Booker T. Washington's *Up from Slavery*.[21] Washington saw racial progress at every turn and wrote of having faith in God, taking personal responsibility, working mightily hard, and overcoming incredible hardship.

With the publication of *Up from Slavery* in February 1901, Washington was at the height of his career. Praise and dona-tions rained down on him while Du Bois was starving for fund-ing and praise. As Du Bois looked up at the lonely Washington on the white pedestal of black leadership, it had all become too much for him to bear in silence. In his review of *Up from Slav-ery* in *Dial* on July 16, 1901, Du Bois "fired the opening salvo," explained his biographer, "in the war between the Tuskegee Machine"—those publicly accommodating politicos, scholars, philanthropists, and editors loyal to Washington—"and the Tal-ented Tenth."[22]

Despite Du Bois's criticism, *Up from Slavery* remains an American classic. But another book, released weeks before, re-ceived as much praise in 1901: William Hannibal Thomas's *The American Negro: What He Was, What He Is, and What He May Become*. An enthusiastic *New York Times* reviewer placed its author "next to Mr. Booker T. Washington" as "the best American authority on the negro question."[23] Another reviewer jointly reviewed *The American Negro* and Du Bois's previously published *The Philadelphia Negro* and argued that *The Amer-ican Negro* was better.[24]

For years the biracial William Hannibal Thomas had worked as a preacher, teacher, journalist, and politician to eliminate racial distinctions and to be accepted by white people. Nothing had worked. And so he turned to the pen, pleading furiously for white acceptance in one of the most furious attacks on black people in history. His "list of negative qualities of Negroes seemed limitless," according to his biographer. Blacks, Thomas wrote, are an "intrinsically inferior type of humanity." Black history is a "record of lawless existence, led by every impulse and passion." Blacks are mentally retarded, immoral beasts, "unable practically to discern between right and wrong." Ninety percent of black women are "lascivious by instinct and in bondage to physical pleasure."[25]

While white readers almost unanimously praised *The American Negro*, black readers felt so betrayed by Thomas that they dubbed him "Black Judas."[26] But no one's review hit as hard as Du Bois's in *Dial*, titled "The Storm and Stress in the Black World"—an essay he may have considered for inclusion in *Souls*. "Mr. Thomas's book," Du Bois wrote, "is a sinister symptom" of the age that desires nothing less for "the Negro" than to "kindly go to the devil and make haste about it" so the "American conscience can justify three centuries of shameful history."[27] Even though it is forgotten today, Thomas's book incited Du Bois, as well as Washington.

Decades later, James Weldon Johnson, the composer of the "Black National Anthem," lifted every voice and sang the praises of *The Souls of Black Folk*, for having a "greater" impact "upon and within the Negro race than any other single book published in this country since *Uncle Tom's Cabin*."[28] It is difficult to understand where Du Bois was coming from in *Souls* without having traveled with Harriet Beecher Stowe to *Uncle Tom's Cabin*, published fifty years earlier, in 1852. "The scenes of this story," Stowe wrote, "lie among . . . an exotic race, whose . . . character" was "so essentially unlike the hard and dominant Anglo-Saxon race." In black people's "lowly docility of heart, their aptitude to repose on a superior mind and rest on a higher power, their childlike simplicity of affection, and facility of forgiveness," she wrote, in "all these they will exhibit the highest form of the peculiarly Christian life."[29]

Uncle Tom's Cabin put forward the racist idea of complementary biological race traits, of the humble, *soulful* African complementing the hard, *rational* European.[30] The fourteen essays in *The Souls of Black Folk* reinforced this idea. From Du Bois's title, to his writing style—pairing the verses of Negro spirituals with those of European poets—to his content, Du Bois carried the idea of complementary race traits into the twentieth century. It would be a few decades before he would renounce this thinking.[31]

Du Bois ends *Soul*'s first and most enduring essay, "Of Our Spiritual Strivings," by expressing his dream "that some day on American soil two world-races may give each to each those characteristics both so sadly lack." He adds, "we black men seem the sole oasis of simple faith and reverence in a dusty desert of dollars and smartness" (12, 13). But it is racist to assert that a race lacks characteristics. White people do not lack "simple faith and reverence," and black people do not lack materialism and "smartness."

Educated in a New England influenced by the myths of *Uncle Tom's Cabin*, Du Bois had been professing these ideas since his graduate school days at Harvard.[32] In *Souls*, Du Bois tries to transform the dividing ideal of race into the "unifying ideal of race," which would heal the split souls of black folk, and the split souls of America, split by the Veil (12). "It is a peculiar sensation, this double consciousness, this sense of always looking at one's self through the eyes of others, of measuring one's soul by the tape of a world that looks on in amused contempt and pity," Du Bois writes. "One ever feels his two-ness,—an American, a Negro; two souls, two thoughts, two unreconciled strivings; two warring ideals in one dark body, whose dogged strength alone keeps it from being torn asunder" (7).

For many of his black readers—in 1903 and thereafter—Du Bois's double consciousness finally gave them the glasses they needed to see their own inner struggles. What has made this concept so enduringly popular among black people for more than a century after the publication of *Souls*? Du Bois met many black people where many of them were, and where many have remained—at the warring crossroads between assimilationist and antiracist ideas. He believed in both the antiracist concept of cultural relativity, of everyone looking at one's self through the eyes of one's group, and the assimilationist idea of "looking at one's self through the eyes" of white people. In his mind, this double desire, this double consciousness, yielded an inner strife between pride in equal blackness and assimilation into superior whiteness, and an outer strife from the Veil of American racism denying both. "He would not Africanize America, for America has too much to teach the world and Africa," Du Bois writes. "He would not bleach his Negro soul in a flood of white Americanism, for he knows that Negro blood has a message for the world" (7).

Du Bois's opening essay on *his* double consciousness of antiracist and assimilationist ideas set the conceptual stage for the rest of *The Souls of Black Folk*. But what sold books in 1903 was the third chapter, "Of Mr. Booker T. Washington and Others," a refined and expanded version of his *Dial* review. "Two classes of colored Americans" have criticized "Mr. Washington's position," Du Bois explains. He dismissed those bent on "revolt and revenge" and Washington's class of accommodators to make way for his elite class of doubly conscious colored Americans, advocating civil rights and higher education (38). He called this class "The Talented Tenth" and wrote about it in another essay—not part of *Souls* but included in this volume.

Du Bois emphasizes education and character for entry into the Talented Tenth. "The Negro race, like all races, is going to be saved by its exceptional men," he writes. He asks Americans if they "ever stop to reflect that there are in this land a million men of Negro blood . . . who, judged by any standard, have reached the full measure of the best type of modern European culture?" It was an assimilationist idea to measure the Negro against the best type of modern European, but that is how Du Bois came to frame the untalented ninetieth, those black masses that were inferior to the Talented Tenth and to white people. He described their spirituals, their religion, their economic lives, but he did not equalize the souls of the mass of black folk.

Before he died, though, he did. In 1948 Du Bois called for a "Guiding One Hundredth" whose "passport to leadership" would be their "expert knowledge of modern economics" and "willingness to sacrifice." He had assumed in 1903 "that with knowledge, sacrifice would automatically follow. In my youth and idealism, I did not realize that selfishness is ever more natural than sacrifice."[33]

But among those doubly conscious black folk willing to sacrifice in 1903, *The Souls of Black Folk* became their manifesto, and in 1920 Du Bois's *Darkwater* recharged them in battle, especially the essay "The Souls of White Folk," included in this volume. In it, Du Bois advocates for a "fight for freedom which black and brown and yellow men must and will make unless their oppression and humiliation and insult at the hands of the White World cease" (241). But before these men and women could meet Jim Crow on the battlefield, they first had to fight Washington's Tuskegee Machine. Du Bois's dismantling of those, like Washington, who were apparently accommodating to Jim Crow is as insightful and impassioned and intrepid as the abolitionist dismantling of those accommodating to slavery in the 1830s, or the Black Lives Matter dismantling of those accommodating to mass incarceration and black death since 2013.

And the accommodators instantly knew it in 1903. "This book is indeed dangerous for the negro to read," admitted the *Nashville American*. The Tuskegee Machine tried to suppress it, to no avail. Black newspapers, done with Washington, typically shouted in unison, "SHOULD BE READ AND STUDIED BY EVERY PERSON, WHITE AND BLACK," to quote one, the *Ohio Enterprise*. And today it still SHOULD BE READ AND STUDIED BY EVERY PERSON.[34]

Du Bois lived another sixty years after the publication of *Souls*, dying in 1963, on the eve of the March on Washington. He was thirty-four years old when he assembled *Soul's* essays in 1902, the same age I am as I write this. He did not bare his soul and then devour the acclaim, trash the criticism, and close the door on his thinking. He evolved as black thought evolved over the course of the twentieth century. Or did black thought evolve as he evolved? We should remember *Souls* not only as the poetry that so many black folk could relate to in 1903, like the spirituals they often sang in church, but also as the foundation on which Du Bois built a lifetime of ideas, and on which the black and antiracist intelligentsia continues to build today.

"Let there spring, Gentle One, from out its leaves vigor of thought and thoughtful deep to reap the harvest wonderful," Du Bois prayed at the end of *Souls*, in the section he called an afterthought. "Let the ears of a guilty people tingle with truth, and seventy millions sigh for the righteousness which exalteth nations, in this drear day when human brotherhood is a mockery and a snare" (199). Looking at the harvest of black thought since *Souls*, his prayers have been answered. But looking at our drear days when human unity remains a farce, his prayers have yet to be answered.

Du Bois could not save Sam Hose from the noose. He could not prevent the death of his firstborn. But with the poetry of *Souls*, we should never forget his courageous rescue of black folk from the Veil of the beast.

IBRAM X. KENDI

NOTES

1. For studies on the Hose lynching, see Ida B. Wells-Barnett, *Lynch Law in Georgia* (Chicago: Chicago Colored Citizens, 1899); Donald G. Mathews, *At the Altar of Lynching: Burning Sam Hose in the American South* (New York: Cambridge University Press, 2017); and Edwin T. Arnold, *What Virtue There Is in Fire: Cultural Memory and the Lynching of Sam Hose* (Athens: University of Georgia Press, 2012).

2. C. Vann Woodward, *The Strange Career of Jim Crow* (New York: Oxford University Press, 1966).

3. For scholarship on the Wilmington massacre, see David S. Cecelski and Timothy B. Tyson, *Democracy Betrayed: The Wilmington Race Riot of 1898 and Its Legacy* (Chapel Hill: University of North Carolina Press, 1998); and LeRae Umfleet, *1898 Wilmington Race Riot Report* (Raleigh: North Carolina Office of Archives and History and North Carolina Department of Cultural Resources, 2006).

4. W. Fitzhugh Brundage, "The Darien 'Insurrection' of 1899: Black Protest During the Nadir of Race Relations," *The Georgia Historical Quarterly* 74, no. 2 (1990).

5. Ida B. Wells-Barnett, "Southern Horrors: Lynch Law in All Its Phases," in *Selected Works of Ida B. Wells-Barnett* (New York: Oxford University Press, 1991), 44.

6. Gomes Eanes de Zurara, *The Chronicle of the Discovery and Conquest of Guinea*, volume 1 (New York: Burt Franklin, 1896), 84.

7. Joseph R. Washington, *Anti-Blackness in English Religion, 1500–1800* (New York: E. Mellen Press, 1984), 105–111.

8. Richard Wormser, *The Rise and Fall of Jim Crow* (New York: Macmillan, 2004), 84.

9. Charles Carroll, *The Mystery Solved: The Negro a Beast* (St. Louis: American Book and Bible House, 1900).

10. Thomas Dixon, *The Leopard's Spots: A Romance of the White Man's Burden, 1865–1900* (New York: A. Wessels, 1906).

11. See Hose literature above, and W. E. B. Du Bois, *The Autobiography of W. E. B. Du Bois* (New York: International Publishers, 1968), 222.

12. David Levering Lewis, *W. E. B. Du Bois: Biography of a Race, 1868–1919* (New York: Henry Holt, 1993), 226–228.

13. Du Bois, *The Autobiography*, 197.

14. Ibid., 222.

15. W. E. B. Du Bois, "My Evolving Program for Negro Freedom," in *What the Negro Wants*, ed. Rayford Logan (New York: Agathon Press, 1969), 70.

16. W. E. B. Du Bois, *Dusk of Dawn: An Essay Toward an Autobiography of a Race Concept* (New York: Oxford University Press, 1940), 41.

17. Roxane Gay, *Bad Feminist* (New York: HarperCollins, 2014).

18. "Why 2014 Was the Year of the Essay," Electric Literature, December 16, 2014. See https://electricliterature.com/why-2014-was-the-year-of-the-essay-2cf1fbc499e4.

19. Roxane Gay, "Discomfort Zone," *New York Times*, December 14, 2014.

20. George H. White, "A Defense of the Negro Race," in *Masterpieces of Negro Eloquence*, ed. Alice Moore Dunbar (New York: Bookery, 1914), 241.

21. Booker T. Washington, *Up from Slavery* (London: Oxford University Press, 1945).

22. Lewis, *W. E. B. Du Bois*, 262–264.

23. William Hannibal Thomas, *The American Negro: What He Was, What He Is, and What He May Become* (New York: Macmillan,

1901); "The Negro Arraigned," *New York Times*, February 23, 1901.

24. "Book Notes," *Political Science Quarterly* 17:3 (1902), 547.

25. John David Smith, *Black Judas: William Hannibal Thomas and the American Negro* (Athens: University of Georgia Press, 2000), 77–78, 85–89, 161–64; Thomas, *The American Negro*.

26. That is why his biographer above titled his biography *Black Judas*.

27. W. E. B. Du Bois, "The Storm and Stress in the Black World," *Dial*, April 16, 1901.

28. James Weldon Johnson, *Along This Way: The Autobiography of James Weldon Johnson* (Boston: Da Capo Press, 1933), 203.

29. Harriet Beecher Stowe, *Uncle Tom's Cabin* (London: John Cassell, 1852), iii, 154.

30. For more analysis of this construct, see Ibram X. Kendi, *Stamped from the Beginning: The Definitive History of Racist Ideas in America* (New York: Nation Books, 2016), 193–195.

31. For insight into Du Bois's race concepts, see Joel Olson, "W. E. B. Du Bois and the Race Concept," in *Souls: A Critical Journal of Black Politics, Culture and Society* 7:3–4 (2005), 118–128.

32. For better clarity, see Du Bois's commencement address at Harvard in 1890: "Jefferson Davis as a Representative of Civilization," in *W. E. B. Du Bois: Writings* (New York: Penguin, 1986), 811–814.

33. W. E. B. Du Bois, "The Talented Tenth: Memorial Address," *Boulé Journal* 15 (October 1948), 347–353.

34. Lewis, *W. E. B. Du Bois*, 291–293.

Suggestions for Further Reading

Cooper, Anna Julia. *A Voice from the South*. Mineola, NY: Dover, 2016.

Du Bois, W. E. B. *Darkwater: Voices from Within the Veil*. Mineola, NY: Dover, 1999.

———. "My Evolving Program for Negro Freedom." In *What the Negro Wants*. Edited by Rayford Logan. New York: Agathon Press, 1969.

———. *The Autobiography of W. E. B. Du Bois*. New York: International Publishers, 1968.

———. *The Philadelphia Negro: A Social Study*. Philadelphia: University of Pennsylvania Press, 1995.

———. "The Talented Tenth: Memorial Address." *Boulé Journal* 15 (October 1948): 347–353.

Harlan, Louis R. *Booker T. Washington: The Making of a Black Leader, 1856–1901*. New York: Oxford University Press, 1972.

———. *Booker T. Washington: The Wizard of Tuskegee, 1901–1915*. New York: Oxford University Press, 1983.

Lewis, David Levering. *W. E. B. Du Bois: Biography of a Race, 1868–1919*. New York: Henry Holt, 1993.

———. *W. E. B. Du Bois: The Fight for Equality and the American Century, 1919–1963*. New York: Henry Holt, 2000.

Morris, Aldon. *The Scholar Denied: W. E. B. Du Bois and the Birth of Modern Sociology*. Berkeley: University of California Press, 2015.

Olson, Joel. "W. E. B. Du Bois and the Race Concept." *Souls: A Critical Journal of Black Politics, Culture and Society* 7:3–4 (2005): 118–128.

Smith, John David. *Black Judas: William Hannibal Thomas and the American Negro*. Athens: University of Georgia Press, 2000.

Stowe, Harriet Beecher. *Uncle Tom's Cabin*. London: John Cassell, 1852.

Washington, Booker T. *Up from Slavery*. London: Oxford University Press, 1945.

THE SOULS OF
BLACK FOLK

To
Burghardt and Yolande,
the Lost and the Found

THE FORETHOUGHT

Herein lie buried many things which if read with patience may show the strange meaning of being black here in the dawning of the Twentieth Century. This meaning is not without interest to you, Gentle Reader; for the problem of the Twentieth Century is the problem of the color-line.

I pray you, then, receive my little book in all charity, studying my words with me, forgiving mistake and foible for sake of the faith and passion that is in me, and seeking the grain of truth hidden there.

I have sought here to sketch, in vague, uncertain outline, the spiritual world in which ten thousand thousand Americans live and strive. First, in two chapters I have tried to show what Emancipation meant to them, and what was its aftermath. In a third chapter I have pointed out the slow rise of personal leadership, and criticised candidly the leader who bears the chief burden of his race to-day. Then, in two other chapters I have sketched in swift outline the two worlds within and without the Veil, and thus have come to the central problem of training men for life. Venturing now into deeper detail, I have in two chapters studied the struggles of the massed millions of the black peasantry, and in another have sought to make clear the present relations of the sons of master and man.

Leaving, then, the world of the white man, I have stepped within the Veil, raising it that you may view faintly its deeper recesses,—the meaning of its religion, the passion of its human sorrow, and the struggle of its greater souls. All this I have ended with a tale twice told but seldom written.

Some of these thoughts of mine have seen the light before in other guise. For kindly consenting to their republication here, in altered and extended form, I must thank the publishers of *The Atlantic Monthly, The World's Work, The Dial, The New World,* and the *Annals of the American Academy of Political and Social Science.*

Before each chapter, as now printed, stands a bar of the Sorrow Songs,—some echo of haunting melody from the only American music which welled up from black souls in the dark past. And, finally, need I add that I who speak here am bone of the bone and flesh of the flesh of them that live within the Veil?

W. E. B. DU B.
Atlanta, Ga., Feb. 1, 1903.

I

OF OUR SPIRITUAL STRIVINGS

O water, voice of my heart, crying in the sand,
  All night long crying with a mournful cry,
As I lie and listen, and cannot understand
    The voice of my heart in my side or the voice of the sea,
  O water, crying for rest, is it I, is it I?
    All night long the water is crying to me.

Unresting water, there shall never be rest
  Till the last moon droop and the last tide fail,
And the fire of the end begin to burn in the west;
    And the heart shall be weary and wonder and cry like the
      sea,
  All life long crying without avail,
    As the water all night long is crying to me.

ARTHUR SYMONS

Between me and the other world there is ever an unasked question: unasked by some through feelings of delicacy; by others through the difficulty of rightly framing it. All, nevertheless, flutter round it. They approach me in a half-hesitant sort of way, eye me curiously or compassionately, and then, instead of saying directly, How does it feel to be a problem? they say, I know an excellent colored man in my town; or, I fought at Mechanicsville; or, Do not these Southern outrages make your blood boil? At these I smile, or am interested, or reduce the boiling to a simmer, as the occasion may require. To the real question, How does it feel to be a problem? I answer seldom a word.

And yet, being a problem is a strange experience,—peculiar even for one who has never been anything else, save perhaps in babyhood and in Europe. It is in the early days of rollicking boyhood that the revelation first bursts upon one, all in a day, as it were. I remember well when the shadow swept across me. I was a little thing, away up in the hills of New England, where the dark Housatonic winds between Hoosac and Taghkanic to the sea. In a wee wooden schoolhouse, something put it into the boys' and girls' heads to buy gorgeous visiting-cards—ten cents a package—and exchange. The exchange was merry, till one girl, a tall newcomer, refused my card,—refused it peremptorily, with a glance. Then it dawned upon me with a certain suddenness that I was different from the others; or like, mayhap, in heart and life and longing, but shut out from their world by a vast veil. I had thereafter no desire to tear down that veil, to creep through; I held all beyond it in common contempt, and lived above it in a region of blue sky and great wandering shadows. That sky was bluest when I could beat my mates at examination-time, or beat them at a foot-race, or even beat their stringy heads. Alas, with the years all this fine contempt began to fade; for the worlds I longed for, and all their dazzling opportunities, were theirs, not mine. But they should not keep these prizes, I said; some, all, I would wrest from them. Just how I would do it I could never decide: by reading law, by healing the sick, by telling the wonderful tales that swam in my head,—some way. With other black boys the strife was not so fiercely sunny: their youth shrunk into tasteless sycophancy, or into silent hatred of the pale world about them and mocking distrust of everything white; or wasted itself in a bitter cry, Why did God make me an outcast and a stranger in mine own house? The shades of the prison-house closed round about us all: walls strait and stubborn to the whitest, but relentlessly narrow, tall, and unscalable to sons of night who must plod darkly on in resignation, or beat unavailing palms against the stone, or steadily, half hopelessly, watch the streak of blue above.

After the Egyptian and Indian, the Greek and Roman, the Teuton and Mongolian, the Negro is a sort of seventh son, born with a veil, and gifted with second-sight in this American world,—a world which yields him no true self-consciousness, but only lets him see himself through the revelation of the other world. It is a peculiar sensation, this double-consciousness, this sense of always looking at one's self through the eyes of others, of measuring one's soul by the tape of a world that looks on in amused contempt and pity. One ever feels his twoness,—an American, a Negro; two souls, two thoughts, two unreconciled strivings; two warring ideals in one dark body, whose dogged strength alone keeps it from being torn asunder.

The history of the American Negro is the history of this strife—this longing to attain self-conscious manhood, to merge his double self into a better and truer self. In this merging he wishes neither of the older selves to be lost. He would not Africanize America, for America has too much to teach the world and Africa. He would not bleach his Negro soul in a flood of white Americanism, for he knows that Negro blood has a message for the world. He simply wishes to make it possible for a man to be both a Negro and an American, without being cursed and spit upon by his fellows, without having the doors of Opportunity closed roughly in his face.

This, then, is the end of his striving: to be a co-worker in the kingdom of culture, to escape both death and isolation, to husband and use his best powers and his latent genius. These powers of body and mind have in the past been strangely wasted, dispersed, or forgotten. The shadow of a mighty Negro past flits through the tale of Ethiopia the Shadowy and of Egypt the Sphinx. Throughout history, the powers of single black men flash here and there like falling stars, and die sometimes before the world has rightly gauged their brightness. Here in America, in the few days since Emancipation, the black man's turning hither and thither in hesitant and doubtful striving has often made his very strength to lose effectiveness, to seem like absence of power, like weakness. And yet it is not weakness,—it is the contradiction of double aims. The double-aimed struggle of the black artisan—on the one hand to escape white contempt for a nation of mere hewers of wood and drawers of water, and on the other hand to plough and nail and dig for a poverty-stricken horde—could only result in making him a poor craftsman, for he had but half a heart in either cause. By the poverty and ignorance of his people, the Negro minister or doctor was tempted toward quackery and demagogy; and by the criticism of the other world, toward ideals that made him ashamed of his lowly tasks. The would-be black savant was confronted by the paradox that the knowledge his people needed was a twice-told tale to his white neighbors, while the knowledge which would teach the white world was Greek to his own flesh and blood. The innate love of harmony and beauty that set the ruder souls of his people a-dancing and a-singing raised but confusion and doubt in the soul of the black artist; for the beauty revealed to him was the soul-beauty of a race which his larger audience despised, and he could not articulate the message of another people. This waste of double aims, this seeking to satisfy two unreconciled ideals, has wrought sad havoc with the courage and faith and deeds of ten thousand thousand people,—has sent them often wooing false gods and invoking false means of salvation, and at times has even seemed about to make them ashamed of themselves.

Away back in the days of bondage they thought to see in one divine event the end of all doubt and disappointment; few men ever worshipped Freedom with half such unquestioning faith as did the American Negro for two centuries. To him, so far as he thought and dreamed, slavery was indeed the sum of all villainies, the cause of all sorrow, the root of all prejudice; Emancipation was the key to a promised land of sweeter beauty than ever stretched before the eyes of wearied Israelites. In song and exhortation swelled one refrain—Liberty; in his tears and curses the God he implored had Freedom in his right hand. At last it came,—suddenly, fearfully, like a dream. With one wild

carnival of blood and passion came the message in his own
plaintive cadences:—

> "Shout, O children!
>   Shout, you're free!
>   For God has bought your liberty!"

Years have passed away since then,—ten, twenty, forty; forty
years of national life, forty years of renewal and development,
and yet the swarthy spectre sits in its accustomed seat at
the Nation's feast. In vain do we cry to this our vastest social
problem:—

> "Take any shape but that, and my firm nerves
>   Shall never tremble!"

The Nation has not yet found peace from its sins; the freedman
has not yet found in freedom his promised land. Whatever of
good may have come in these years of change, the shadow of a
deep disappointment rests upon the Negro people,—a disappointment all the more bitter because the unattained ideal was
unbounded save by the simple ignorance of a lowly people.

The first decade was merely a prolongation of the vain search
for freedom, the boon that seemed ever barely to elude their
grasp,—like a tantalizing will-o'-the-wisp, maddening and mis-
leading the headless host. The holocaust of war, the terrors of
the Ku-Klux Klan, the lies of carpet-baggers, the disorganiza-
tion of industry, and the contradictory advice of friends and
foes, left the bewildered serf with no new watch-word beyond
the old cry for freedom. As the time flew, however, he began to
grasp a new idea. The ideal of liberty demanded for its attain-
ment powerful means, and these the Fifteenth Amendment gave
him. The ballot, which before he had looked upon as a visible
sign of freedom, he now regarded as the chief means of gaining
and perfecting the liberty with which war had partially endowed
him. And why not? Had not votes made war and emancipated
millions? Had not votes enfranchised the freedmen? Was

anything impossible to a power that had done all this? A million black men started with renewed zeal to vote themselves
into the kingdom. So the decade flew away, the revolution of
1876 came, and left the half-free serf weary, wondering, but
still inspired. Slowly but steadily, in the following years, a new
vision began gradually to replace the dream of political power,—
a powerful movement, the rise of another ideal to guide the
unguided, another pillar of fire by night after a clouded day. It
was the ideal of "book-learning"; the curiosity, born of com-
pulsory ignorance, to know and test the power of the cabalistic
letters of the white man, the longing to know. Here at last
seemed to have been discovered the mountain path to Canaan;
longer than the highway of Emancipation and law, steep and
rugged, but straight, leading to heights high enough to over-
look life.

Up the new path the advance guard toiled, slowly, heavily,
doggedly; only those who have watched and guided the falter-
ing feet, the misty minds, the dull understandings, of the dark
pupils of these schools know how faithfully, how piteously, this
people strove to learn. It was weary work. The cold statistician
wrote down the inches of progress here and there, noted also
where here and there a foot had slipped or some one had fallen.
To the tired climbers, the horizon was ever dark, the mists were
often cold, the Canaan was always dim and far away. If, however, the vistas disclosed as yet no goal, no resting-place, little
but flattery and criticism, the journey at least gave leisure for
reflection and self-examination; it changed the child of Emancipation to the youth with dawning self-consciousness, self-
realization, self-respect. In those sombre forests of his striving
his own soul rose before him, and he saw himself,—darkly as
through a veil; and yet he saw in himself some faint revelation
of his power, of his mission. He began to have a dim feeling
that, to attain his place in the world, he must be himself, and
not another. For the first time he sought to analyze the burden
he bore upon his back, that dead-weight of social degradation
partially masked behind a half-named Negro problem. He felt
his poverty; without a cent, without a home, without land, tools,
or savings, he had entered into competition with rich, landed,

skilled neighbors. To be a poor man is hard, but to be a poor race in a land of dollars is the very bottom of hardships. He felt the weight of his ignorance,—not simply of letters, but of life, of business, of the humanities; the accumulated sloth and shirking and awkwardness of decades and centuries shackled his hands and feet. Nor was his burden all poverty and ignorance. The red stain of bastardy, which two centuries of systematic legal defilement of Negro women had stamped upon his race, meant not only the loss of ancient African chastity, but also the hereditary weight of a mass of corruption from white adulterers, threatening almost the obliteration of the Negro home.

A people thus handicapped ought not to be asked to race with the world, but rather allowed to give all its time and thought to its own social problems. But alas! while sociologists gleefully count his bastards and his prostitutes, the very soul of the toiling, sweating black man is darkened by the shadow of a vast despair. Men call the shadow prejudice, and learnedly explain it as the natural defence of culture against barbarism, learning against ignorance, purity against crime, the "higher" against the "lower" races. To which the Negro cries Amen! and swears that to so much of this strange prejudice as is founded on just homage to civilization, culture, righteousness, and progress, he humbly bows and meekly does obeisance. But before that nameless prejudice that leaps beyond all this he stands helpless, dismayed, and well-nigh speechless; before that personal disrespect and mockery, the ridicule and systematic humiliation, the distortion of fact and wanton license of fancy, the cynical ignoring of the better and the boisterous welcoming of the worse, the all-pervading desire to inculcate disdain for everything black, from Toussaint to the devil,—before this there rises a sickening despair that would disarm and discourage any nation save that black host to whom "discouragement" is an unwritten word.

But the facing of so vast a prejudice could not but bring the inevitable self-questioning, self-disparagement, and lowering of ideals which ever accompany repression and breed in an atmosphere of contempt and hate. Whisperings and portents came borne upon the four winds: Lo! we are diseased and dying, cried the dark hosts; we cannot write, our voting is vain; what need of education, since we must always cook and serve? And the Nation echoed and enforced this self-criticism, saying: Be content to be servants, and nothing more; what need of higher culture for half-men? Away with the black man's ballot, by force or fraud,—and behold the suicide of a race! Nevertheless, out of the evil came something of good,—the more careful adjustment of education to real life, the clearer perception of the Negroes' social responsibilities, and the sobering realization of the meaning of progress.

So dawned the time of *Sturm und Drang*: storm and stress to-day rocks our little boat on the mad waters of the world-sea; there is within and without the sound of conflict, the burning of body and rending of soul; inspiration strives with doubt, and faith with vain questionings. The bright ideals of the past,— physical freedom, political power, the training of brains and the training of hands,—all these in turn have waxed and waned, until even the last grows dim and overcast. Are they all wrong,— all false? No, not that, but each alone was over-simple and incomplete,—the dreams of a credulous race-childhood, or the fond imaginings of the other world which does not know and does not want to know our power. To be really true, all these ideals must be melted and welded into one. The training of the schools we need to-day more than ever,—the training of deft hands, quick eyes and ears, and above all the broader, deeper, higher culture of gifted minds and pure hearts. The power of the ballot we need in sheer self-defence,—else what shall save us from a second slavery? Freedom, too, the long-sought, we still seek,—the freedom of life and limb, the freedom to work and think, the freedom to love and aspire. Work, culture, liberty,— all these we need, not singly but together, not successively but together, each growing and aiding each, and all striving toward that vaster ideal that swims before the Negro people, the ideal of human brotherhood, gained through the unifying ideal of Race; the ideal of fostering and developing the traits and talents of the Negro, not in opposition to or contempt for other races, but rather in large conformity to the greater ideals of the American Republic, in order that some day on American soil two world-races may give each to each those characteristics both so sadly lack. We the darker ones come even now not altogether empty-handed: there are to-day no truer exponents of the pure human spirit of the Declaration of Independence than the American Negroes; there is no true American music but the wild sweet melodies of the Negro slave; the American fairy tales and folklore are Indian and African; and, all in all, we black men seem the sole oasis of simple faith and reverence in a dusty desert of dollars and smartness. Will America be poorer if she replace her brutal dyspeptic blundering with light-hearted but determined Negro humility? or her coarse and cruel wit with loving jovial good humor? or her vulgar music with the soul of the Sorrow Songs?

Merely a concrete test of the underlying principles of the great republic is the Negro Problem, and the spiritual striving of the freedmen's sons is the travail of souls whose burden is almost beyond the measure of their strength, but who bear it in the name of an historic race, in the name of this the land of their fathers' fathers, and in the name of human opportunity.

And now what I have briefly sketched in large outline let me on coming pages tell again in many ways, with loving emphasis and deeper detail, that men may listen to the striving in the souls of black folk.

II

OF THE DAWN OF
FREEDOM

Careless seems the great Avenger;
  History's lessons but record
One death-grapple in the darkness
  'Twixt old systems and the Word;
Truth forever on the scaffold,
  Wrong forever on the throne;
Yet that scaffold sways the future,
  And behind the dim unknown
Standeth God within the shadow
  Keeping watch above His own.

LOWELL

The problem of the twentieth century is the problem of the color-line,—the relation of the darker to the lighter races of men in Asia and Africa, in America and the islands of the sea. It was a phase of this problem that caused the Civil War; and however much they who marched South and North in 1861 may have fixed on the technical points of union and local autonomy as a shibboleth, all nevertheless knew, as we know, that the question of Negro slavery was the real cause of the conflict. Curious it was, too, how this deeper question ever forced itself to the surface despite effort and disclaimer. No sooner had Northern armies touched Southern soil than this old question, newly guised, sprang from the earth,—What shall be done with Negroes? Peremptory military commands, this way and that, could not answer the query; the Emancipation Proclamation seemed but to broaden and intensify the difficulties; and the War Amendments made the Negro problems of to-day.

It is the aim of this essay to study the period of history from 1861 to 1872 so far as it relates to the American Negro. In effect, this tale of the dawn of Freedom is an account of that government of men called the Freedmen's Bureau,—one of the most singular and interesting of the attempts made by a great nation to grapple with vast problems of race and social condition.

The war has naught to do with slaves, cried Congress, the President, and the Nation; and yet no sooner had the armies, East and West, penetrated Virginia and Tennessee than fugitive slaves appeared within their lines. They came at night, when the flickering camp-fires shone like vast unsteady stars along the black horizon: old men and thin, with gray and tufted hair; women, with frightened eyes, dragging whimpering hungry children; men and girls, stalwart and gaunt,—a horde of starving vagabonds, homeless, helpless, and pitiable, in their dark distress. Two methods of treating these newcomers seemed equally logical to opposite sorts of minds. Ben Butler, in Virginia, quickly declared slave property contraband of war, and put the fugitives to work; while Fremont, in Missouri, declared the slaves free under martial law. Butler's action was approved, but Fremont's was hastily countermanded, and his successor, Halleck, saw things differently. "Hereafter," he commanded, "no slaves should be allowed to come into your lines at all; if any come without your knowledge, when owners call for them deliver them." Such a policy was difficult to enforce; some of the black refugees declared themselves freedmen, others showed that their masters had deserted them, and still others were captured with forts and plantations. Evidently, too, slaves were a source of strength to the Confederacy, and were being used as laborers and producers. "They constitute a military resource," wrote Secretary Cameron, late in 1861; "and being such, that they should not be turned over to the enemy is too plain to discuss." So gradually the tone of the army chiefs changed; Congress forbade the rendition of fugitives, and Butler's "contrabands" were welcomed as military laborers. This complicated rather than solved the problem, for now the scattering fugitives became a steady stream, which flowed faster as the armies marched.

Then the long-headed man with care-chiselled face who sat in the White House saw the inevitable, and emancipated the slaves of rebels on New Year's, 1863. A month later Congress called earnestly for the Negro soldiers whom the act of July, 1862, had half grudgingly allowed to enlist. Thus the barriers were levelled and the deed was done. The stream of fugitives swelled to a flood, and anxious army officers kept inquiring: "What must be done with slaves, arriving almost daily? Are we to find food and shelter for women and children?"

It was a Pierce of Boston who pointed out the way, and thus became in a sense the founder of the Freedmen's Bureau. He was a firm friend of Secretary Chase; and when, in 1861, the care of slaves and abandoned lands devolved upon the Treasury officials, Pierce was specially detailed from the ranks to study the conditions. First, he cared for the refugees at Fortress Monroe; and then, after Sherman had captured Hilton Head, Pierce was sent there to found his Port Royal experiment of making free workingmen out of slaves. Before his experiment was barely started, however, the problem of the fugitives had assumed such proportions that it was taken from the hands of the overburdened Treasury Department and given to the army officials. Already centres of massed freedmen were forming at Fortress Monroe, Washington, New Orleans, Vicksburg and Corinth, Columbus, Ky., and Cairo, Ill., as well as at Port Royal. Army chaplains found here new and fruitful fields; "superintendents of contrabands" multiplied, and some attempt at systematic work was made by enlisting the able-bodied men and giving work to the others.

Then came the Freedmen's Aid societies, born of the touching appeals from Pierce and from these other centres of distress. There was the American Missionary Association, sprung from the *Amistad*, and now full-grown for work; the various church organizations, the National Freedmen's Relief Association, the American Freedmen's Union, the Western Freedmen's Aid Commission,—in all fifty or more active organizations, which sent clothes, money, school-books, and teachers southward. All they did was needed, for the destitution of the freedmen was often reported as "too appalling for belief," and the situation was daily growing worse rather than better.

And daily, too, it seemed more plain that this was no ordinary matter of temporary relief, but a national crisis; for here loomed a labor problem of vast dimensions. Masses of Negroes stood idle, or, if they worked spasmodically, were never sure of pay; and if perchance they received pay, squandered the new thing thoughtlessly. In these and other ways were camp-life and the new liberty demoralizing the freedmen. The broader economic organization thus clearly demanded sprang up here and there as accident and local conditions determined. Here it was that Pierce's Port Royal plan of leased plantations and guided workmen pointed out the rough way. In Washington the military governor, at the urgent appeal of the superintendent, opened confiscated estates to the cultivation of the fugitives, and there in the shadow of the dome gathered black farm villages. General Dix gave over estates to the freedmen of Fortress Monroe, and so on, South and West. The government and benevolent societies furnished the means of cultivation, and the Negro turned again slowly to work. The systems of control, thus started, rapidly grew, here and there, into strange little governments, like that of General Banks in Louisiana, with its ninety thousand black subjects, its fifty thousand guided laborers, and its annual budget of one hundred thousand dollars and more. It made out four thousand pay-rolls a year, registered all freedmen, inquired into grievances and redressed them, laid and collected taxes, and established a system of public schools. So, too, Colonel Eaton, the superintendent of Tennessee and Arkansas, ruled over one hundred thousand freedmen, leased and cultivated seven thousand acres of cotton land, and fed ten thousand paupers a year.

In South Carolina was General Saxton, with his deep interest in
black folk. He succeeded Pierce and the Treasury officials, and
sold forfeited estates, leased abandoned plantations, encouraged
schools, and received from Sherman, after that terribly picturesque march to the sea, thousands of the wretched camp followers.

Three characteristic things one might have seen in Sherman's
raid through Georgia, which threw the new situation in shadowy relief: the Conqueror, the Conquered, and the Negro. Some
see all significance in the grim front of the destroyer, and some
in the bitter sufferers of the Lost Cause. But to me neither soldier nor fugitive speaks with so deep a meaning as that dark
human cloud that clung like remorse on the rear of those swift
columns, swelling at times to half their size, almost engulfing
and choking them. In vain were they ordered back, in vain were
bridges hewn from beneath their feet; on they trudged and
writhed and surged, until they rolled into Savannah, a starved
and naked horde of tens of thousands. There too came the characteristic military remedy: "The islands from Charleston south,
the abandoned rice-fields along the rivers for thirty miles back
from the sea, and the country bordering the St. John's River,
Florida, are reserved and set apart for the settlement of Negroes
now made free by act of war." So read the celebrated "Field-
order Number Fifteen."

All these experiments, orders, and systems were bound to at-
tract and perplex the government and the nation. Directly after
the Emancipation Proclamation, Representative Eliot had introduced a bill creating a Bureau of Emancipation; but it was
never reported. The following June a committee of inquiry, appointed by the Secretary of War, reported in favor of a temporary bureau for the "improvement, protection, and employment
of refugee freedmen," on much the same lines as were afterwards followed. Petitions came in to President Lincoln from
distinguished citizens and organizations, strongly urging a com-
prehensive and unified plan of dealing with the freedmen, under
a bureau which should be "charged with the study of plans and
execution of measures for easily guiding, and in every way ju-
diciously and humanely aiding, the passage of our emancipated

and yet to be emancipated blacks from the old condition of forced labor to their new state of voluntary industry."

Some half-hearted steps were taken to accomplish this, in part, by putting the whole matter again in charge of the special Treasury agents. Laws of 1863 and 1864 directed them to take charge of and lease abandoned lands for periods not exceeding twelve months, and to "provide in such leases, or otherwise, for the employment and general welfare" of the freedmen. Most of the army officers greeted this as a welcome relief from perplexing "Negro affairs," and Secretary Fessenden, July 29, 1864, issued an excellent system of regulations, which were afterward closely followed by General Howard. Under Treasury agents, large quantities of land were leased in the Mississippi Valley, and many Negroes were employed; but in August, 1864, the new regulations were suspended for reasons of "public policy," and the army was again in control.

Meanwhile Congress had turned its attention to the subject; and in March the House passed a bill by a majority of two establishing a Bureau for Freedmen in the War Department. Charles Sumner, who had charge of the bill in the Senate, argued that freedmen and abandoned lands ought to be under the same department, and reported a substitute for the House bill attaching the Bureau to the Treasury Department. This bill passed, but too late for action by the House. The debates wandered over the whole policy of the administration and the general question of slavery, without touching very closely the specific merits of the measure in hand. Then the national election took place; and the administration, with a vote of renewed confidence from the country, addressed itself to the matter more seriously. A conference between the two branches of Congress agreed upon a carefully drawn measure which contained the chief provisions of Sumner's bill, but made the proposed organization a department independent of both the War and the Treasury officials. The bill was conservative, giving the new department "general superintendence of all freedmen." Its purpose was to "establish regulations" for them, protect them, lease them lands, adjust their wages, and appear in civil and military courts as their "next friend." There were many limitations attached to the powers thus granted, and the organization was made permanent. Nevertheless, the Senate defeated the bill, and a new conference committee was appointed. This committee reported a new bill, February 28, which was whirled through just as the session closed, and became the act of 1865 establishing in the War Department a "Bureau of Refugees, Freedmen, and Abandoned Lands."

This last compromise was a hasty bit of legislation, vague and uncertain in outline. A Bureau was created, "to continue during the present War of Rebellion, and for one year thereafter," to which was given "the supervision and management of all abandoned lands and the control of all subjects relating to refugees and freedmen," under "such rules and regulations as may be presented by the head of the Bureau and approved by the President." A Commissioner, appointed by the President and Senate, was to control the Bureau, with an office force not exceeding ten clerks. The President might also appoint assistant commissioners in the seceded States, and to all these offices military officials might be detailed at regular pay. The Secretary of War could issue rations, clothing, and fuel to the destitute, and all abandoned property was placed in the hands of the Bureau for eventual lease and sale to ex-slaves in forty-acre parcels.

Thus did the United States government definitely assume charge of the emancipated Negro as the ward of the nation. It was a tremendous undertaking. Here at a stroke of the pen was erected a government of millions of men,—and not ordinary men either, but black men emasculated by a peculiarly complete system of slavery, centuries old; and now, suddenly, violently, they come into a new birthright, at a time of war and passion, in the midst of the stricken and embittered population of their former masters. Any man might well have hesitated to assume charge of such a work, with vast responsibilities, indefinite powers, and limited resources. Probably no one but a soldier would have answered such a call promptly; and, indeed, no one but a soldier could be called, for Congress had appropriated no money for salaries and expenses.

Less than a month after the weary Emancipator passed to his rest, his successor assigned Major-Gen. Oliver O. Howard to duty as Commissioner of the new Bureau. He was a Maine man, then only thirty-five years of age. He had marched with Sherman to the sea, had fought well at Gettysburg, and but the year before had been assigned to the command of the Department of Tennessee. An honest man, with too much faith in human nature, little aptitude for business and intricate detail, he had had large opportunity of becoming acquainted at first hand with much of the work before him. And of that work it has been truly said that "no approximately correct history of civilization can ever be written which does not throw out in bold relief, as one of the great landmarks of political and social progress, the organization and administration of the Freedmen's Bureau."

On May 12, 1865, Howard was appointed; and he assumed the duties of his office promptly on the 15th, and began examining the field of work. A curious mess he looked upon: little despotisms, communistic experiments, slavery, peonage, business speculations, organized charity, unorganized almsgiving,— all reeling on under the guise of helping the freedmen, and all enshrined in the smoke and blood of war and the cursing and silence of angry men. On May 19 the new government—for a government it really was—issued its constitution; commissioners were to be appointed in each of the seceded States, who were to take charge of "all subjects relating to refugees and freedmen," and all relief and rations were to be given by their consent alone. The Bureau invited continued cooperation with benevolent societies, and declared: "It will be the object of all commissioners to introduce practicable systems of compensated labor," and to establish schools. Forthwith nine assistant commissioners were appointed. They were to hasten to their fields of work; seek gradually to close relief establishments, and make the destitute self-supporting; act as courts of law where there were no courts, or where Negroes were not recognized in them as free; establish the institution of marriage among ex-slaves, and keep records; see that freedmen were free to choose their employers, and help in making fair contracts for them; and finally, the circular said: "Simple good faith, for which we hope on all hands for those concerned in the passing away of slavery, will especially relieve the assistant commissioners in the discharge of their duties toward the freedmen, as well as promote the general welfare."

No sooner was the work thus started, and the general system and local organization in some measure begun, than two grave difficulties appeared which changed largely the theory and outcome of Bureau work. First, there were the abandoned lands of the South. It had long been the more or less definitely expressed theory of the North that all the chief problems of Emancipation might be settled by establishing the slaves on the forfeited lands of their masters,—a sort of poetic justice, said some. But this poetry done into solemn prose meant either wholesale confiscation of private property in the South, or vast appropriations. Now Congress had not appropriated a cent, and no sooner did the proclamations of general amnesty appear than the eight hundred thousand acres of abandoned lands in the hands of the Freedmen's Bureau melted quickly away. The second difficulty lay in perfecting the local organization of the Bureau throughout the wide field of work. Making a new machine and sending out officials of duly ascertained fitness for a great work of social reform is no child's task; but this task was even harder, for a new central organization had to be fitted on a heterogeneous and confused but already existing system of relief and control of ex-slaves; and the agents available for this work must be sought for in an army still busy with war operations,—men in the very nature of the case ill fitted for delicate social work,—or among the questionable camp followers of an invading host. Thus, after a year's work, vigorously as it was pushed, the problem looked even more difficult to grasp and solve than at the beginning. Nevertheless, three things that year's work did, well worth the doing: it relieved a vast amount of physical suffering; it transported seven thousand fugitives from congested centres back to the farm; and, best of all, it inaugurated the crusade of the New England school-ma'am.

The annals of this Ninth Crusade are yet to be written,—the tale of a mission that seemed to our age far more quixotic than the quest of St. Louis seemed to his. Behind the mists of ruin and rapine waved the calico dresses of women who dared, and after the hoarse mouthings of the field guns rang the rhythm of the alphabet. Rich and poor they were, serious and curious. Bereaved now of a father, now of a brother, now of more than these, they came seeking a life work in planting New England schoolhouses among the white and black of the South. They did their work well. In that first year they taught one hundred thousand souls, and more.

Evidently, Congress must soon legislate again on the hastily organized Bureau, which had so quickly grown into wide significance and vast possibilities. An institution such as that was well-nigh as difficult to end as to begin. Early in 1866 Congress took up the matter, when Senator Trumbull, of Illinois, introduced a bill to extend the Bureau and enlarge its powers. This measure received, at the hands of Congress, far more thorough discussion and attention than its predecessor. The war cloud had thinned enough to allow a clearer conception of the work of Emancipation. The champions of the bill argued that the strengthening of the Freedmen's Bureau was still a military necessity; that it was needed for the proper carrying out of the Thirteenth Amendment, and was a work of sheer justice to the ex-slave, at a trifling cost to the government. The opponents of the measure declared that the war was over, and the necessity for war measures past; that the Bureau, by reason of its extraordinary powers, was clearly unconstitutional in time of peace, and was destined to irritate the South and pauperize the freedmen, at a final cost of possibly hundreds of millions. These two arguments were unanswered, and indeed unanswerable: the one that the extraordinary powers of the Bureau threatened the civil rights of all citizens; and the other that the government must have power to do what manifestly must be done, and that present abandonment of the freedmen meant their practical reenslavement. The bill which finally passed enlarged and made permanent the Freedmen's Bureau. It was promptly vetoed by President Johnson as "unconstitutional," "unnecessary," and "extrajudicial," and failed of passage over the veto. Meantime, however, the breach between Congress and the President began to broaden, and a modified form of the lost bill was finally passed over the President's second veto, July 16.

The act of 1866 gave the Freedmen's Bureau its final

form,—the form by which it will be known to posterity and judged of men. It extended the existence of the Bureau to July, 1868; it authorized additional assistant commissioners, the retention of army officers mustered out of regular service, the sale of certain forfeited lands to freedmen on nominal terms, the sale of Confederate public property for Negro schools, and a wider field of judicial interpretation and cognizance. The government of the unreconstructed South was thus put very largely in the hands of the Freedmen's Bureau, especially as in many cases the departmental military commander was now made also assistant commissioner. It was thus that the Freedmen's Bureau became a full-fledged government of men. It made laws, executed them and interpreted them; it laid and collected taxes, defined and punished crime, maintained and used military force, and dictated such measures as it thought necessary and proper for the accomplishment of its varied ends. Naturally, all these powers were not exercised continuously nor to their fullest extent; and yet, as General Howard has said, "scarcely any subject that has to be legislated upon in civil society failed, at one time or another, to demand the action of this singular Bureau."

To understand and criticise intelligently so vast a work, one must not forget an instant the drift of things in the later sixties. Lee had surrendered, Lincoln was dead, and Johnson and Congress were at loggerheads; the Thirteenth Amendment was adopted, the Fourteenth pending, and the Fifteenth declared in force in 1870. Guerrilla raiding, the ever-present flickering afterflame of war, was spending its force against the Negroes, and all the Southern land was awakening as from some wild dream to poverty and social revolution. In a time of perfect calm, amid willing neighbors and streaming wealth, the social uplifting of four million slaves to an assured and self-sustaining place in the body politic and economic would have been a herculean task; but when to the inherent difficulties of so delicate and nice a social operation were added the spite and hate of conflict, the hell of war; when suspicion and cruelty were rife, and gaunt Hunger wept beside Bereavement,—in such a case, the work of any instrument of social regeneration was in large part foredoomed to failure. The very name of the Bureau stood for a thing in the South which for two centuries and better men had refused even to argue,—that life amid free Negroes was simply unthinkable, the maddest of experiments.

The agents that the Bureau could command varied all the way from unselfish philanthropists to narrow-minded busybodies and thieves; and even though it be true that the average was far better than the worst, it was the occasional fly that helped spoil the ointment.

Then amid all crouched the freed slave, bewildered between friend and foe. He had emerged from slavery,—not the worst slavery in the world, not a slavery that made all life unbearable, rather a slavery that had here and there something of kindliness, fidelity, and happiness,—but withal slavery, which, so far as human aspiration and desert were concerned, classed the black man and the ox together. And the Negro knew full well that, whatever their deeper convictions may have been, Southern men had fought with desperate energy to perpetuate this slavery under which the black masses, with half-articulate thought, had writhed and shivered. They welcomed freedom with a cry. They shrank from the master who still strove for their chains; they fled to the friends that had freed them, even though those friends stood ready to use them as a club for driving the recalcitrant South back into loyalty. So the cleft between the white and black South grew. Idle to say it never should have been; it was as inevitable as its results were pitiable. Curiously incongruous elements were left arrayed against each other,—the North, the government, the carpet-bagger, and the slave, here; and there, all the South that was white, whether gentleman or vagabond, honest man or rascal, lawless murderer or martyr to duty.

Thus it is doubly difficult to write of this period calmly, so intense was the feeling, so mighty the human passions that swayed and blinded men. Amid it all, two figures ever stand to typify that day to coming ages,—the one, a gray-haired gentleman, whose fathers had quit themselves like men, whose sons lay in nameless graves; who bowed to the evil of slavery because its abolition threatened untold ill to all; who stood at last, in the evening of life, a blighted, ruined form, with hate in his eyes;—and the other, a form hovering dark and mother-like, her awful face black with the mists of centuries, had aforetime quailed at that white master's command, had bent in love over the cradles of his sons and daughters, and closed in death the sunken eyes of his wife,—aye, too, at his behest had laid herself low to his lust, and borne a tawny man-child to the world, only to see her dark boy's limbs scattered to the winds by midnight marauders riding after "cursed Niggers." These were the saddest sights of that woful day; and no man clasped the hands of these two passing figures of the present-past; but, hating, they went to their long home, and, hating, their children's children live to-day.

Here, then, was the field of work for the Freedmen's Bureau; and since, with some hesitation, it was continued by the act of 1868 until 1869, let us look upon four years of its work as a whole. There were, in 1868, nine hundred Bureau officials scattered from Washington to Texas, ruling, directly and indirectly, many millions of men. The deeds of these rulers fall mainly under seven heads: the relief of physical suffering, the overseeing of the beginnings of free labor, the buying and selling of land, the establishment of schools, the paying of bounties, the administration of justice, and the financiering of all these activities.

Up to June, 1869, over half a million patients had been treated by Bureau physicians and surgeons, and sixty hospitals and asylums had been in operation. In fifty months twenty-one million free rations were distributed at a cost of over four million dollars. Next came the difficult question of labor. First, thirty thousand black men were transported from the refuges and relief stations back to the farms, back to the critical trial of a new way of working. Plain instructions went out from Washington: the laborers must be free to choose their employers, no fixed rate of wages was prescribed, and there was to be no peonage or forced labor. So far, so good; but where local agents differed *toto cœlo* in capacity and character, where the personnel was continually changing, the outcome was necessarily varied. The largest element of success lay in the fact that the majority of the freedmen were willing, even eager, to work. So labor contracts were written,—fifty thousand in a single State,—laborers advised, wages guaranteed, and employers supplied. In truth, the organization became a vast labor bureau,—not perfect, indeed, notably defective here and there, but on the whole successful beyond the dreams of thoughtful men. The two great obstacles which confronted the officials were the tyrant and the idler,—the slave-holder who was determined to perpetuate slavery under another name; and the freedman who regarded freedom as perpetual rest,—the Devil and the Deep Sea.

In the work of establishing the Negroes as peasant proprietors, the Bureau was from the first handicapped and at last absolutely checked. Something was done, and larger things were planned; abandoned lands were leased so long as they remained in the hands of the Bureau, and a total revenue of nearly half a million dollars derived from black tenants. Some other lands to which the nation had gained title were sold on easy terms, and public lands were opened for settlement to the very few freedmen who had tools and capital. But the vision of "forty acres and a mule"—the righteous and reasonable ambition to become a landholder, which the nation had all but categorically promised the freedmen—was destined in most cases to bitter disappointment. And those men of marvellous hindsight who are to-day seeking to preach the Negro back to the present peonage of the soil know well, or ought to know, that the opportunity of binding the Negro peasant willingly to the soil was lost on that day when the Commissioner of the Freedmen's Bureau had to go to South Carolina and tell the weeping freedmen, after their years of toil, that their land was not theirs, that there was a mistake—somewhere. If by 1874 the Georgia Negro alone owned three hundred and fifty thousand acres of land, it was by grace of his thrift rather than by bounty of the government.

The greatest success of the Freedmen's Bureau lay in the planting of the free school among Negroes, and the idea of free elementary education among all classes in the South. It not only called the schoolmistresses through the benevolent agencies and built them schoolhouses, but it helped discover and support such apostles of human culture as Edmund Ware, Samuel Armstrong, and Erastus Cravath. The opposition to Negro education in the South was at first bitter, and showed itself in ashes, insult, and blood; for the South believed an educated Negro to be a dangerous Negro. And the South was not wholly wrong; for education among all kinds of men always has had, and always will have, an element of danger and revolution, of dissatisfaction and discontent. Nevertheless, men strive to know. Perhaps some inkling of this paradox, even in the unquiet days of the Bureau, helped the bayonets allay an opposition to human training which still to-day lies smouldering in the South, but not flaming. Fisk, Atlanta, Howard, and Hampton were founded in these days, and six million dollars were expended for educational work, seven hundred and fifty thousand dollars of which the freedmen themselves gave of their poverty.

Such contributions, together with the buying of land and various other enterprises, showed that the ex-slave was handling some free capital already. The chief initial source of this was labor in the army, and his pay and bounty as a soldier. Payments to Negro soldiers were at first complicated by the ignorance of the recipients, and the fact that the quotas of colored regiments from Northern States were largely filled by recruits from the South, unknown to their fellow soldiers. Consequently, payments were accompanied by such frauds that Congress, by joint resolution in 1867, put the whole matter in the hands of the Freedmen's Bureau. In two years six million dollars was thus distributed to five thousand claimants, and in the end the sum exceeded eight million dollars. Even in this system fraud was frequent; but still the work put needed capital in the hands of practical paupers, and some, at least, was well spent.

The most perplexing and least successful part of the Bureau's work lay in the exercise of its judicial functions. The regular Bureau court consisted of one representative of the employer, one of the Negro, and one of the Bureau. If the Bureau could have maintained a perfectly judicial attitude, this arrangement would have been ideal, and must in time have gained confidence; but the nature of its other activities and the character of its personnel prejudiced the Bureau in favor of the black litigants, and led without doubt to much injustice and annoyance. On the other hand, to leave the Negro in the hands of Southern courts was impossible. In a distracted land where slavery had hardly fallen, to keep the strong from wanton abuse of the weak, and the weak from gloating insolently over the half-shorn strength of the strong, was a thankless, hopeless task. The former masters of the land were peremptorily ordered about, seized, and imprisoned, and punished over and again, with scant courtesy from army officers. The former slaves were intimidated, beaten, raped, and butchered by angry and revengeful men. Bureau courts tended to become centres simply for punishing whites, while the regular civil courts tended to become solely institutions for perpetuating the slavery of blacks. Almost every law and method ingenuity could devise was employed by the legislatures to reduce the Negroes to serfdom,—to make them the slaves of the State, if not of individual owners; while the Bureau officials too often were found striving to put the "bottom rail on top," and give the freedmen a power and independence which they could not yet use. It is all well enough for us of another generation to wax wise with advice to those who bore the burden in the heat of the day. It is full easy now to see that the man who lost home, fortune, and family at a stroke, and saw his land ruled by "mules and niggers," was really benefited by the passing of slavery. It is not difficult now to say to the young freedman, cheated and cuffed about, who has seen his father's head beaten to a jelly and his own mother namelessly assaulted, that the meek shall inherit the earth. Above all, nothing is more convenient than to heap on the Freedmen's Bureau all the evils of that evil day, and damn it utterly for every mistake and blunder that was made.

All this is easy, but it is neither sensible nor just. Some one had blundered, but that was long before Oliver Howard was born; there was criminal aggression and heedless neglect, but without some system of control there would have been far more than there was. Had that control been from within, the Negro would have been re-enslaved, to all intents and purposes. Coming as the control did from without, perfect men and methods would have bettered all things; and even with imperfect agents and questionable methods, the work accomplished was not undeserving of commendation.

Such was the dawn of Freedom; such was the work of the Freedmen's Bureau, which, summed up in brief, may be

epitomized thus: For some fifteen million dollars, beside the
sums spent before 1865, and the dole of benevolent societies,
this Bureau set going a system of free labor, established a beginning of peasant proprietorship, secured the recognition of
black freedmen before courts of law, and founded the free common school in the South. On the other hand, it failed to begin
the establishment of good-will between ex-masters and freedmen, to guard its work wholly from paternalistic methods which
discouraged self-reliance, and to carry out to any considerable
extent its implied promises to furnish the freedmen with land.
Its successes were the result of hard work, supplemented by the
aid of philanthropists and the eager striving of black men. Its
failures were the result of bad local agents, the inherent difficulties of the work, and national neglect.

Such an institution, from its wide powers, great responsibilities, large control of moneys, and generally conspicuous position,
was naturally open to repeated and bitter attack. It sustained a
searching Congressional investigation at the instance of Fer-
nando Wood in 1870. Its archives and few remaining functions
were with blunt discourtesy transferred from Howard's control,
in his absence, to the supervision of Secretary of War Belknap
in 1872, on the Secretary's recommendation. Finally, in conse-
quence of grave intimations of wrongdoing made by the Secretary and his subordinates, General Howard was court-martialed
in 1874. In both of these trials the Commissioner of the Freedmen's Bureau was officially exonerated from any wilful misdo-
ing, and his work commended. Nevertheless, many unpleasant
things were brought to light,—the methods of transacting the
business of the Bureau were faulty; several cases of defalcation
were proved, and other frauds strongly suspected; there were
some business transactions which savored of dangerous specula-
tion, if not dishonesty; and around it all lay the smirch of the
Freedmen's Bank.

Morally and practically, the Freedmen's Bank was part of the
Freedmen's Bureau, although it had no legal connection with
it. With the prestige of the government back of it, and a direct-
ing board of unusual respectability and national reputation,
this banking institution had made a remarkable start in the

development of that thrift among black folk which slavery had kept them from knowing. Then in one sad day came the crash,— all the hard-earned dollars of the freedmen disappeared; but that was the least of the loss,—all the faith in saving went too, and much of the faith in men; and that was a loss that a Nation which to-day sneers at Negro shiftlessness has never yet made good. Not even ten additional years of slavery could have done so much to throttle the thrift of the freedmen as the mismanagement and bankruptcy of the series of savings banks chartered by the Nation for their especial aid. Where all the blame should rest, it is hard to say; whether the Bureau and the Bank died chiefly by reason of the blows of its selfish friends or the dark machinations of its foes, perhaps even time will never reveal, for here lies unwritten history.

Of the foes without the Bureau, the bitterest were those who attacked not so much its conduct or policy under the law as the necessity for any such institution at all. Such attacks came primarily from the Border States and the South; and they were summed up by Senator Davis, of Kentucky, when he moved to entitle the act of 1866 a bill "to promote strife and conflict between the white and black races . . . by a grant of unconstitutional power." The argument gathered tremendous strength South and North; but its very strength was its weakness. For, argued the plain common-sense of the nation, if it is unconstitutional, unpractical, and futile for the nation to stand guardian over its helpless wards, then there is left but one alternative,—to make those wards their own guardians by arming them with the ballot. Moreover, the path of the practical politician pointed the same way; for, argued this opportunist, if we cannot peacefully reconstruct the South with white votes, we certainly can with black votes. So justice and force joined hands.

The alternative thus offered the nation was not between full and restricted Negro suffrage; else every sensible man, black and white, would easily have chosen the latter. It was rather a choice between suffrage and slavery, after endless blood and gold had flowed to sweep human bondage away. Not a single Southern legislature stood ready to admit a Negro, under any conditions, to the polls; not a single Southern legislature

believed free Negro labor was possible without a system of restrictions that took all its freedom away; there was scarcely a
white man in the South who did not honestly regard Emancipation as a crime, and its practical nullification as a duty. In such
a situation, the granting of the ballot to the black man was a
necessity, the very least a guilty nation could grant a wronged
race, and the only method of compelling the South to accept
the results of the war. Thus Negro suffrage ended a civil war
by beginning a race feud. And some felt gratitude toward the
race thus sacrificed in its swaddling clothes on the altar of national integrity; and some felt and feel only indifference and
contempt.

Had political exigencies been less pressing, the opposition to
government guardianship of Negroes less bitter, and the attach-
ment to the slave system less strong, the social seer can well
imagine a far better policy,—a permanent Freedmen's Bureau,
with a national system of Negro schools; a carefully supervised
employment and labor office; a system of impartial protection
before the regular courts; and such institutions for social betterment as savings-banks, land and building associations, and
social settlements. All this vast expenditure of money and brains
might have formed a great school of prospective citizenship, and
solved in a way we have not yet solved the most perplexing and
persistent of the Negro problems.

That such an institution was unthinkable in 1870 was due in
part to certain acts of the Freedmen's Bureau itself. It came to
regard its work as merely temporary, and Negro suffrage as a
final answer to all present perplexities. The political ambition
of many of its agents and *protégés* led it far afield into questionable activities, until the South, nursing its own deep prejudices,
came easily to ignore all the good deeds of the Bureau and hate
its very name with perfect hatred. So the Freedmen's Bureau
died, and its child was the Fifteenth Amendment.

The passing of a great human institution before its work is
done, like the untimely passing of a single soul, but leaves a
legacy of striving for other men. The legacy of the Freedmen's
Bureau is the heavy heritage of this generation. To-day, when
new and vaster problems are destined to strain every fibre of

the national mind and soul, would it not be well to count this legacy honestly and carefully? For this much all men know: despite compromise, war, and struggle, the Negro is not free. In the backwoods of the Gulf States, for miles and miles, he may not leave the plantation of his birth; in well-nigh the whole rural South the black farmers are peons, bound by law and custom to an economic slavery, from which the only escape is death or the penitentiary. In the most cultured sections and cities of the South the Negroes are a segregated servile caste, with restricted rights and privileges. Before the courts, both in law and custom, they stand on a different and peculiar basis. Taxation without representation is the rule of their political life. And the result of all this is, and in nature must have been, lawlessness and crime. That is the large legacy of the Freedmen's Bureau, the work it did not do because it could not.

I have seen a land right merry with the sun, where children sing, and rolling hills lie like passioned women wanton with harvest. And there in the King's Highway sat and sits a figure veiled and bowed, by which the traveller's footsteps hasten as they go. On the tainted air broods fear. Three centuries' thought has been the raising and unveiling of that bowed human heart, and now behold a century new for the duty and the deed. The problem of the Twentieth Century is the problem of the color-line.

III

OF MR. BOOKER T.
WASHINGTON AND OTHERS

From birth till death enslaved; in word, in deed, unmanned!
Hereditary bondsmen! Know ye not
Who would be free themselves must strike the blow?

BYRON

Easily the most striking thing in the history of the American
Negro since 1876 is the ascendancy of Mr. Booker T. Washington. It began at the time when war memories and ideals were
rapidly passing; a day of astonishing commercial development
was dawning; a sense of doubt and hesitation overtook the
freedmen's sons,—then it was that his leading began. Mr. Washington came, with a simple definite programme, at the psychological moment when the nation was a little ashamed of having
bestowed so much sentiment on Negroes, and was concentrat-
ing its energies on Dollars. His programme of industrial education, conciliation of the South, and submission and silence as
to civil and political rights, was not wholly original; the Free
Negroes from 1830 up to wartime had striven to build

industrial schools, and the American Missionary Association had from the first taught various trades; and Price and others had sought a way of honorable alliance with the best of the Southerners. But Mr. Washington first indissolubly linked these things; he put enthusiasm, unlimited energy, and perfect faith into this programme, and changed it from a by-path into a veritable Way of Life. And the tale of the methods by which he did this is a fascinating study of human life.

It startled the nation to hear a Negro advocating such a programme after many decades of bitter complaint; it startled and won the applause of the South, it interested and won the admiration of the North; and after a confused murmur of protest, it silenced if it did not convert the Negroes themselves.

To gain the sympathy and cooperation of the various elements comprising the white South was Mr. Washington's first task; and this, at the time Tuskegee was founded, seemed, for a black man, well-nigh impossible. And yet ten years later it was done in the word spoken at Atlanta: "In all things purely social we can be as separate as the five fingers, and yet one as the hand in all things essential to mutual progress." This "Atlanta Compromise" is by all odds the most notable thing in Mr. Washington's career. The South interpreted it in different ways: the radicals received it as a complete surrender of the demand for civil and political equality; the conservatives, as a generously conceived working basis for mutual understanding. So both approved it, and to-day its author is certainly the most distinguished Southerner since Jefferson Davis, and the one with the largest personal following.

Next to this achievement comes Mr. Washington's work in gaining place and consideration in the North. Others less shrewd and tactful had formerly essayed to sit on these two stools and had fallen between them; but as Mr. Washington knew the heart of the South from birth and training, so by singular insight he intuitively grasped the spirit of the age which was dominating the North. And so thoroughly did he learn the speech and thought of triumphant commercialism, and the ideals of material prosperity, that the picture of a lone black boy poring over a French grammar amid the weeds and dirt of a neglected home soon seemed to him the acme of absurdities. One wonders what Socrates and St. Francis of Assisi would say to this.

And yet this very singleness of vision and thorough oneness with his age is a mark of the successful man. It is as though Nature must needs make men narrow in order to give them force. So Mr. Washington's cult has gained unquestioning followers, his work has wonderfully prospered, his friends are legion, and his enemies are confounded. To-day he stands as the one recognized spokesman of his ten million fellows, and one of the most notable figures in a nation of seventy millions. One hesitates, therefore, to criticise a life which, beginning with so little, has done so much. And yet the time is come when one may speak in all sincerity and utter courtesy of the mistakes and shortcomings of Mr. Washington's career, as well as of his triumphs, without being thought captious or envious, and without forgetting that it is easier to do ill than well in the world.

The criticism that has hitherto met Mr. Washington has not always been of this broad character. In the South especially has he had to walk warily to avoid the harshest judgments,—and naturally so, for he is dealing with the one subject of deepest sensitiveness to that section. Twice—once when at the Chicago celebration of the Spanish-American War he alluded to the color-prejudice that is "eating away the vitals of the South," and once when he dined with President Roosevelt—has the resulting Southern criticism been violent enough to threaten seriously his popularity. In the North the feeling has several times forced itself into words, that Mr. Washington's counsels of submission overlooked certain elements of true manhood, and that his educational programme was unnecessarily narrow. Usually, however, such criticism has not found open expression, although, too, the spiritual sons of the Abolitionists have not been prepared to acknowledge that the schools founded before Tuskegee, by men of broad ideals and self sacrificing spirit, were wholly failures or worthy of ridicule. While, then, criticism has not failed to follow Mr. Washington, yet the prevailing public opinion of the land has been but too willing to deliver the solution of a wearisome problem into his hands, and say, "If that is all you and your race ask, take it."

Among his own people, however, Mr. Washington has encountered the strongest and most lasting opposition, amounting at times to bitterness, and even to-day continuing strong and insistent even though largely silenced in outward expression by the public opinion of the nation. Some of this opposition is, of course, mere envy; the disappointment of displaced demagogues and the spite of narrow minds. But aside from this, there is among educated and thoughtful colored men in all parts of the land a feeling of deep regret, sorrow, and apprehension at the wide currency and ascendancy which some of Mr. Washington's theories have gained. These same men admire his sincerity of purpose, and are willing to forgive much to honest endeavor which is doing something worth the doing. They cooperate with Mr. Washington as far as they conscientiously can; and, indeed, it is no ordinary tribute to this man's tact and power that, steering as he must between so many diverse interests and opinions, he so largely retains the respect of all.

But the hushing of the criticism of honest opponents is a dangerous thing. It leads some of the best of the critics to unfortunate silence and paralysis of effort, and others to burst into speech so passionately and intemperately as to lose listeners. Honest and earnest criticism from those whose interests are most nearly touched,—criticism of writers by readers, of government by those governed, of leaders by those led,—this is the soul of democracy and the safeguard of modern society. If the best of the American Negroes receive by outer pressure a leader whom they had not recognized before, manifestly there is here a certain palpable gain. Yet there is also irreparable loss,—a loss of that peculiarly valuable education which a group receives when by search and criticism it finds and commissions its own leaders. The way in which this is done is at once the most elementary and the nicest problem of social growth. History is but the record of such group-leadership; and yet how infinitely changeful is its type and character! And of all types and kinds, what can be more instructive than the leadership of a group within a group?—that curious double movement where real

progress may be negative and actual advance be relative retrogression. All this is the social student's inspiration and despair.

Now in the past the American Negro has had instructive
experience in the choosing of group leaders, founding thus a
peculiar dynasty which in the light of present conditions is
worth while studying. When sticks and stones and beasts form
the sole environment of a people, their attitude is largely one of
determined opposition to and conquest of natural forces. But
when to earth and brute is added an environment of men and
ideas, then the attitude of the imprisoned group may take three
main forms,—a feeling of revolt and revenge; an attempt to adjust all thought and action to the will of the greater group; or,
finally, a determined effort at self-realization and self-development
despite environing opinion. The influence of all of these attitudes
at various times can be traced in the history of the American
Negro, and in the evolution of his successive leaders.

Before 1750, while the fire of African freedom still burned in
the veins of the slaves, there was in all leadership or attempted
leadership but the one motive of revolt and revenge,—typified
in the terrible Maroons, the Danish blacks, and Cato of Stono,
and veiling all the Americas in fear of insurrection. The liberal-
izing tendencies of the latter half of the eighteenth century
brought, along with kindlier relations between black and white,
thoughts of ultimate adjustment and assimilation. Such aspiration was especially voiced in the earnest songs of Phyllis, in the
martyrdom of Attucks, the fighting of Salem and Poor, the intellectual accomplishments of Banneker and Derham, and the
political demands of the Cuffes.

Stern financial and social stress after the war cooled much of
the previous humanitarian ardor. The disappointment and impatience of the Negroes at the persistence of slavery and serfdom
voiced itself in two movements. The slaves in the South, aroused
undoubtedly by vague rumors of the Haytian revolt, made three
fierce attempts at insurrection,—in 1800 under Gabriel in Virginia, in 1822 under Vesey in Carolina, and in 1831 again in
Virginia under the terrible Nat Turner. In the Free States, on
the other hand, a new and curious attempt at self-development
was made. In Philadelphia and New York color-prescription led

to a withdrawal of Negro communicants from white churches and the formation of a peculiar socio-religious institution among the Negroes known as the African Church,—an organization still living and controlling in its various branches over a million of men.

Walker's wild appeal against the trend of the times showed how the world was changing after the coming of the cotton-gin. By 1830 slavery seemed hopelessly fastened on the South, and the slaves thoroughly cowed into submission. The free Negroes of the North, inspired by the mulatto immigrants from the West Indies, began to change the basis of their demands; they recognized the slavery of slaves, but insisted that they themselves were freemen, and sought assimilation and amalgamation with the nation on the same terms with other men. Thus, Forten and Purvis of Philadelphia, Shad of Wilmington, Du Bois of New Haven, Barbadoes of Boston, and others, strove singly and together as men, they said, not as slaves; as "people of color," not as "Negroes." The trend of the times, however, refused them recognition save in individual and exceptional cases, considered them as one with all the despised blacks, and they soon found themselves striving to keep even the rights they formerly had of voting and working and moving as freemen. Schemes of migration and colonization arose among them; but these they refused to entertain, and they eventually turned to the Abolition movement as a final refuge.

Here, led by Remond, Nell, Wells-Brown, and Douglass, a new period of self-assertion and self-development dawned. To be sure, ultimate freedom and assimilation was the ideal before the leaders, but the assertion of the manhood rights of the Negro by himself was the main reliance, and John Brown's raid was the extreme of its logic. After the war and emancipation, the great form of Frederick Douglass, the greatest of American Negro leaders, still led the host. Self-assertion, especially in political lines, was the main programme, and behind Douglass came Elliot, Bruce, and Langston, and the Reconstruction politicians, and, less conspicuous but of greater social significance Alexander Crummell and Bishop Daniel Payne.

Then came the Revolution of 1876, the suppression of the

Negro votes, the changing and shifting of ideals, and the seeking of new lights in the great night. Douglass, in his old age,
still bravely stood for the ideals of his early manhood,—ultimate
assimilation through self-assertion, and on no other terms. For
a time Price arose as a new leader, destined, it seemed, not to
give up, but to re-state the old ideals in a form less repugnant
to the white South. But he passed away in his prime. Then came
the new leader. Nearly all the former ones had become leaders
by the silent suffrage of their fellows, had sought to lead their
own people alone, and were usually, save Douglass, little known
outside their race. But Booker T. Washington arose as essentially
the leader not of one race but of two,—a compromiser between
the South, the North, and the Negro. Naturally the Negroes
resented, at first bitterly, signs of compromise which surrendered
their civil and political rights, even though this was to be ex-
changed for larger chances of economic development. The rich
and dominating North, however, was not only weary of the
race problem, but was investing largely in Southern enterprises,
and welcomed any method of peaceful cooperation. Thus, by
national opinion, the Negroes began to recognize Mr. Washington's leadership; and the voice of criticism was hushed.

Mr. Washington represents in Negro thought the old attitude
of adjustment and submission; but adjustment at such a peculiar
time as to make his programme unique. This is an age of unusual economic development, and Mr. Washington's programme
naturally takes an economic cast, becoming a gospel of Work
and Money to such an extent as apparently almost completely
to overshadow the higher aims of life. Moreover, this is an age
when the more advanced races are coming in closer contact with
the less developed races, and the race-feeling is therefore intensified; and Mr. Washington's programme practically accepts the
alleged inferiority of the Negro races. Again, in our own land,
the reaction from the sentiment of war time has given impetus
to race-prejudice against Negroes, and Mr. Washington with-
draws many of the high demands of Negroes as men and American citizens. In other periods of intensified prejudice all the
Negro's tendency to self-assertion has been called forth; at this
period a policy of submission is advocated. In the history of

nearly all other races and peoples the doctrine preached at such crises has been that manly self-respect is worth more than lands and houses, and that a people who voluntarily surrender such respect, or cease striving for it, are not worth civilizing.

In answer to this, it has been claimed that the Negro can survive only through submission. Mr. Washington distinctly asks that black people give up, at least for the present, three things,—

First, political power,

Second, insistence on civil rights,

Third, higher education of Negro youth,—and concentrate all their energies on industrial education, the accumulation of wealth, and the conciliation of the South. This policy has been courageously and insistently advocated for over fifteen years, and has been triumphant for perhaps ten years. As a result of this tender of the palm-branch, what has been the return? In these years there have occurred:

1. The disfranchisement of the Negro.
2. The legal creation of a distinct status of civil inferiority for the Negro.
3. The steady withdrawal of aid from institutions for the higher training of the Negro.

These movements are not, to be sure, direct results of Mr. Washington's teachings; but his propaganda has, without a shadow of doubt, helped their speedier accomplishment. The question then comes: Is it possible, and probable, that nine millions of men can make effective progress in economic lines if they are deprived of political rights, made a servile caste, and allowed only the most meagre chance for developing their exceptional men? If history and reason give any distinct answer to these questions, it is an emphatic No. And Mr. Washington thus faces the triple paradox of his career:

1. He is striving nobly to make Negro artisans business men and property-owners; but it is utterly impossible, under modern competitive methods, for workingmen and

property-owners to defend their rights and exist without the right of suffrage.

2. He insists on thrift and self-respect, but at the same time counsels a silent submission to civic inferiority such as is bound to sap the manhood of any race in the long run.

3. He advocates common-school and industrial training, and depreciates institutions of higher learning; but neither the Negro common-schools, nor Tuskegee itself, could remain open a day were it not for teachers trained in Negro colleges, or trained by their graduates.

This triple paradox in Mr. Washington's position is the object of criticism by two classes of colored Americans. One class is spiritually descended from Toussaint the Savior, through Gabriel, Vesey, and Turner, and they represent the attitude of revolt and revenge; they hate the white South blindly and distrust the white race generally, and so far as they agree on definite action, think that the Negro's only hope lies in emigration beyond the borders of the United States. And yet, by the irony of fate, nothing has more effectually made this programme seem hopeless than the recent course of the United States toward weaker and darker peoples in the West Indies, Hawaii, and the Philippines,—for where in the world may we go and be safe from lying and brute force?

The other class of Negroes who cannot agree with Mr. Washington has hitherto said little aloud. They deprecate the sight of scattered counsels, of internal disagreement; and especially they dislike making their just criticism of a useful and earnest man an excuse for a general discharge of venom from small-minded opponents. Nevertheless, the questions involved are so fundamental and serious that it is difficult to see how men like the Grimkes, Kelly Miller, J. W. E. Bowen, and other representatives of this group, can much longer be silent. Such men feel in conscience bound to ask of this nation three things:

1. The right to vote.
2. Civic equality.
3. The education of youth according to ability.

They acknowledge Mr. Washington's invaluable service in coun-selling patience and courtesy in such demands; they do not ask that ignorant black men vote when ignorant whites are de-barred, or that any reasonable restrictions in the suffrage should not be applied; they know that the low social level of the mass of the race is responsible for much discrimination against it, but they also know, and the nation knows, that relentless color-prejudice is more often a cause than a result of the Negro's deg-radation; they seek the abatement of this relic of barbarism, and not its systematic encouragement and pampering by all agencies of social power from the Associated Press to the Church of Christ. They advocate, with Mr. Washington, a broad system of Negro common schools supplemented by thorough industrial training; but they are surprised that a man of Mr. Washington's insight cannot see that no such educational system ever has rested or can rest on any other basis than that of the well-equipped college and university, and they insist that there is a demand for a few such institutions throughout the South to train the best of the Negro youth as teachers, professional men, and leaders.

This group of men honor Mr. Washington for his attitude of conciliation toward the white South; they accept the "Atlanta Compromise" in its broadest interpretation; they recognize, with him, many signs of promise, many men of high purpose and fair judgment, in this section; they know that no easy task has been laid upon a region already tottering under heavy bur-dens. But, nevertheless, they insist that the way to truth and right lies in straightforward honesty, not in indiscriminate flat-tery; in praising those of the South who do well and criticising uncompromisingly those who do ill; in taking advantage of the opportunities at hand and urging their fellows to do the same, but at the same time in remembering that only a firm adherence to their higher ideals and aspirations will ever keep those ideals within the realm of possibility. They do not expect that the free right to vote, to enjoy civic rights, and to be educated, will come in a moment; they do not expect to see the bias and prejudices of years disappear at the blast of a trumpet; but they are abso-lutely certain that the way for a people to gain their reasonable

rights is not by voluntarily throwing them away and insisting
that they do not want them; that the way for a people to gain
respect is not by continually belittling and ridiculing themselves;
that, on the contrary, Negroes must insist continually, in season
and out of season, that voting is necessary to modern manhood,
that color discrimination is barbarism, and that black boys need
education as well as white boys.

In failing thus to state plainly and unequivocally the legitimate demands of their people, even at the cost of opposing an
honored leader, the thinking classes of American Negroes would
shirk a heavy responsibility,—a responsibility to themselves, a
responsibility to the struggling masses, a responsibility to the
darker races of men whose future depends so largely on this
American experiment, but especially a responsibility to this
nation,—this common Fatherland. It is wrong to encourage a
man or a people in evil-doing; it is wrong to aid and abet a national crime simply because it is unpopular not to do so. The
growing spirit of kindliness and reconciliation between the
North and South after the frightful differences of a generation
ago ought to be a source of deep congratulation to all, and especially to those whose mistreatment caused the war; but if that
reconciliation is to be marked by the industrial slavery and civic
death of those same black men, with permanent legislation into
a position of inferiority, then those black men, if they are really
men, are called upon by every consideration of patriotism and
loyalty to oppose such a course by all civilized methods, even
though such opposition involves disagreement with Mr. Booker
T. Washington. We have no right to sit silently by while the inevitable seeds are sown for a harvest of disaster to our children,
black and white.

First, it is the duty of black men to judge the South discrimi-
natingly. The present generation of Southerners are not responsible for the past, and they should not be blindly hated or blamed
for it. Furthermore, to no class is the indiscriminate endorse-
ment of the recent course of the South toward Negroes more
nauseating than to the best thought of the South. The South is
not "solid"; it is a land in the ferment of social change, wherein
forces of all kinds are fighting for supremacy; and to praise the

ill the South is to-day perpetrating is just as wrong as to condemn the good. Discriminating and broad-minded criticism is what the South needs,—needs it for the sake of her own white sons and daughters, and for the insurance of robust, healthy mental and moral development.

To-day even the attitude of the Southern whites toward the blacks is not, as so many assume, in all cases the same; the ignorant Southerner hates the Negro, the workingmen fear his competition, the money-makers wish to use him as a laborer, some of the educated see a menace in his upward development, while others—usually the sons of the masters—wish to help him to rise. National opinion has enabled this last class to maintain the Negro common schools, and to protect the Negro partially in property, life, and limb. Through the pressure of the money-makers, the Negro is in danger of being reduced to semi-slavery, especially in the country districts; the workingmen, and those of the educated who fear the Negro, have united to disfranchise him, and some have urged his deportation; while the passions of the ignorant are easily aroused to lynch and abuse any black man. To praise this intricate whirl of thought and prejudice is nonsense; to inveigh indiscriminately against "the South" is unjust; but to use the same breath in praising Governor Aycock, exposing Senator Morgan, arguing with Mr. Thomas Nelson Page, and denouncing Senator Ben Tillman, is not only sane, but the imperative duty of thinking black men.

It would be unjust to Mr. Washington not to acknowledge that in several instances he has opposed movements in the South which were unjust to the Negro; he sent memorials to the Louisiana and Alabama constitutional conventions, he has spoken against lynching, and in other ways has openly or silently set his influence against sinister schemes and unfortunate happenings. Notwithstanding this, it is equally true to assert that on the whole the distinct impression left by Mr. Washington's propaganda is, first, that the South is justified in its present attitude toward the Negro because of the Negro's degradation; secondly, that the prime cause of the Negro's failure to rise more quickly is his wrong education in the past; and, thirdly, that his future rise depends primarily on his own efforts. Each of these

propositions is a dangerous half-truth. The supplementary
truths must never be lost sight of: first, slavery and race-prejudice
are potent if not sufficient causes of the Negro's position; second, industrial and common-school training were necessarily
slow in planting because they had to await the black teachers
trained by higher institutions,—it being extremely doubtful if
any essentially different development was possible, and certainly
a Tuskegee was unthinkable before 1880; and, third, while it is
a great truth to say that the Negro must strive and strive mightily to help himself, it is equally true that unless his striving be
not simply seconded, but rather aroused and encouraged, by
the initiative of the richer and wiser environing group, he cannot hope for great success.

In his failure to realize and impress this last point, Mr. Washington is especially to be criticised. His doctrine has tended to
make the whites, North and South, shift the burden of the
Negro problem to the Negro's shoulders and stand aside as
critical and rather pessimistic spectators; when in fact the burden belongs to the nation, and the hands of none of us are clean
if we bend not our energies to righting these great wrongs.

The South ought to be led, by candid and honest criticism,
to assert her better self and do her full duty to the race she has
cruelly wronged and is still wronging. The North—her copart-
ner in guilt—cannot salve her conscience by plastering it with
gold. We cannot settle this problem by diplomacy and suave-
ness, by "policy" alone. If worse comes to worst, can the moral
fibre of this country survive the slow throttling and murder of
nine millions of men?

The black men of America have a duty to perform, a duty
stern and delicate,—a forward movement to oppose a part of
the work of their greatest leader. So far as Mr. Washington
preaches Thrift, Patience, and Industrial Training for the
masses, we must hold up his hands and strive with him, rejoic-
ing in his honors and glorying in the strength of this Joshua
called of God and of man to lead the headless host. But so far
as Mr. Washington apologizes for injustice, North or South,
does not rightly value the privilege and duty of voting, belittles
the emasculating effects of caste distinctions, and opposes the

higher training and ambition of our brighter minds,—so far as he, the South, or the Nation, does this,—we must unceasingly and firmly oppose them. By every civilized and peaceful method we must strive for the rights which the world accords to men, clinging unwaveringly to those great words which the sons of the Fathers would fain forget: "We hold these truths to be self-evident: That all men are created equal; that they are endowed by their Creator with certain unalienable rights; that among these are life, liberty, and the pursuit of happiness."

IV

OF THE MEANING OF PROGRESS

Willst Du Deine Macht verkünden,
Wähle sie die frei von Sünden,
Steh'n in Deinem ew'gen Haus!
Deine Geister sende aus!
Die Unsterblichen, die Reinen,
Die nicht fühlen, die nicht weinen!
Nicht die zarte Jungfrau wähle,
Nicht der Hirtin weiche Seele!

SCHILLER

Once upon a time I taught school in the hills of Tennessee,
where the broad dark vale of the Mississippi begins to roll and
crumple to greet the Alleghanies. I was a Fisk student then, and
all Fisk men thought that Tennessee—beyond the Veil—was
theirs alone, and in vacation time they sallied forth in lusty
bands to meet the county school-commissioners. Young and
happy, I too went, and I shall not soon forget that summer, seventeen years ago.

First, there was a Teachers' Institute at the county-seat; and there distinguished guests of the superintendent taught the teachers fractions and spelling and other mysteries,—white teachers in the morning, Negroes at night. A picnic now and then, and a supper, and the rough world was softened by laughter and song. I remember how— But I wander.

There came a day when all the teachers left the Institute and began the hunt for schools. I learn from hearsay (for my mother was mortally afraid of fire-arms) that the hunting of ducks and bears and men is wonderfully interesting, but I am sure that the man who has never hunted a country school has something to learn of the pleasures of the chase. I see now the white, hot roads lazily rise and fall and wind before me under the burning July sun; I feel the deep weariness of heart and limb as ten, eight, six miles stretch relentlessly ahead; I feel my heart sink heavily as I hear again and again, "Got a teacher? Yes." So I walked on and on—horses were too expensive—until I had wandered beyond railways, beyond stage lines, to a land of "varmints" and rattlesnakes, where the coming of a stranger was an event, and men lived and died in the shadow of one blue hill.

Sprinkled over hill and dale lay cabins and farmhouses, shut out from the world by the forests and the rolling hills toward the east. There I found at last a little school. Josie told me of it; she was a thin, homely girl of twenty, with a dark-brown face and thick, hard hair. I had crossed the stream at Watertown, and rested under the great willows; then I had gone to the little cabin in the lot where Josie was resting on her way to town. The gaunt farmer made me welcome, and Josie, hearing my errand, told me anxiously that they wanted a school over the hill; that but once since the war had a teacher been there; that she herself longed to learn,—and thus she ran on, talking fast and loud, with much earnestness and energy.

Next morning I crossed the tall round hill, lingered to look at the blue and yellow mountains stretching toward the Carolinas, then plunged into the wood, and came out at Josie's home. It was a dull frame cottage with four rooms, perched just below the brow of the hill, amid peach-trees. The father was a quiet,

simple soul, calmly ignorant, with no touch of vulgarity. The
mother was different,—strong, bustling, and energetic, with a
quick, restless tongue, and an ambition to live "like folks."
There was a crowd of children. Two boys had gone away. There
remained two growing girls; a shy midget of eight; John, tall,
awkward, and eighteen; Jim, younger, quicker, and better looking; and two babies of indefinite age. Then there was Josie herself. She seemed to be the centre of the family: always busy at
service, or at home, or berry-picking; a little nervous and inclined to scold, like her mother, yet faithful, too, like her father.
She had about her a certain fineness, the shadow of an uncon-
scious moral heroism that would willingly give all of life to make
life broader, deeper, and fuller for her and hers. I saw much of
this family afterwards, and grew to love them for their honest
efforts to be decent and comfortable, and for their knowledge
of their own ignorance. There was with them no affectation.
The mother would scold the father for being so "easy"; Josie
would roundly berate the boys for carelessness; and all knew
that it was a hard thing to dig a living out of a rocky side-hill.

I secured the school. I remember the day I rode horseback out
to the commissioner's house with a pleasant young white fellow
who wanted the white school. The road ran down the bed of a
stream; the sun laughed and the water jingled, and we rode on.
"Come in," said the commissioner,—"come in. Have a seat.
Yes, that certificate will do. Stay to dinner. What do you want
a month?" "Oh," thought I, "this is lucky"; but even then fell
the awful shadow of the Veil, for they ate first, then I—alone.

The schoolhouse was a log hut, where Colonel Wheeler used
to shelter his corn. It sat in a lot behind a rail fence and thorn
bushes, near the sweetest of springs. There was an entrance
where a door once was, and within, a massive rickety fireplace;
great chinks between the logs served as windows. Furniture was
scarce. A pale blackboard crouched in the corner. My desk was
made of three boards, reinforced at critical points, and my chair,
borrowed from the landlady, had to be returned every night.
Seats for the children—these puzzled me much. I was haunted
by a New England vision of neat little desks and chairs, but,

alas! the reality was rough plank benches without backs, and at times without legs. They had the one virtue of making naps dangerous,—possibly fatal, for the floor was not to be trusted.

It was a hot morning late in July when the school opened. I trembled when I heard the patter of little feet down the dusty road, and saw the growing row of dark solemn faces and bright eager eyes facing me. First came Josie and her brothers and sisters. The longing to know, to be a student in the great school at Nashville, hovered like a star above this child-woman amid her work and worry, and she studied doggedly. There were the Dowells from their farm over toward Alexandria,—Fanny, with her smooth black face and wondering eyes; Martha, brown and dull; the pretty girl-wife of a brother, and the younger brood.

There were the Burkes,—two brown and yellow lads, and a tiny haughty-eyed girl. Fat Reuben's little chubby girl came, with golden face and old-gold hair, faithful and solemn. 'Thenie was on hand early,—a jolly, ugly, good-hearted girl, who slyly dipped snuff and looked after her little bow-legged brother. When her mother could spare her, 'Tildy came,—a midnight beauty, with starry eyes and tapering limbs; and her brother, correspondingly homely. And then the big boys,—the hulking Lawrences; the lazy Neills, unfathered sons of mother and daughter; Hickman, with a stoop in his shoulders; and the rest.

There they sat, nearly thirty of them, on the rough benches, their faces shading from a pale cream to a deep brown, the little feet bare and swinging, the eyes full of expectation, with here and there a twinkle of mischief, and the hands grasping Webster's blue-back spelling-book. I loved my school, and the fine faith the children had in the wisdom of their teacher was truly marvellous. We read and spelled together, wrote a little, picked flowers, sang, and listened to stories of the world beyond the hill. At times the school would dwindle away, and I would start out. I would visit Mun Eddings, who lived in two very dirty rooms, and ask why little Lugene, whose flaming face seemed ever ablaze with the dark-red hair uncombed, was absent all last week, or why I missed so often the inimitable rags of Mack and Ed. Then the father, who worked Colonel

Wheeler's farm on shares, would tell me how the crops needed the boys; and the thin, slovenly mother, whose face was pretty when washed, assured me that Lugene must mind the baby. "But we'll start them again next week." When the Lawrences stopped, I knew that the doubts of the old folks about book-learning had conquered again, and so, toiling up the hill, and getting as far into the cabin as possible, I put Cicero "pro Archia Poeta" into the simplest English with local applications, and usually convinced them—for a week or so.

On Friday nights I often went home with some of the children,—sometimes to Doc Burke's farm. He was a great, loud, thin Black, ever working, and trying to buy the seventy-five acres of hill and dale where he lived; but people said that he would surely fail, and the "white folks would get it all." His wife was a magnificent Amazon, with saffron face and shining hair, uncorseted and barefooted, and the children were strong and beautiful. They lived in a one-and-a-half-room cabin in the hollow of the farm, near the spring. The front room was full of great fat white beds, scrupulously neat; and there were bad chromos on the walls, and a tired centre-table. In the tiny back kitchen I was often invited to "take out and help" myself to fried chicken and wheat biscuit, "meat" and corn pone, string-beans and berries. At first I used to be a little alarmed at the approach of bedtime in the one lone bedroom, but embarrassment was very deftly avoided. First, all the children nodded and slept, and were stowed away in one great pile of goose feathers; next, the mother and the father discreetly slipped away to the kitchen while I went to bed; then, blowing out the dim light, they retired in the dark. In the morning all were up and away before I thought of awaking. Across the road, where fat Reuben lived, they all went outdoors while the teacher retired, because they did not boast the luxury of a kitchen.

I liked to stay with the Dowells, for they had four rooms and plenty of good country fare. Uncle Bird had a small, rough farm, all woods and hills, miles from the big road; but he was full of tales,—he preached now and then,—and with his children, ber-ries, horses, and wheat he was happy and prosperous. Often, to keep the peace, I must go where life was less lovely; for instance, 'Tildy's mother was incorrigibly dirty, Reuben's larder was limited seriously, and herds of untamed insects wandered over the Eddingses' beds. Best of all I loved to go to Josie's, and sit on the porch, eating peaches, while the mother bustled and talked: how Josie had bought the sewing-machine; how Josie worked at service in winter, but that four dollars a month was "mighty little" wages; how Josie longed to go away to school, but that it "looked like" they never could get far enough ahead to let her; how the crops failed and the well was yet unfinished; and, finally, how "mean" some of the white folks were.

For two summers I lived in this little world; it was dull and humdrum. The girls looked at the hill in wistful longing, and the boys fretted and haunted Alexandria. Alexandria was "town,"—a straggling, lazy village of houses, churches, and shops, and an aristocracy of Toms, Dicks, and Captains. Cuddled on the hill to the north was the village of the colored folks, who lived in three- or four-room unpainted cottages, some neat and homelike, and some dirty. The dwellings were scattered rather aimlessly, but they centered about the twin temples of the hamlet, the Methodist, and the Hard-Shell Baptist churches. These, in turn, leaned gingerly on a sad-colored schoolhouse. Hither my little world wended its crooked way on Sunday to meet other worlds, and gossip, and wonder, and make the weekly sacrifice with frenzied priest at the altar of the "old-time religion." Then the soft melody and mighty cadences of Negro song fluttered and thundered.

I have called my tiny community a world, and so its isolation made it; and yet there was among us but a half-awakened common consciousness, sprung from common joy and grief, at burial, birth, or wedding; from a common hardship in poverty, poor land, and low wages; and, above all, from the sight of the Veil that hung between us and Opportunity. All this caused us to think some thoughts together; but these, when ripe for speech, were spoken in various languages. Those whose eyes twenty-five and more years before had seen "the glory of the coming of the Lord," saw in every present hindrance or help a dark fatalism bound to bring all things right in His own good time. The mass of those to whom slavery was a dim recollection of childhood found the world a puzzling thing: it asked little of them, and they answered with little, and yet it ridiculed their offering. Such a paradox they could not understand, and therefore sank into listless indifference, or shiftlessness, or reckless bravado. There were, however, some—such as Josie, Jim, and Ben—to whom War, Hell, and Slavery were but childhood tales, whose young appetites had been whetted to an edge by school and story and half-awakened thought. Ill could they be content, born without and beyond the World. And their weak wings beat against their barriers,—barriers of caste, of youth, of life; at last, in dangerous moments, against everything that opposed even a whim.

The ten years that follow youth, the years when first the realization comes that life is leading somewhere,—these were the years that passed after I left my little school. When they were past, I came by chance once more to the walls of Fisk University, to the halls of the chapel of melody. As I lingered there in the joy and pain of meeting old school-friends, there swept over me a sudden longing to pass again beyond the blue hill, and to see the homes and the school of other days, and to learn how life had gone with my school-children; and I went.

Josie was dead, and the gray-haired mother said simply, "We've had a heap of trouble since you've been away." I had feared for Jim. With a cultured parentage and a social caste to uphold him, he might have made a venturesome merchant or a West Point cadet. But here he was, angry with life and reckless; and when Farmer Durham charged him with stealing wheat, the old man had to ride fast to escape the stones which the furious fool hurled after him. They told Jim to run away; but he would not run, and the constable came that afternoon. It grieved Josie, and great awkward John walked nine miles every day to see his little brother through the bars of Lebanon jail. At last the two came back together in the dark night. The mother cooked supper, and Josie emptied her purse, and the boys stole away. Josie grew thin and silent, yet worked the more. The hill became steep for the quiet old father, and with the boys away there was little to do in the valley. Josie helped them to sell the old farm, and they moved nearer town. Brother Dennis, the carpenter, built a new house with six rooms; Josie toiled a year in Nashville, and brought back ninety dollars to furnish the house and change it to a home.

When the spring came, and the birds twittered, and the stream ran proud and full, little sister Lizzie, bold and thoughtless, flushed with the passion of youth, bestowed herself on the tempter, and brought home a nameless child. Josie shivered and worked on, with the vision of schooldays all fled, with a face wan and tired,—worked until, on a summer's day, some one married another; then Josie crept to her mother like a hurt child, and slept—and sleeps.

I paused to scent the breeze as I entered the valley. The Lawrences have gone,—father and son forever,—and the other son lazily digs in the earth to live. A new young widow rents out their cabin to fat Reuben. Reuben is a Baptist preacher now, but I fear as lazy as ever, though his cabin has three rooms; and little Ella has grown into a bouncing woman, and is ploughing corn on the hot hillside. There are babies a-plenty, and one half-witted girl. Across the valley is a house I did not know before, and there I found, rocking one baby and expecting another, one of my schoolgirls, a daughter of Uncle Bird Dowell. She looked somewhat worried with her new duties, but soon bristled into pride over her neat cabin and the tale of her thrifty husband, the horse and cow, and the farm they were planning to buy.

My log schoolhouse was gone. In its place stood Progress; and Progress, I understand, is necessarily ugly. The crazy foundation stones still marked the former site of my poor little cabin, and not far away, on six weary boulders, perched a jaunty board house, perhaps twenty by thirty feet, with three windows and a door that locked. Some of the window-glass was broken, and part of an old iron stove lay mournfully under the house. I peeped through the window half reverently, and found things that were more familiar. The blackboard had grown by about two feet, and the seats were still without backs. The county owns the lot now, I hear, and every year there is a session of school. As I sat by the spring and looked on the Old and the New I felt glad, very glad, and yet—

After two long drinks I started on. There was the great double log-house on the corner. I remembered the broken, blighted family that used to live there. The strong, hard face of the mother, with its wilderness of hair, rose before me. She had driven her husband away, and while I taught school a strange man lived there, big and jovial, and people talked. I felt sure that Ben and 'Tildy would come to naught from such a home. But this is an odd world; for Ben is a busy farmer in Smith County, "doing well, too," they say, and he had cared for little 'Tildy until last spring, when a lover married her. A hard life the lad had led, toiling for meat, and laughed at because he was homely and crooked. There was Sam Carlon, an impudent old skinflint, who had definite notions about "niggers," and hired Ben a summer and would not pay him. Then the hungry boy gathered his sacks together, and in broad daylight went into Carlon's corn; and when the hard-fisted farmer set upon him, the angry boy flew at him like a beast. Doc Burke saved a murder and a lynching that day.

The story reminded me again of the Burkes, and an impatience seized me to know who won in the battle, Doc or the seventy-five acres. For it is a hard thing to make a farm out of nothing, even in fifteen years. So I hurried on, thinking of the Burkes. They used to have a certain magnificent barbarism about them that I liked. They were never vulgar, never immoral, but rather rough and primitive, with an unconventionality that spent itself in loud guffaws, slaps on the back, and naps in the corner. I hurried by the cottage of the misborn Neill boys. It was empty, and they were grown into fat, lazy farm-hands. I saw the home of the Hickmans, but Albert, with his stooping shoulders, had passed from the world. Then I came to the Burkes' gate and peered through; the inclosure looked rough and untrimmed, and yet there were the same fences around the old farm save to the left, where lay twenty-five other acres. And lo! the cabin in the hollow had climbed the hill and swollen to a half-finished six-room cottage.

The Burkes held a hundred acres, but they were still in debt. Indeed, the gaunt father who toiled night and day would scarcely be happy out of debt, being so used to it. Some day he must stop, for his massive frame is showing decline. The mother wore shoes, but the lion-like physique of other days was broken. The children had grown up. Rob, the image of his father, was loud and rough with laughter. Birdie, my school baby of six, had grown to a picture of maiden beauty, tall and tawny. "Edgar is gone," said the mother, with head half bowed,—"gone to work in Nashville; he and his father couldn't agree."

Little Doc, the boy born since the time of my school, took me horseback down the creek next morning toward Farmer Dowell's. The road and the stream were battling for mastery, and the stream had the better of it. We splashed and waded, and the merry boy, perched behind me, chattered and laughed. He showed me where Simon Thompson had bought a bit of ground and a home; but his daughter Lana, a plump, brown, slow girl, was not there. She had married a man and a farm twenty miles away. We wound on down the stream till we came to a gate that I did not recognize, but the boy insisted that it was "Uncle Bird's." The farm was fat with the growing crop. In that little valley was a strange stillness as I rode up; for death and marriage had stolen youth and left age and childhood there. We sat and talked that night after the chores were done. Uncle Bird was grayer, and his eyes did not see so well, but he was still jovial. We talked of the acres bought,—one hundred and twenty-five,—of the new guest-chamber added, of Martha's marrying. Then we talked of death: Fanny and Fred were gone; a shadow hung over the other daughter, and when it lifted she was to go to Nashville to school. At last we spoke of the neighbors, and as night fell, Uncle Bird told me how, on a night like that, 'Thenie came wandering back to her home over yonder, to escape the blows of her husband. And next morning she died in the home that her little bow-legged brother, working and saving, had bought for their widowed mother.

My journey was done, and behind me lay hill and dale, and

Life and Death. How shall man measure Progress there where the dark-faced Josie lies? How many heartfuls of sorrow shall balance a bushel of wheat? How hard a thing is life to the lowly, and yet how human and real! And all this life and love and strife and failure,—is it the twilight of nightfall or the flush of some faint-dawning day?

Thus sadly musing, I rode to Nashville in the Jim Crow car.

V

OF THE WINGS OF
ATALANTA

O black boy of Atlanta!
  But half was spoken;
The slave's chains and the master's
  like are broken;
The one curse of the races
  Held both in tether;
They are rising—all are rising—
  The black and white together.

WHITTIER

South of the North, yet north of the South, lies the City of a
Hundred Hills, peering out from the shadows of the past into
the promise of the future. I have seen her in the morning, when
the first flush of day had half-roused her; she lay gray and still
on the crimson soil of Georgia; then the blue smoke began to
curl from her chimneys, the tinkle of bell and scream of whistle
broke the silence, the rattle and roar of busy life slowly gathered
and swelled, until the seething whirl of the city seemed a strange
thing in a sleepy land.

Once, they say, even Atlanta slept dull and drowsy at the

foot-hills of the Alleghanies, until the iron baptism of war awakened her with its sullen waters, aroused and maddened her, and
left her listening to the sea. And the sea cried to the hills and the
hills answered the sea, till the city rose like a widow and cast
away her weeds, and toiled for her daily bread; toiled steadily,
toiled cunningly,—perhaps with some bitterness, with a touch
of *réclame*,—and yet with real earnestness, and real sweat.

It is a hard thing to live haunted by the ghost of an untrue
dream; to see the wide vision of empire fade into real ashes and
dirt; to feel the pang of the conquered, and yet know that with
all the Bad that fell on one black day, something was vanquished
that deserved to live, something killed that in justice had not
dared to die; to know that with the Right that triumphed, triumphed something of Wrong, something sordid and mean,
something less than the broadest and best. All this is bitter hard;
and many a man and city and people have found in it excuse
for sulking, and brooding, and listless waiting.

Such are not men of the sturdier make; they of Atlanta turned
resolutely toward the future; and that future held aloft vistas of
purple and gold:—Atlanta, Queen of the cotton kingdom; Atlanta, Gateway to the Land of the Sun; Atlanta, the new Lachesis, spinner of web and woof for the world. So the city crowned
her hundred hills with factories, and stored her shops with cunning handiwork, and stretched long iron ways to greet the busy
Mercury in his coming. And the Nation talked of her striving.

Perhaps Atlanta was not christened for the winged maiden of
dull Bœotia; you know the tale,—how swarthy Atalanta, tall
and wild, would marry only him who out-raced her; and how
the wily Hippomenes laid three apples of gold in the way. She
fled like a shadow, paused, startled over the first apple, but even
as he stretched his hand, fled again; hovered over the second,
then, slipping from his hot grasp, flew over river, vale, and hill;
but as she lingered over the third, his arms fell round her, and
looking on each other, the blazing passion of their love profaned
the sanctuary of Love, and they were cursed. If Atlanta be not
named for Atalanta, she ought to have been.

Atalanta is not the first or the last maiden whom greed of

gold has led to defile the temple of Love; and not maids alone, but men in the race of life, sink from the high and generous ideals of youth to the gambler's code of the Bourse; and in all our Nation's striving is not the Gospel of Work befouled by the Gospel of Pay? So common is this that one-half think it normal; so unquestioned, that we almost fear to question if the end of racing is not gold, if the aim of man is not rightly to be rich. And if this is the fault of America, how dire a danger lies before a new land and a new city, lest Atlanta, stooping for mere gold, shall find that gold accursed!

It was no maiden's idle whim that started this hard racing; a fearful wilderness lay about the feet of that city after the War,— feudalism, poverty, the rise of the Third Estate, serfdom, the re-birth of Law and Order, and above and between all, the Veil of Race. How heavy a journey for weary feet! what wings must Atalanta have to flit over all this hollow and hill, through sour wood and sullen water, and by the red waste of sun-baked clay! How fleet must Atalanta be if she will not be tempted by gold to profane the Sanctuary!

The Sanctuary of our fathers has, to be sure, few Gods,— some sneer, "all too few." There is the thrifty Mercury of New England, Pluto of the North, and Ceres of the West; and there, too, is the half-forgotten Apollo of the South, under whose ægis the maiden ran,—and as she ran she forgot him, even as there in Bœotia Venus was forgot. She forgot the old ideal of the Southern gentleman,—that new-world heir of the grace and courtliness of patrician, knight, and noble; forgot his honor with his foibles, his kindliness with his carelessness, and stooped to apples of gold,—to men busier and sharper, thriftier and more unscrupulous. Golden apples are beautiful—I remember the lawless days of boyhood, when orchards in crimson and gold tempted me over fence and field—and, too, the merchant who has dethroned the planter is no despicable *parvenu*. Work and wealth are the mighty levers to lift this old new land; thrift and toil and saving are the highways to new hopes and new possibilities; and yet the warning is needed lest the wily Hippomenes tempt Atalanta to thinking that golden apples are the goal of racing, and not mere incidents by the way.

Atlanta must not lead the South to dream of material prosperity as the touchstone of all success; already the fatal might
of this idea is beginning to spread; it is replacing the finer type
of Southerner with vulgar money-getters; it is burying the
sweeter beauties of Southern life beneath pretence and ostenta-
tion. For every social ill the panacea of Wealth has been urged,—
wealth to overthrow the remains of the slave feudalism; wealth
to raise the "cracker" Third Estate; wealth to employ the black
serfs, and the prospect of wealth to keep them working; wealth
as the end and aim of politics, and as the legal tender for law
and order; and, finally, instead of Truth, Beauty, and Goodness,
wealth as the ideal of the Public School.

Not only is this true in the world which Atlanta typifies, but
it is threatening to be true of a world beneath and beyond that
world,—the Black World beyond the Veil. To-day it makes little
difference to Atlanta, to the South, what the Negro thinks or
dreams or wills. In the soul-life of the land he is to-day, and
naturally will long remain, unthought of, half forgotten; and yet
when he does come to think and will and do for himself,—and
let no man dream that day will never come,—then the part he
plays will not be one of sudden learning, but words and thoughts
he has been taught to lisp in his race-childhood. To day the ferment of his striving toward self-realization is to the strife of the
white world like a wheel within a wheel: beyond the Veil are
smaller but like problems of ideals, of leaders and the led, of
serfdom, of poverty, of order and subordination, and, through
all, the Veil of Race. Few know of these problems, few who know
notice them; and yet there they are, awaiting student, artist, and
seer,—a field for somebody sometime to discover. Hither has the
temptation of Hippomenes penetrated; already in this smaller
world, which now indirectly and anon directly must influence
the larger for good or ill, the habit is forming of interpreting the
world in dollars. The old leaders of Negro opinion, in the little
groups where there is a Negro social consciousness, are being
replaced by new; neither the black preacher nor the black teacher
leads as he did two decades ago. Into their places are pushing
the farmers and gardeners, the well-paid porters and artisans,

the businessmen,—all those with property and money. And with all this change, so curiously parallel to that of the Other-world, goes too the same inevitable change in ideals. The South laments to-day the slow, steady disappearance of a certain type of Negro,—the faithful, courteous slave of other days, with his incorruptible honesty and dignified humility. He is passing away just as surely as the old type of Southern gentleman is passing, and from not dissimilar causes,—the sudden transformation of a fair far-off ideal of Freedom into the hard reality of bread-winning and the consequent deification of Bread.

In the Black World, the Preacher and Teacher embodied once the ideals of this people,—the strife for another and a juster world, the vague dream of righteousness, the mystery of know-ing; but to-day the danger is that these ideals, with their simple beauty and weird inspiration, will suddenly sink to a question of cash and a lust for gold. Here stands this black young Ata-lanta, girding herself for the race that must be run; and if her eyes be still toward the hills and sky as in the days of old, then we may look for noble running; but what if some ruthless or wily or even thoughtless Hippomenes lay golden apples before her? What if the Negro people be wooed from a strife for righ-teousness, from a love of knowing, to regard dollars as the be-all and end-all of life? What if to the Mammonism of America be added the rising Mammonism of the reborn South, and the Mammonism of this South be reinforced by the budding Mam-monism of its half-awakened black millions? Whither, then, is the new-world quest of Goodness and Beauty and Truth gone glimmering? Must this, and that fair flower of Freedom which, despite the jeers of latter-day striplings, sprung from our fathers' blood, must that too degenerate into a dusty quest of gold,—into lawless lust with Hippomenes?

The hundred hills of Atlanta are not all crowned with factories. On one, toward the west, the setting sun throws three buildings in bold relief against the sky. The beauty of the group lies in its simple unity:—a broad lawn of green rising from the red street with mingled roses and peaches; north and south, two plain

and stately halls; and in the midst, half hidden in ivy, a larger
building, boldly graceful, sparingly decorated, and with one
low spire. It is a restful group,—one never looks for more; it is
all here, all intelligible. There I live, and there I hear from day
to day the low hum of restful life. In winter's twilight, when the
red sun glows, I can see the dark figures pass between the halls
to the music of the night-bell. In the morning, when the sun is
golden, the clang of the day-bell brings the hurry and laughter
of three hundred young hearts from hall and street, and from
the busy city below,—children all dark and heavy-haired,—to
join their clear young voices in the music of the morning sacrifice. In a half-dozen class-rooms they gather then,—here to follow the love-song of Dido, here to listen to the tale of Troy
divine; there to wander among the stars, there to wander among
men and nations,—and elsewhere other well-worn ways of knowing this queer world. Nothing new, no time-saving devices,—
simply old time-glorified methods of delving for Truth, and
searching out the hidden beauties of life, and learning the good
of living. The riddle of existence is the college curriculum that
was laid before the Pharaohs, that was taught in the groves by
Plato, that formed the *trivium* and *quadrivium*, and is to-day
laid before the freedmen's sons by Atlanta University. And this
course of study will not change; its methods will grow more
deft and effectual, its content richer by toil of scholar and sight
of seer; but the true college will ever have one goal,—not to
earn meat, but to know the end and aim of that life which meat
nourishes.

The vision of life that rises before these dark eyes has in it
nothing mean or selfish. Not at Oxford or at Leipsic, not at Yale
or Columbia, is there an air of higher resolve or more unfettered
striving; the determination to realize for men, both black and
white, the broadest possibilities of life, to seek the better and the
best, to spread with their own hands the Gospel of Sacrifice,—
all this is the burden of their talk and dream. Here, amid a wide
desert of caste and proscription, amid the heart-hurting slights
and jars and vagaries of a deep race-dislike, lies this green oasis,
where hot anger cools, and the bitterness of disappointment is
sweetened by the springs and breezes of Parnassus; and here

men may lie and listen, and learn of a future fuller than the past, and hear the voice of Time:

"Entbehren sollst du, sollst entbehren."

They made their mistakes, those who planted Fisk and Howard and Atlanta before the smoke of battle had lifted; they made their mistakes, but those mistakes were not the things at which we lately laughed somewhat uproariously. They were right when they sought to found a new educational system upon the University: where, forsooth, shall we ground knowledge save on the broadest and deepest knowledge? The roots of the tree, rather than the leaves, are the sources of its life; and from the dawn of history, from Academus to Cambridge, the culture of the University has been the broad foundation-stone on which is built the kindergarten's ABC.

But these builders did make a mistake in minimizing the gravity of the problem before them; in thinking it a matter of years and decades; in therefore building quickly and laying their foundation carelessly, and lowering the standard of knowing, until they had scattered haphazard through the South some dozen poorly equipped high schools and miscalled them universities. They forgot, too, just as their successors are forgetting, the rule of inequality:—that of the million black youth, some were fitted to know and some to dig; that some had the talent and capacity of university men, and some the talent and capacity of blacksmiths; and that true training meant neither that all should be college men nor all artisans, but that the one should be made a missionary of culture to an untaught people, and the other a free workman among serfs. And to seek to make the blacksmith a scholar is almost as silly as the more modern scheme of making the scholar a blacksmith; almost, but not quite.

The function of the university is not simply to teach bread-winning, or to furnish teachers for the public schools, or to be a centre of polite society; it is, above all, to be the organ of that fine adjustment between real life and the growing knowledge of life, an adjustment which forms the secret of civilization.

Such an institution the South of to-day sorely needs. She has religion, earnest, bigoted:—religion that on both sides the Veil often omits the sixth, seventh, and eighth commandments, but substitutes a dozen supplementary ones. She has, as Atlanta shows, growing thrift and love of toil; but she lacks that broad knowledge of what the world knows and knew of human living and doing, which she may apply to the thousand problems of real life to-day confronting her. The need of the South is knowledge and culture,—not in dainty limited quantity, as before the war, but in broad busy abundance in the world of work; and until she has this, not all the Apples of Hesperides, be they golden and bejewelled, can save her from the curse of the Bœotian lovers.

The Wings of Atalanta are the coming universities of the South. They alone can bear the maiden past the temptation of golden fruit. They will not guide her flying feet away from the cotton and gold; for—ah, thoughtful Hippomenes!—do not the apples lie in the very Way of Life? But they will guide her over and beyond them, and leave her kneeling in the Sanctuary of Truth and Freedom and broad Humanity, virgin and undefiled. Sadly did the Old South err in human education, despising the education of the masses, and niggardly in the support of colleges. Her ancient university foundations dwindled and withered under the foul breath of slavery; and even since the war they have fought a failing fight for life in the tainted air of social unrest and commercial selfishness, stunted by the death of criticism, and starving for lack of broadly cultured men. And if this is the white South's need and danger, how much heavier the danger and need of the freedmen's sons! how pressing here the need of broad ideals and true culture, the conservation of soul from sordid aims and petty passions! Let us build the Southern university—William and Mary, Trinity, Georgia, Texas, Tulane, Vanderbilt, and the others—fit to live; let us build, too, the Negro universities:—Fisk, whose foundation was ever broad; Howard, at the heart of the Nation; Atlanta at Atlanta, whose ideal of scholarship has been held above the temptation of numbers. Why not here, and perhaps elsewhere, plant deeply and for all time centres of learning and living, colleges that yearly would send into the life of the South a few white men and a few black men of broad culture, catholic tolerance, and trained ability, joining their hands to other hands, and giving to this squabble of the Races a decent and dignified peace?

Patience, Humility, Manners, and Taste, common schools and kindergartens, industrial and technical schools, literature and tolerance,—all these spring from knowledge and culture, the children of the university. So must men and nations build, not otherwise, not upside down.

Teach workers to work,—a wise saying; wise when applied to German boys and American girls; wiser when said of Negro boys, for they have less knowledge of working and none to teach them. Teach thinkers to think,—a needed knowledge in a day of loose and careless logic; and they whose lot is gravest must have the carefulest training to think aright. If these things are so, how foolish to ask what is the best education for one or seven, or sixty million souls! shall we teach them trades, or train them in liberal arts? Neither and both: teach the workers to work and the thinkers to think; make carpenters of carpenters, and philosophers of philosophers, and fops of fools. Nor can we pause here. We are training not isolated men but a living group of men,—nay, a group within a group. And the final product of our training must be neither a psychologist nor a brickmason, but a man. And to make men, we must have ideals, broad, pure, and inspiring ends of living,—not sordid money-getting, not apples of gold. The worker must work for the glory of his handiwork, not simply for pay; the thinker must think for truth, not for fame. And all this is gained only by human strife and longing; by ceaseless training and education; by founding Right on righteousness and Truth on the unhampered search for Truth; by founding the common school on the university, and the industrial school on the common school; and weaving thus a system, not a distortion, and bringing a birth, not an abortion.

When night falls on the City of a Hundred Hills, a wind gathers itself from the seas and comes murmuring westward. And at its bidding, the smoke of the drowsy factories sweeps down upon the mighty city and covers it like a pall, while yonder at the University the stars twinkle above Stone Hall. And they say that yon gray mist is the tunic of Atalanta pausing over her golden apples. Fly, my maiden, fly, for yonder comes Hippomenes!

VI

OF THE TRAINING OF
BLACK MEN

Why, if the Soul can fling the Dust aside,
And naked on the Air of Heaven ride,
     Were't not a Shame—were't not a Shame for him
In this clay carcase crippled to abide?
                    OMAR KHAYYAM (FITZGERALD)

From the shimmering swirl of waters where many, many thoughts ago the slave-ship first saw the square tower of Jamestown, have flowed down to our day three streams of thinking; one swollen from the larger world here and over-seas, saying, the multiplying of human wants in culture-lands calls for the world-wide cooperation of men in satisfying them. Hence arises a new human unity, pulling the ends of earth nearer, and all men, black, yellow, and white. The larger humanity strives to feel in this contact of living Nations and sleeping hordes a thrill of new life in the world, crying, "If the contact of Life and Sleep by Death, shame on such Life." To be sure, behind this thought lurks the afterthought of force and dominion,—the making of brown men to delve when the temptation of beads and red calico cloys.

The second thought streaming from the death-ship and the curving river is the thought of the older South,—the sincere and passionate belief that somewhere between men and cattle, God created a *tertium quid*, and called it a Negro,—a clownish, simple creature, at times even lovable within its limitations, but straitly foreordained to walk within the Veil. To be sure, behind the thought lurks the afterthought,—some of them with favoring chance might become men, but in sheer self-defence we dare not let them, and we build about them walls so high, and hang between them and the light a veil so thick, that they shall not even think of breaking through.

And last of all there trickles down that third and darker thought,—the thought of the things themselves, the confused, half-conscious mutter of men who are black and whitened, crying "Liberty, Freedom, Opportunity—vouchsafe to us, O boastful World, the chance of living men!" To be sure, behind the thought lurks the afterthought,—suppose, after all, the World is right and we are less than men? Suppose this mad impulse within is all wrong, some mock mirage from the untrue?

So here we stand among thoughts of human unity, even through conquest and slavery; the inferiority of black men, even if forced by fraud; a shriek in the night for the freedom of men who themselves are not yet sure of their right to demand it. This is the tangle of thought and afterthought wherein we are called to solve the problem of training men for life.

Behind all its curiousness, so attractive alike to sage and *dilettante*, lie its dim dangers, throwing across us shadows at once grotesque and awful. Plain it is to us that what the world seeks through desert and wild we have within our threshold,—a stalwart laboring force, suited to the semi-tropics; if, deaf to the voice of the Zeitgeist, we refuse to use and develop these men, we risk poverty and loss. If, on the other hand, seized by the brutal afterthought, we debauch the race thus caught in our talons, selfishly sucking their blood and brains in the future as in the past, what shall save us from national decadence? Only that saner selfishness, which Education teaches men, can find the rights of all in the whirl of work.

Again, we may decry the color-prejudice of the South, yet it remains a heavy fact. Such curious kinks of the human mind exist and must be reckoned with soberly. They cannot be laughed away, nor always successfully stormed at, nor easily abolished by act of legislature. And yet they must not be encouraged by being let alone. They must be recognized as facts, but unpleasant facts; things that stand in the way of civilization and religion and common decency. They can be met in but one way,—by the breadth and broadening of human reason, by catholicity of taste and culture. And so, too, the native ambition and aspiration of men, even though they be black, backward, and ungraceful, must not lightly be dealt with. To stimulate wildly weak and untrained minds is to play with mighty fires; to flout their striving idly is to welcome a harvest of brutish crime and shameless lethargy in our very laps. The guiding of thought and the deft coordination of deed is at once the path of honor and humanity.

And so, in this great question of reconciling three vast and partially contradictory streams of thought, the one panacea of Education leaps to the lips of all:—such human training as will best use the labor of all men without enslaving or brutalizing; such training as will give us poise to encourage the prejudices that bulwark society, and to stamp out those that in sheer barbarity deafen us to the wail of prisoned souls within the Veil, and the mounting fury of shackled men.

But when we have vaguely said that Education will set this tangle straight, what have we uttered but a truism? Training for life teaches living; but what training for the profitable living together of black men and white? A hundred and fifty years ago our task would have seemed easier. Then Dr. Johnson blandly assured us that education was needful solely for the embellishments of life, and was useless for ordinary vermin. To-day we have climbed to heights where we would open at least the outer courts of knowledge to all, display its treasures to many, and select the few to whom its mystery of Truth is revealed, not wholly by birth or the accidents of the stock market, but at least in part according to deftness and aim, talent and character. This programme, however, we are sorely puzzled in carrying out through that part of the land where the blight of slavery fell hardest, and where we are dealing with two backward peoples. To make here in human education that ever necessary combination of the permanent and the contingent—of the ideal and the practical in workable equilibrium—has been there, as it ever must be in every age and place, a matter of infinite experiment and frequent mistakes.

In rough approximation we may point out four varying decades of work in Southern education since the Civil War. From the close of the war until 1876, was the period of uncertain groping and temporary relief. There were army schools, mission schools, and schools of the Freedmen's Bureau in chaotic disarrangement seeking system and cooperation. Then followed ten years of constructive definite effort toward the building of complete school systems in the South. Normal schools and colleges were founded for the freedmen, and teachers trained there to man the public schools. There was the inevitable tendency of war to underestimate the prejudices of the master and the ignorance of the slave, and all seemed clear sailing out of the wreckage of the storm. Meantime, starting in this decade yet especially developing from 1885 to 1895, began the industrial revolution of the South. The land saw glimpses of a new destiny and the stirring of new ideals. The educational system striving to complete itself saw new obstacles and a field of work ever broader and deeper. The Negro colleges, hurriedly founded, were inadequately equipped, illogically distributed, and of varying efficiency and grade; the normal and high schools were doing little more than common-school work, and the common schools were training but a third of the children who ought to be in them, and training these too often poorly. At the same time the white South, by reason of its sudden conversion from the slavery ideal, by so much the more became set and strengthened in its racial prejudice, and crystallized it into harsh law and harsher custom; while the marvellous pushing forward of the poor white daily threatened to take even bread and butter from the mouths of the heavily handicapped sons of the freedmen. In the midst, then, of the larger problem of Negro education sprang up the more practical question of work, the inevitable economic quandary that faces a people in the transition from slavery to freedom, and especially those who make that change amid hate and prejudice, lawlessness and ruthless competition.

The industrial school springing to notice in this decade, but coming to full recognition in the decade beginning with 1895, was the proffered answer to this combined educational and economic crisis, and an answer of singular wisdom and timeliness. From the very first in nearly all the schools some attention had been given to training in handiwork, but now was this training first raised to a dignity that brought it in direct touch with the South's magnificent industrial development, and given an emphasis which reminded black folk that before the Temple of Knowledge swing the Gates of Toil.

Yet after all they are but gates, and when turning our eyes from the temporary and the contingent in the Negro problem to the broader question of the permanent uplifting and civilization of black men in America, we have a right to inquire, as this enthusiasm for material advancement mounts to its height, if after all the industrial school is the final and sufficient answer in the training of the Negro race; and to ask gently, but in all sincerity, the ever-recurring query of the ages, Is not life more than meat, and the body more than raiment? And men ask this to-day all the more eagerly because of sinister signs in recent educational movements. The tendency is here, born of slavery and quickened to renewed life by the crazy imperialism of the day, to regard human beings as among the material resources of a land to be trained with an eye single to future dividends. Race-prejudices, which keep brown and black men in their "places," we are coming to regard as useful allies with such a theory, no matter how much they may dull the ambition and sicken the hearts of struggling human beings. And above all, we daily hear that an education that encourages aspiration, that sets the loftiest of ideals and seeks as an end culture and character rather than bread-winning, is the privilege of white men and the danger and delusion of black.

Especially has criticism been directed against the former educational efforts to aid the Negro. In the four periods I have mentioned, we find first, boundless, planless enthusiasm and sacrifice; then the preparation of teachers for a vast public-school system; then the launching and expansion of that school system amid increasing difficulties; and finally the training of workmen for the new and growing industries. This development has been sharply ridiculed as a logical anomaly and flat reversal of nature. Soothly we have been told that first industrial and manual training should have taught the Negro to work, then simple schools should have taught him to read and write, and finally, after years, high and normal schools could have completed the system, as intelligence and wealth demanded.

That a system logically so complete was historically impossible, it needs but a little thought to prove. Progress in human affairs is more often a pull than a push, surging forward of the exceptional man, and the lifting of his duller brethren slowly and painfully to his vantage-ground. Thus it was no accident that gave birth to universities centuries before the common schools, that made fair Harvard the first flower of our wilderness. So in the South: the mass of the freedmen at the end of the war lacked the intelligence so necessary to modern workingmen. They must first have the common school to teach them to read, write, and cipher; and they must have higher schools to teach teachers for the common schools. The white teachers who flocked South went to establish such a common-school system. Few held the idea of founding colleges; most of them at first would have laughed at the idea. But they faced, as all men since them have faced, that central paradox of the South,—the social separation of the races. At that time it was the sudden volcanic rupture of nearly all relations between black and white, in work and government and family life. Since then a new adjustment of relations in economic and political affairs has grown up,—an adjustment subtle and difficult to grasp, yet singularly ingenious, which leaves still that frightful chasm at the color-line across which men pass at their peril. Thus, then and now, there stand in the South two separate worlds; and separate not simply in the higher realms of social intercourse, but also in church and school, on railway and street-car, in hotels and theatres, in streets and city sections, in books and newspapers, in asylums and jails, in hospitals and graveyards. There is still enough of contact for large economic and group cooperation, but the separation is so thorough and deep that it absolutely precludes for the present between the races anything like that sympathetic and effective group-training and leadership of the one by the other, such as the American Negro and all backward peoples must have for effectual progress.

This the missionaries of '68 soon saw; and if effective industrial and trade schools were impracticable before the establishment of a common-school system, just as certainly no adequate common schools could be founded until there were teachers to teach them. Southern whites would not teach them; Northern whites in sufficient numbers could not be had. If the Negro was to learn, he must teach himself, and the most effective help that could be given him was the establishment of schools to train Negro teachers. This conclusion was slowly but surely reached by every student of the situation until simultaneously, in widely separated regions, without consultation or systematic plan, there arose a series of institutions designed to furnish teachers for the untaught. Above the sneers of critics at the obvious defects of this procedure must ever stand its one crushing rejoinder: in a single generation they put thirty thousand black teachers in the South; they wiped out the illiteracy of the majority of the black people of the land, and they made Tuskegee possible.

Such higher training-schools tended naturally to deepen broader development: at first they were common and grammar schools, then some became high schools. And finally, by 1900, some thirty-four had one year or more of studies of college grade. This development was reached with different degrees of speed in different institutions: Hampton is still a high school, while Fisk University started her college in 1871, and Spelman Seminary about 1896. In all cases the aim was identical,—to maintain the standards of the lower training by giving teachers and leaders the best practicable training; and above all, to furnish the black world with adequate standards of human culture and lofty ideals of life. It was not enough that the teachers of teachers should be trained in technical normal methods; they must also, so far as possible, be broad-minded, cultured men and women, to scatter civilization among a people whose ignorance was not simply of letters, but of life itself.

It can thus be seen that the work of education in the South began with higher institutions of training, which threw off as their foliage common schools, and later industrial schools, and at the same time strove to shoot their roots ever deeper toward college and university training. That this was an inevitable and necessary development, sooner or later, goes without saying; but there has been, and still is, a question in many minds if the natural growth was not forced, and if the higher training was not either overdone or done with cheap and unsound methods. Among white Southerners this feeling is widespread and positive. A prominent Southern journal voiced this in a recent editorial.

> "The experiment that has been made to give the colored students classical training has not been satisfactory. Even though many were able to pursue the course, most of them did so in a parrot-like way, learning what was taught, but not seeming to appropriate the truth and import of their instruction, and graduating without sensible aim or valuable occupation for their future. The whole scheme has proved a waste of time, efforts, and the money of the state."

While most fair-minded men would recognize this as extreme and overdrawn, still without doubt many are asking, Are there a sufficient number of Negroes ready for college training to warrant the undertaking? Are not too many students prematurely forced into this work? Does it not have the effect of dissatisfying the young Negro with his environment? And do these graduates succeed in real life? Such natural questions cannot be evaded, nor on the other hand must a Nation naturally skeptical as to Negro ability assume an unfavorable answer without careful inquiry and patient openness to conviction. We must not forget that most Americans answer all queries regarding the Negro *a priori*, and that the least that human courtesy can do is to listen to evidence.

The advocates of the higher education of the Negro would be the last to deny the incompleteness and glaring defects of the present system: too many institutions have attempted to do college work, the work in some cases has not been thoroughly done, and quantity rather than quality has sometimes been sought. But all this can be said of higher education throughout the land; it is the almost inevitable incident of educational growth, and leaves the deeper question of the legitimate demand for the higher training of Negroes untouched. And this latter question can be settled in but one way,—by a first-hand study of the facts. If we leave out of view all institutions which have not actually graduated students from a course higher than that of a New England high school, even though they be called colleges; if then we take the thirty-four remaining institutions, we may clear up many misapprehensions by asking searchingly, What kind of institutions are they? what do they teach? and what sort of men do they graduate?

And first we may say that this type of college, including Atlanta, Fisk, and Howard, Wilberforce and Lincoln, Biddle, Shaw, and the rest, is peculiar, almost unique. Through the shining trees that whisper before me as I write, I catch glimpses of a boulder of New England granite, covering a grave, which graduates of Atlanta University have placed there, with this inscription:

> "IN GRATEFUL MEMORY OF THEIR
> FORMER TEACHER AND FRIEND
> AND OF THE UNSELFISH LIFE HE
> LIVED, AND THE NOBLE WORK HE
> WROUGHT; THAT THEY, THEIR
> CHILDREN, AND THEIR CHILDREN'S
> CHILDREN MIGHT BE
> BLESSED."

This was the gift of New England to the freed Negro: not alms, but a friend; not cash, but character. It was not and is not money these seething millions want, but love and sympathy, the pulse of hearts beating with red blood;—a gift which to-day only their own kindred and race can bring to the masses, but which once saintly souls brought to their favored children in the crusade of the sixties, that finest thing in American history, and one of the few things untainted by sordid greed and cheap vainglory. The teachers in these institutions came not to keep the Negroes in their place, but to raise them out of the defilement of the places where slavery had wallowed them. The colleges they founded were social settlements; homes where the best of the sons of the freedmen came in close and sympathetic touch with the best traditions of New England. They lived and ate together, studied and worked, hoped and harkened in the dawning light. In actual formal content their curriculum was doubtless old-fashioned, but in educational power it was supreme, for it was the contact of living souls.

From such schools about two thousand Negroes have gone forth with the bachelor's degree. The number in itself is enough to put at rest the argument that too large a proportion of Negroes are receiving higher training. If the ratio to population of all Negro students throughout the land, in both college and secondary training, be counted, Commissioner Harris assures us "it must be increased to five times its present average" to equal the average of the land.

Fifty years ago the ability of Negro students in any appreciable numbers to master a modern college course would have been difficult to prove. To-day it is proved by the fact that four hundred Negroes, many of whom have been reported as brilliant students, have received the bachelor's degree from Harvard, Yale, Oberlin, and seventy other leading colleges. Here we have, then, nearly twenty-five hundred Negro graduates, of whom the crucial query must be made, How far did their training fit them for life? It is of course extremely difficult to collect satisfactory data on such a point,—difficult to reach the men, to get trustworthy testimony, and to gauge that testimony by any generally acceptable criterion of success. In 1900, the Conference at Atlanta University undertook to study these graduates, and published the results. First they sought to know what these graduates were doing, and succeeded in getting answers from nearly two-thirds of the living. The direct testimony was in almost all cases corroborated by the reports of the colleges where they graduated, so that in the main the reports were worthy of credence. Fifty-three per cent of these graduates were teachers,—presidents of institutions, heads of normal schools, principals of city school-systems, and the like. Seventeen per cent were clergymen; another seventeen per cent were in the professions, chiefly as physicians. Over six per cent were merchants, farmers, and artisans, and four per cent were in the government civil-service. Granting even that a considerable proportion of the third unheard from are unsuccessful, this is a record of usefulness. Personally I know many hundreds of these graduates, and have corresponded with more than a thousand; through others I have followed carefully the life-work of scores; I have taught some of them and some of the pupils whom they have taught, lived in homes which they have builded, and looked at life through their eyes. Comparing them as a class with my fellow students in New England and in Europe, I cannot hesitate in saying that nowhere have I met men and women with a broader spirit of helpfulness, with deeper devotion to their life-work, or with more consecrated determination to succeed in the face of bitter difficulties than among Negro college-bred men. They have, to be sure, their proportion of ne'er-do-wells, their pedants and lettered fools, but they have a surprisingly small proportion of them; they have not that culture of manner which we instinctively associate with university men, forgetting that in reality it is the heritage from cultured homes, and that no people a generation removed from slavery can escape a certain unpleasant rawness and *gaucherie*, despite the best of training.

With all their larger vision and deeper sensibility, these men have usually been conservative, careful leaders. They have seldom been agitators, have withstood the temptation to head the mob, and have worked steadily and faithfully in a thousand communities in the South. As teachers, they have given the South a commendable system of city schools and large numbers of private normal-schools and academies. Colored college-bred men have worked side by side with white college graduates at Hampton; almost from the beginning the backbone of Tuskegee's teaching force has been formed of graduates from Fisk and Atlanta. And to-day the institute is filled with college graduates, from the energetic wife of the principal down to the teacher of agriculture, including nearly half of the executive council and a majority of the heads of departments. In the professions, college men are slowly but surely leavening the Negro church, are healing and preventing the devastations of disease, and beginning to furnish legal protection for the liberty and property of the toiling masses. All this is needful work. Who would do it if Negroes did not? How could Negroes do it if they were not trained carefully for it? If white people need colleges to furnish teachers, ministers, lawyers, and doctors, do black people need nothing of the sort?

If it is true that there are an appreciable number of Negro youth in the land capable by character and talent to receive that higher training, the end of which is culture, and if the two and a half thousand who have had something of this training in the past have in the main proved themselves useful to their race and generation, the question then comes, What place in the future development of the South ought the Negro college and college-bred man to occupy? That the present social separation and acute race-sensitiveness must eventually yield to the influences of culture, as the South grows civilized, is clear. But such transformation calls for singular wisdom and patience. If, while the healing of this vast sore is progressing, the races are to live for many years side by side, united in economic effort, obeying a common government, sensitive to mutual thought and feeling, yet subtly and silently separate in many matters of deeper human intimacy,—if this unusual and dangerous development is to progress amid peace and order, mutual respect and growing intelligence, it will call for social surgery at once the delicatest and nicest in modern history. It will demand broad-minded, upright men, both white and black, and in its final accomplishment American civilization will triumph. So far as white men are concerned, this fact is to-day being recognized in the South,

and a happy renaissance of university education seems immi-
nent. But the very voices that cry hail to this good work are,
strange to relate, largely silent or antagonistic to the higher
education of the Negro.

Strange to relate! for this is certain, no secure civilization can
be built in the South with the Negro as an ignorant, turbulent
proletariat. Suppose we seek to remedy this by making them
laborers and nothing more: they are not fools, they have tasted
of the Tree of Life, and they will not cease to think, will not
cease attempting to read the riddle of the world. By taking away
their best equipped teachers and leaders, by slamming the door
of opportunity in the faces of their bolder and brighter minds,
will you make them satisfied with their lot? or will you not
rather transfer their leading from the hands of men taught to
think to the hands of untrained demagogues? We ought not to
forget that despite the pressure of poverty, and despite the active discouragement and even ridicule of friends, the demand
for higher training steadily increases among Negro youth: there
were, in the years from 1875 to 1880, 22 Negro graduates from
Northern colleges; from 1885 to 1890 there were 43, and from
1895 to 1900, nearly 100 graduates. From Southern Negro colleges there were, in the same three periods, 143, 413, and over
500 graduates. Here, then, is the plain thirst for training; by
refusing to give this Talented Tenth the key to knowledge,
can any sane man imagine that they will lightly lay aside their
yearning and contentedly become hewers of wood and drawers
of water?

No. The dangerously clear logic of the Negro's position will
more and more loudly assert itself in that day when increasing
wealth and more intricate social organization preclude the South
from being, as it so largely is, simply an armed camp for in-
timidating black folk. Such waste of energy cannot be spared
if the South is to catch up with civilization. And as the black
third of the land grows in thrift and skill, unless skilfully guided
in its larger philosophy, it must more and more brood over the
red past and the creeping, crooked present, until it grasps a
gospel of revolt and revenge and throws its new-found energies

athwart the current of advance. Even to-day the masses of the
Negroes see all too clearly the anomalies of their position and
the moral crookedness of yours. You may marshal strong in-
dictments against them, but their counter-cries, lacking though
they be in formal logic, have burning truths within them which
you may not wholly ignore, O Southern Gentlemen! If you de-
plore their presence here, they ask, Who brought us? When you
cry, Deliver us from the vision of intermarriage, they answer
that legal marriage is infinitely better than systematic concubi-
nage and prostitution. And if in just fury you accuse their vagabonds of violating women, they also in fury quite as just may
reply: The wrong which your gentlemen have done against helpless black women in defiance of your own laws is written on
the foreheads of two millions of mulattoes, and written in inef-
faceable blood. And finally, when you fasten crime upon this
race as its peculiar trait, they answer that slavery was the arch-
crime, and lynching and lawlessness its twin abortion; that
color and race are not crimes, and yet they it is which in this
land receives most unceasing condemnation, North, East, South,
and West.

I will not say such arguments are wholly justified,—I will not
insist that there is no other side to the shield; but I do say that
of the nine millions of Negroes in this nation, there is scarcely
one out of the cradle to whom these arguments do not daily
present themselves in the guise of terrible truth. I insist that the
question of the future is how best to keep these millions from
brooding over the wrongs of the past and the difficulties of the
present, so that all their energies may be bent toward a cheerful
striving and co-operation with their white neighbors toward a
larger, juster, and fuller future. That one wise method of doing
this lies in the closer knitting of the Negro to the great industrial possibilities of the South is a great truth. And this the common schools and the manual training and trade schools are
working to accomplish. But these alone are not enough. The
foundations of knowledge in this race, as in others, must be
sunk deep in the college and university if we would build a solid,
permanent structure. Internal problems of social advance must
inevitably come,—problems of work and wages, of families and

homes, of morals and the true valuing of the things of life; and all these and other inevitable problems of civilization the Negro must meet and solve largely for himself, by reason of his isolation; and can there be any possible solution other than by study and thought and an appeal to the rich experience of the past? Is there not, with such a group and in such a crisis, infinitely more danger to be apprehended from half-trained minds and shallow thinking than from over-education and over-refinement? Surely we have wit enough to found a Negro college so manned and equipped as to steer successfully between the *dilettante* and the fool. We shall hardly induce black men to believe that if their stomachs be full, it matters little about their brains. They already dimly perceive that the paths of peace winding between honest toil and dignified manhood call for the guidance of skilled thinkers, the loving, reverent comradeship between the black lowly and the black men emancipated by training and culture.

The function of the Negro college, then, is clear: it must maintain the standards of popular education, it must seek the social regeneration of the Negro, and it must help in the solution of problems of race contact and co-operation. And finally, beyond all this, it must develop men. Above our modern socialism, and out of the worship of the mass, must persist and evolve that higher individualism which the centres of culture protect; there must come a loftier respect for the sovereign human soul that seeks to know itself and the world about it; that seeks a freedom for expansion and self-development; that will love and hate and labor in its own way, untrammeled alike by old and new. Such souls aforetime have inspired and guided worlds, and if we be not wholly bewitched by our Rhine-gold, they shall again. Herein the longing of black men must have respect: the rich and bitter depth of their experience, the unknown treasures of their inner life, the strange rendings of nature they have seen, may give the world new points of view and make their loving, living, and doing precious to all human hearts. And to themselves in these the days that try their souls, the chance to soar in the dim blue air above the smoke is to their finer spirits boon and guerdon for what they lose on earth by being black.

———

I sit with Shakespeare and he winces not. Across the color-line I move arm in arm with Balzac and Dumas, where smiling men and welcoming women glide in gilded halls. From out the caves of evening that swing between the strong-limbed earth and the tracery of the stars, I summon Aristotle and Aurelius and what soul I will, and they come all graciously with no scorn nor condescension. So, wed with Truth, I dwell above the Veil. Is this the life you grudge us, O knightly America? Is this the life you long to change into the dull red hideousness of Georgia? Are you so afraid lest peering from this high Pisgah, between Philistine and Amalekite, we sight the Promised Land?

VII

OF THE BLACK BELT

I am black but comely, O ye daughters of Jerusalem,
As the tents of Kedar, as the curtains of Solomon.
Look not upon me, because I am black,
Because the sun hath looked upon me:
My mother's children were angry with me;
They made me the keeper of the vineyards;
But mine own vineyard have I not kept.

THE SONG OF SOLOMON

Out of the North the train thundered, and we woke to see
the crimson soil of Georgia stretching away bare and monotonous right and left. Here and there lay straggling, unlovely villages, and lean men loafed leisurely at the depots; then again
came the stretch of pines and clay. Yet we did not nod, nor
weary of the scene; for this is historic ground. Right across our
track, three hundred and sixty years ago, wandered the

cavalcade of Hernando de Soto, looking for gold and the Great Sea; and he and his foot-sore captives disappeared yonder in the grim forests to the west. Here sits Atlanta, the city of a hundred hills, with something Western, something Southern, and something quite its own, in its busy life. And a little past Atlanta, to the southwest, is the land of the Cherokees, and there, not far from where Sam Hose was crucified, you may stand on a spot which is to-day the centre of the Negro problem,—the centre of those nine million men who are America's dark heritage from slavery and the slave-trade.

Not only is Georgia thus the geographical focus of our Negro population, but in many other respects, both now and yesterday, the Negro problems have seemed to be centered in this State. No other State in the Union can count a million Negroes among its citizens,—a population as large as the slave population of the whole Union in 1800; no other State fought so long and strenuously to gather this host of Africans. Oglethorpe thought slavery against law and gospel; but the circumstances which gave Georgia its first inhabitants were not calculated to furnish citizens over-nice in their ideas about rum and slaves. Despite the prohibitions of the trustees, these Georgians, like some of their descendants, proceeded to take the law into their own hands; and so pliant were the judges, and so flagrant the smuggling, and so earnest were the prayers of Whitefield, that by the middle of the eighteenth century all restrictions were swept away, and the slave-trade went merrily on for fifty years and more.

Down in Darien, where the Delegal riots took place some summers ago, there used to come a strong protest against slavery from the Scotch Highlanders; and the Moravians of Ebenezer did not like the system. But not till the Haytian Terror of Toussaint was the trade in men even checked; while the national statute of 1808 did not suffice to stop it. How the Africans poured in!—fifty thousand between 1790 and 1810, and then, from Virginia and from smugglers, two thousand a year for many years more. So the thirty thousand Negroes of Georgia in 1790 were doubled in a decade,—were over a hundred thousand in 1810, had reached two hundred thousand in 1820, and half a million at the time of the war. Thus like a snake the black population writhed upward.

But we must hasten on our journey. This that we pass as we leave Atlanta is the ancient land of the Cherokees,—that brave Indian nation which strove so long for its fatherland, until Fate and the United States Government drove them beyond the Mississippi. If you wish to ride with me you must come into the "Jim Crow Car." There will be no objection,—already four other white men, and a little white girl with her nurse, are in there. Usually the races are mixed in there; but the white coach is all white. Of course this car is not so good as the other, but it is fairly clean and comfortable. The discomfort lies chiefly in the hearts of those four black men yonder—and in mine.

We rumble south in quite a business-like way. The bare red clay and pines of Northern Georgia begin to disappear, and in their place appears a rich rolling land, luxuriant, and here and there well tilled. This is the land of the Creek Indians; and a hard time the Georgians had to seize it. The towns grow more frequent and more interesting, and brand-new cotton mills rise on every side. Below Macon the world grows darker; for now we approach the Black Belt,—that strange land of shadows, at which even slaves paled in the past, and whence come now only faint and half-intelligible murmurs to the world beyond. The "Jim Crow Car" grows larger and a shade better; three rough field-hands and two or three white loafers accompany us, and the newsboy still spreads his wares at one end. The sun is setting, but we can see the great cotton country as we enter it,—the soil now dark and fertile, now thin and gray, with fruit-trees and dilapidated buildings,—all the way to Albany.

At Albany, in the heart of the Black Belt, we stop. Two hundred miles south of Atlanta, two hundred miles west of the Atlantic, and one hundred miles north of the Great Gulf lies Dougherty County, with ten thousand Negroes and two thousand whites. The Flint River winds down from Andersonville, and, turning suddenly at Albany, the county-seat, hurries on to join the Chattahoochee and the sea. Andrew Jackson knew the Flint well, and marched across it once to avenge the Indian Massacre at Fort Mims. That was in 1814, not long before the

battle of New Orleans; and by the Creek treaty that followed
this campaign, all Dougherty County, and much other rich land,
was ceded to Georgia. Still, settlers fought shy of this land, for
the Indians were all about, and they were unpleasant neighbors
in those days. The panic of 1837, which Jackson bequeathed to
Van Buren, turned the planters from the impoverished lands of
Virginia, the Carolinas, and east Georgia, toward the West.
The Indians were removed to Indian Territory, and settlers
poured into these coveted lands to retrieve their broken fortunes. For a radius of a hundred miles about Albany, stretched
a great fertile land, luxuriant with forests of pine, oak, ash,
hickory, and poplar; hot with the sun and damp with the rich
black swamp-land; and here the corner-stone of the Cotton
Kingdom was laid.

Albany is to-day a wide-streeted, placid, Southern town, with
a broad sweep of stores and saloons, and flanking rows of
homes,—whites usually to the north, and blacks to the south.
Six days in the week the town looks decidedly too small for itself, and takes frequent and prolonged naps. But on Saturday
suddenly the whole county disgorges itself upon the place, and
a perfect flood of black peasantry pours through the streets, fills
the stores, blocks the sidewalks, chokes the thoroughfares, and
takes full possession of the town. They are black, sturdy, uncouth country folk, good-natured and simple, talkative to a degree, and yet far more silent and brooding than the crowds of
the Rhine-pfalz, or Naples, or Cracow. They drink considerable
quantities of whiskey, but do not get very drunk; they talk and
laugh loudly at times, but seldom quarrel or fight. They walk up
and down the streets, meet and gossip with friends, stare at the
shop windows, buy coffee, cheap candy, and clothes, and at dusk
drive home—happy? well no, not exactly happy, but much hap-
pier than as though they had not come.

Thus Albany is a real capital,—a typical Southern county
town, the centre of the life of ten thousand souls; their point of
contact with the outer world, their centre of news and gossip,
their market for buying and selling, borrowing and lending,
their fountain of justice and law. Once upon a time we knew
country life so well and city life so little, that we illustrated city

life as that of a closely crowded country district. Now the world has well-nigh forgotten what the country is, and we must imagine a little city of black people scattered far and wide over three hundred lonesome square miles of land, without train or trolley, in the midst of cotton and corn, and wide patches of sand and gloomy soil.

It gets pretty hot in Southern Georgia in July,—a sort of dull, determined heat that seems quite independent of the sun; so it took us some days to muster courage enough to leave the porch and venture out on the long country roads, that we might see this unknown world. Finally we started. It was about ten in the morning, bright with a faint breeze, and we jogged leisurely southward in the valley of the Flint. We passed the scattered box-like cabins of the brick-yard hands, and the long tenement-row facetiously called "The Ark," and were soon in the open country, and on the confines of the great plantations of other days. There is the "Joe Fields place"; a rough old fellow was he, and had killed many a "nigger" in his day. Twelve miles his plantation used to run,—a regular barony. It is nearly all gone now; only straggling bits belong to the family, and the rest has passed to Jews and Negroes. Even the bits which are left are heavily mortgaged, and, like the rest of the land, tilled by tenants. Here is one of them now,—a tall brown man, a hard worker and a hard drinker, illiterate, but versed in farm-lore, as his nodding crops declare. This distressingly new board house is his, and he has just moved out of yonder moss-grown cabin with its one square room.

From the curtains in Benton's house, down the road, a dark comely face is staring at the strangers; for passing carriages are not every-day occurrences here. Benton is an intelligent yellow man with a good-sized family, and manages a plantation blasted by the war and now the broken staff of the widow. He might be well-to-do, they say; but he carouses too much in Albany. And the half-desolate spirit of neglect born of the very soil seems to have settled on these acres. In times past there were cotton-gins and machinery here; but they have rotted away.

The whole land seems forlorn and forsaken. Here are the remnants of the vast plantations of the Sheldons, the Pellots,

and the Rensons; but the souls of them are passed. The houses
lie in half ruin, or have wholly disappeared; the fences have
flown, and the families are wandering in the world. Strange vi-
cissitudes have met these whilom masters. Yonder stretch the
wide acres of Bildad Reasor; he died in war-time, but the upstart
overseer hastened to wed the widow. Then he went, and his
neighbors too, and now only the black tenant remains; but the
shadow-hand of the master's grand-nephew or cousin or credi-
tor stretches out of the gray distance to collect the rack-rent
remorselessly, and so the land is uncared-for and poor. Only
black tenants can stand such a system, and they only because
they must. Ten miles we have ridden to-day and have seen no
white face.

A resistless feeling of depression falls slowly upon us, despite
the gaudy sunshine and the green cotton-fields. This, then, is
the Cotton Kingdom,—the shadow of a marvellous dream. And
where is the King? Perhaps this is he,—the sweating plough-
man, tilling his eighty acres with two lean mules, and fighting
a hard battle with debt. So we sit musing, until, as we turn a
corner on the sandy road, there comes a fairer scene suddenly
in view,—a neat cottage snugly ensconced by the road, and near
it a little store. A tall bronzed man rises from the porch as we
hail him, and comes out to our carriage. He is six feet in height,
with a sober face that smiles gravely. He walks too straight to
be a tenant,—yes, he owns two hundred and forty acres. "The
land is run down since the boom-days of eighteen hundred and
fifty," he explains, and cotton is low. Three black tenants live
on his place, and in his little store he keeps a small stock of tobacco, snuff, soap, and soda, for the neighborhood. Here is his
gin-house with new machinery just installed. Three hundred
bales of cotton went through it last year. Two children he has
sent away to school. Yes, he says sadly, he is getting on, but cotton is down to four cents; I know how Debt sits staring at him.

Wherever the King may be, the parks and palaces of the Cotton Kingdom have not wholly disappeared. We plunge even now
into great groves of oak and towering pine, with an undergrowth of myrtle and shrubbery. This was the "home-house"
of the Thompsons,—slave-barons who drove their coach and

four in the merry past. All is silence now, and ashes, and tangled
weeds. The owner put his whole fortune into the rising cotton
industry of the fifties, and with the falling prices of the eighties
he packed up and stole away. Yonder is another grove, with
unkempt lawn, great magnolias, and grass-grown paths. The
Big House stands in half-ruin, its great front door staring
blankly at the street, and the back part grotesquely restored for
its black tenant. A shabby, well-built Negro he is, unlucky and
irresolute. He digs hard to pay rent to the white girl who owns
the remnant of the place. She married a policeman, and lives in
Savannah.

Now and again we come to churches. Here is one now,—
Shepherd's, they call it,—a great whitewashed barn of a thing,
perched on stilts of stone, and looking for all the world as
though it were just resting here a moment and might be expected
to waddle off down the road at almost any time. And yet it is
the centre of a hundred cabin homes; and sometimes, of a Sunday, five hundred persons from far and near gather here and
talk and eat and sing. There is a school-house near,—a very
airy, empty shed; but even this is an improvement, for usually
the school is held in the church. The churches vary from log-
huts to those like Shepherd's, and the schools from nothing to
this little house that sits demurely on the county line. It is a tiny
plank-house, perhaps ten by twenty, and has within a double
row of rough unplaned benches, resting mostly on legs, sometimes on boxes. Opposite the door is a square home-made desk.
In one corner are the ruins of a stove, and in the other a dim
blackboard. It is the cheerfulest schoolhouse I have seen in
Dougherty, save in town. Back of the schoolhouse is a lodge-
house two stories high and not quite finished. Societies meet
there,—societies "to care for the sick and bury the dead"; and
these societies grow and flourish.

We had come to the boundaries of Dougherty, and were about
to turn west along the county line, when all these sights were
pointed out to us by a kindly old man, black, white-haired, and
seventy. Forty-five years he had lived here, and now supports
himself and his old wife by the help of the steer tethered yonder
and the charity of his black neighbors. He shows us the farm

of the Hills just across the county line in Baker,—a widow and
two strapping sons, who raised ten bales (one need not add
"cotton" down here) last year. There are fences and pigs and
cows, and the soft-voiced, velvet-skinned young Memnon, who
sauntered half-bashfully over to greet the strangers, is proud of
his home. We turn now to the west along the county line. Great
dismantled trunks of pines tower above the green cotton-fields,
cracking their naked gnarled fingers toward the border of living
forest beyond. There is little beauty in this region, only a sort
of crude abandon that suggests power,—a naked grandeur, as
it were. The houses are bare and straight; there are no ham-
mocks or easy-chairs, and few flowers. So when, as here at
Rawdon's, one sees a vine clinging to a little porch, and homelike windows peeping over the fences, one takes a long breath.
I think I never before quite realized the place of the Fence in
civilization. This is the Land of the Unfenced, where crouch on
either hand scores of ugly one-room cabins, cheerless and dirty.
Here lies the Negro problem in its naked dirt and penury. And
here are no fences. But now and then the criss cross rails or
straight palings break into view, and then we know a touch of
culture is near. Of course Harrison Gohagen,—a quiet yellow
man, young, smooth-faced, and diligent,—of course he is lord
of some hundred acres, and we expect to see a vision of well-
kept rooms and fat beds and laughing children. For has he not
fine fences? And those over yonder, why should they build fences
on the rack-rented land? It will only increase their rent.

On we wind, through sand and pines and glimpses of old plantations, till there creeps into sight a cluster of buildings,—wood
and brick, mills and houses, and scattered cabins. It seemed quite
a village. As it came nearer and nearer, however, the aspect
changed: the buildings were rotten, the bricks were falling out,
the mills were silent, and the store was closed. Only in the cabins
appeared now and then a bit of lazy life. I could imagine the place
under some weird spell, and was half-minded to search out the
princess. An old ragged black man, honest, simple, and improvident, told us the tale. The Wizard of the North—the Capitalist—
had rushed down in the seventies to woo this coy dark soil. He
bought a square mile or more, and for a time the field-hands sang,

the gins groaned, and the mills buzzed. Then came a change. The agent's son embezzled the funds and ran off with them. Then the agent himself disappeared. Finally the new agent stole even the books, and the company in wrath closed its business and its houses, refused to sell, and let houses and furniture and machinery rust and rot. So the Waters-Loring plantation was stilled by the spell of dishonesty, and stands like some gaunt rebuke to a scarred land.

Somehow that plantation ended our day's journey; for I could not shake off the influence of that silent scene. Back toward town we glided, past the straight and thread-like pines, past a dark tree-dotted pond where the air was heavy with a dead sweet perfume. White slender-legged curlews flitted by us, and the garnet blooms of the cotton looked gay against the green and purple stalks. A peasant girl was hoeing in the field, white-turbaned and black-limbed. All this we saw, but the spell still lay upon us.

How curious a land is this,—how full of untold story, of tragedy and laughter, and the rich legacy of human life; shadowed with a tragic past, and big with future promise! This is the Black Belt of Georgia. Dougherty County is the west end of the Black Belt, and men once called it the Egypt of the Confederacy. It is full of historic interest. First there is the Swamp, to the west, where the Chickasawhatchee flows sullenly southward. The shadow of an old plantation lies at its edge, forlorn and dark. Then comes the pool; pendent gray moss and brackish waters appear, and forests filled with wild-fowl. In one place the wood is on fire, smouldering in dull red anger; but nobody minds. Then the swamp grows beautiful; a raised road, built by chained Negro convicts, dips down into it, and forms a way walled and almost covered in living green. Spreading trees spring from a prodigal luxuriance of undergrowth; great dark green shadows fade into the black background, until all is one mass of tangled semi-tropical foliage, marvellous in its weird savage splendor. Once we crossed a black silent stream, where the sad trees and writhing creepers, all glinting fiery yellow and green, seemed like some vast cathedral,—some green Milan builded of wildwood. And as I crossed, I seemed to see again that fierce tragedy of seventy years ago. Osceola, the Indian-Negro chieftain, had risen in the swamps of Florida, vowing vengeance. His war-cry reached the red Creeks of Dougherty, and their war-cry rang from the Chattahoochee to the sea. Men and women and children fled and fell before them as they swept into Dougherty. In yonder shadows a dark and hideously painted warrior glided stealthily on,—another and another, until three hundred had crept into the treacherous swamp. Then the false slime closing about them called the white men from the east. Waist-deep, they fought beneath the tall trees, until the war-cry was hushed and the Indians glided back into the west. Small wonder the wood is red.

Then came the black slaves. Day after day the clank of chained feet marching from Virginia and Carolina to Georgia was heard in these rich swamp lands. Day after day the songs of the callous, the wail of the motherless, and the muttered curses of the wretched echoed from the Flint to the Chicka-sawhatchee, until by 1860 there had risen in West Dougherty perhaps the richest slave kingdom the modern world ever knew. A hundred and fifty barons commanded the labor of nearly six thousand Negroes, held sway over farms with ninety thousand acres of tilled land, valued even in times of cheap soil at three millions of dollars. Twenty thousand bales of ginned cotton went yearly to England, New and Old; and men that came there bankrupt made money and grew rich. In a single decade the cotton output increased four-fold and the value of lands was tripled. It was the heyday of the *nouveau riche*, and a life of careless extravagance reigned among the masters. Four and six bob-tailed thoroughbreds rolled their coaches to town; open hospitality and gay entertainment were the rule. Parks and groves were laid out, rich with flower and vine, and in the midst stood the low wide-halled "big house," with its porch and columns and great fire-places.

And yet with all this there was something sordid, something forced,—a certain feverish unrest and recklessness; for was not all this show and tinsel built upon a groan? "This land was a little Hell," said a ragged, brown, and grave-faced man to me.

We were seated near a roadside blacksmith-shop, and behind was the bare ruin of some master's home. "I've seen niggers drop dead in the furrow, but they were kicked aside, and the plough never stopped. And down in the guard-house, there's where the blood ran."

With such foundations a kingdom must in time sway and fall. The masters moved to Macon and Augusta, and left only the irresponsible overseers on the land. And the result is such ruin as this, the Lloyd "home-place":—great waving oaks, a spread of lawn, myrtles and chestnuts, all ragged and wild; a solitary gate-post standing where once was a castle entrance; an old rusty anvil lying amid rotting bellows and wood in the ruins of a blacksmith shop; a wide rambling old mansion, brown and dingy, filled now with the grandchildren of the slaves who once waited on its tables; while the family of the master has dwindled to two lone women, who live in Macon and feed hungrily off the remnants of an earldom. So we ride on, past phantom gates and falling homes,—past the once flourishing farms of the Smiths, the Gandys, and the Lagores,—and find all dilapidated and half ruined, even there where a solitary white woman, a relic of other days, sits alone in state among miles of Negroes and rides to town in her ancient coach each day.

This was indeed the Egypt of the Confederacy,—the rich granary whence potatoes and corn and cotton poured out to the famished and ragged Confederate troops as they battled for a cause lost long before 1861. Sheltered and secure, it became the place of refuge for families, wealth, and slaves. Yet even then the hard ruthless rape of the land began to tell. The red-clay sub-soil already had begun to peer above the loam. The harder the slaves were driven the more careless and fatal was their farming. Then came the revolution of war and Emancipation, the bewilderment of Reconstruction,—and now, what is the Egypt of the Confederacy, and what meaning has it for the nation's weal or woe?

It is a land of rapid contrasts and of curiously mingled hope and pain. Here sits a pretty blue-eyed quadroon hiding her bare feet; she was married only last week, and yonder in the field is her dark young husband, hoeing to support her, at thirty cents a day without board. Across the way is Gatesby, brown and tall, lord of two thousand acres shrewdly won and held. There is a store conducted by his black son, a blacksmith-shop, and a ginnery. Five miles below here is a town owned and controlled by one white New Englander. He owns almost a Rhode Island county, with thousands of acres and hundreds of black laborers. Their cabins look better than most, and the farm, with machinery and fertilizers, is much more business-like than any in the county, although the manager drives hard bargains in wages. When now we turn and look five miles above, there on the edge of town are five houses of prostitutes,—two of blacks and three of whites; and in one of the houses of the whites a worthless black boy was harbored too openly two years ago; so he was hanged for rape. And here, too, is the high white-washed fence of the "stockade," as the county prison is called; the white folks say it is ever full of black criminals,—the black folks say that only colored boys are sent to jail, and they not because they are guilty, but because the State needs criminals to eke out its income by their forced labor.

The Jew is the heir of the slave-baron in Dougherty; and as we ride westward, by wide stretching cornfields and stubby orchards of peach and pear, we see on all sides within the circle of dark forest a Land of Canaan. Here and there are tales of projects for money-getting, born in the swift days of Reconstruction,—"improvement" companies, wine companies, mills and factories; nearly all failed, and the Jew fell heir. It is a beautiful land, this Dougherty, west of the Flint. The forests are wonderful, the solemn pines have disappeared, and this is the "Oakey Woods," with its wealth of hickories, beeches, oaks, and palmettos. But a pall of debt hangs over the beautiful land; the merchants are in debt to the wholesalers, the planters are in debt to the merchants, the tenants owe the planters, and laborers bow and bend beneath the burden of it all. Here and there a man has raised his head above these murky waters. We passed one fenced stock-farm, with grass and grazing cattle, that looked very homelike after endless corn and cotton. Here and there are black freeholders: there is the gaunt dull-black

Jackson, with his hundred acres. "I says, 'Look up! If you don't look up you can't get up,'" remarks Jackson, philosophically. And he's gotten up. Dark Carter's neat barns would do credit to New England. His master helped him to get a start, but when the black man died last fall the master's sons immediately laid claim to the estate. "And them white folks will get it, too," said my yellow gossip.

I turn from these well-tended acres with a comfortable feeling that the Negro is rising. Even then, however, the fields, as we proceed, begin to redden and the trees disappear. Rows of old cabins appear filled with renters and laborers,—cheerless, bare, and dirty, for the most part, although here and there the very age and decay makes the scene picturesque. A young black fellow greets us. He is twenty-two, and just married. Until last year he had good luck renting; then cotton fell, and the sheriff seized and sold all he had. So he moved here, where the rent is higher, the land poorer, and the owner inflexible; he rents a forty-dollar mule for twenty dollars a year. Poor lad!—a slave at twenty-two. This plantation, owned now by a Russian Jew, was a part of the famous Bolton estate. After the war it was for many years worked by gangs of Negro convicts,—and black convicts then were even more plentiful than now; it was a way of making Negroes work, and the question of guilt was a minor one. Hard tales of cruelty and mistreatment of the chained freemen are told but the county authorities were deaf until the free-labor market was nearly ruined by wholesale migration. Then they took the convicts from the plantations, but not until one of the fairest regions of the "Oakey Woods" had been ruined and ravished into a red waste, out of which only a Yankee or a Jew could squeeze more blood from debt-cursed tenants.

No wonder that Luke Black, slow, dull, and discouraged, shuffles to our carriage and talks hopelessly. Why should he strive? Every year finds him deeper in debt. How strange that Georgia, the world-heralded refuge of poor debtors, should bind her own to sloth and misfortune as ruthlessly as ever England did! The poor land groans with its birth-pains, and brings forth scarcely a hundred pounds of cotton to the acre, where fifty years ago it yielded eight times as much. Of this meagre yield the tenant pays from a quarter to a third in rent, and most of the rest in interest on food and supplies bought on credit. Twenty years yonder sunken-cheeked, old black man has labored under that system, and now, turned day-laborer, is supporting his wife and boarding himself on his wages of a dollar and a half a week, received only part of the year.

The Bolton convict farm formerly included the neighboring plantation. Here it was that the convicts were lodged in the great log prison still standing. A dismal place it still remains, with rows of ugly huts filled with surly ignorant tenants. "What rent do you pay here?" I inquired. "I don't know,—what is it, Sam?" "All we make," answered Sam. It is a depressing place,—bare, unshaded, with no charm of past association, only a memory of forced human toil,—now, then, and before the war. They are not happy, these black men whom we meet throughout this region. There is little of the joyous abandon and playfulness which we are wont to associate with the plantation Negro. At best, the natural good-nature is edged with complaint or has changed into sullenness and gloom. And now and then it blazes forth in veiled but hot anger. I remember one big red-eyed black whom we met by the roadside. Forty-five years he had labored on this farm, beginning with nothing, and still having nothing. To be sure, he had given four children a common-school training, and perhaps if the new fence-law had not allowed unfenced crops in West Dougherty he might have raised a little stock and kept ahead. As it is, he is hopelessly in debt, disappointed, and embittered. He stopped us to inquire after the black boy in Albany, whom it was said a policeman had shot and killed for loud talking on the sidewalk. And then he said slowly: "Let a white man touch me, and he dies; I don't boast this,—I don't say it around loud, or before the children,—but I mean it. I've seen them whip my father and my old mother in them cotton-rows till the blood ran; by—" and we passed on.

Now Scars, whom we met next lolling under the chubby oak-trees, was of quite different fibre. Happy?—Well, yes; he laughed and flipped pebbles, and thought the world was as it was. He had worked here twelve years and has nothing but a mortgaged mule. Children? Yes, seven; but they hadn't been to school this

year;—couldn't afford books and clothes, and couldn't spare
their work. There go part of them to the fields now,—three big
boys astride mules, and a strapping girl with bare brown legs.
Careless ignorance and laziness here, fierce hate and vindictive-
ness there,—these are the extremes of the Negro problem which
we met that day, and we scarce knew which we preferred.

Here and there we meet distinct characters quite out of the
ordinary. One came out of a piece of newly cleared ground,
making a wide detour to avoid the snakes. He was an old,
hollow-cheeked man, with a drawn and characterful brown
face. He had a sort of self-contained quaintness and rough
humor impossible to describe; a certain cynical earnestness that
puzzled one. "The niggers were jealous of me over on the other
place," he said, "and so me and the old woman begged this
piece of woods, and I cleared it up myself. Made nothing for
two years, but I reckon I've got a crop now." The cotton looked
tall and rich, and we praised it. He curtsied low, and then bowed
almost to the ground, with an imperturbable gravity that seemed
almost suspicious. Then he continued, "My mule died last
week,"—a calamity in this land equal to a devastating fire in
town,—"but a white man loaned me another." Then he added,
eyeing us, "Oh, I gets along with white folks." We turned the
conversation. "Bears? deer?" he answered, "well, I should say
there were," and he let fly a string of brave oaths, as he told
hunting-tales of the swamp. We left him standing still in the
middle of the road looking after us, and yet apparently not no-
ticing us.

The Whistle place, which includes his bit of land, was bought
soon after the war by an English syndicate, the "Dixie Cotton
and Corn Company." A marvellous deal of style their factor put
on, with his servants and coach-and-six; so much so that the
concern soon landed in inextricable bankruptcy. Nobody lives
in the old house now, but a man comes each winter out of the
North and collects his high rents. I know not which are the more
touching,—such old empty houses, or the homes of the masters'
sons. Sad and bitter tales lie hidden back of those white doors,—
tales of poverty, of struggle, of disappointment. A revolution
such as that of '63 is a terrible thing; they that rose rich in the

morning often slept in paupers' beds. Beggars and vulgar spec-
ulators rose to rule over them, and their children went astray.
See yonder sad-colored house, with its cabins and fences and
glad crops? It is not glad within; last month the prodigal son of
the struggling father wrote home from the city for money.
Money! Where was it to come from? And so the son rose in the
night and killed his baby, and killed his wife, and shot himself
dead. And the world passed on.

I remember wheeling around a bend in the road beside a
graceful bit of forest and a singing brook. A long low house
faced us, with porch and flying pillars, great oaken door, and
a broad lawn shining in the evening sun. But the window-panes
were gone, the pillars were worm-eaten, and the moss-grown
roof was falling in. Half curiously I peered through the un-
hinged door, and saw where, on the wall across the hall, was
written in once gay letters a faded "Welcome."

Quite a contrast to the southwestern part of Dougherty
County is the northwest. Soberly timbered in oak and pine, it
has none of that half-tropical luxuriance of the southwest. Then,
too, there are fewer signs of a romantic past, and more of systematic modern land-grabbing and money-getting. White people are more in evidence here, and farmer and hired labor
replace to some extent the absentee landlord and rack-rented
tenant. The crops have neither the luxuriance of the richer land
nor the signs of neglect so often seen, and there were fences and
meadows here and there. More of this land was poor, and beneath the notice of the slave-baron, before the war. Since then
his nephews and the poor whites and the Jews have seized it.
The returns of the farmer are too small to allow much for wages,
and yet he will not sell off small farms. There is the Negro San-
ford; he has worked fourteen years as overseer on the Ladson
place, and "paid out enough for fertilizers to have bought a
farm," but the owner will not sell off a few acres.

Two children—a boy and a girl—are hoeing sturdily in the
fields on the farm where Corliss works. He is smooth-faced and
brown, and is fencing up his pigs. He used to run a successful
cotton-gin, but the Cotton Seed Oil Trust has forced the price
of ginning so low that he says it hardly pays him. He points out

a stately old house over the way as the home of "Pa Willis." We eagerly ride over, for "Pa Willis" was the tall and powerful black Moses who led the Negroes for a generation, and led them well. He was a Baptist preacher, and when he died two thousand black people followed him to the grave; and now they preach his funeral sermon each year. His widow lives here,—a weazened, sharp-featured little woman, who curtsied quaintly as we greeted her. Further on lives Jack Delson, the most prosperous Negro farmer in the county. It is a joy to meet him,—a great broad-shouldered, handsome black man, intelligent and jovial. Six hundred and fifty acres he owns, and has eleven black tenants. A neat and tidy home nestled in a flower-garden, and a little store stands beside it.

We pass the Munson place, where a plucky white widow is renting and struggling; and the eleven hundred acres of the Sennet plantation, with its Negro overseer. Then the character of the farms begins to change. Nearly all the lands belong to Russian Jews; the overseers are white, and the cabins are bare board houses scattered here and there. The rents are high, and day-laborers and "contract" hands abound. It is a keen, hard struggle for living here, and few have time to talk. Tired with the long ride, we gladly drive into Gillonsville. It is a silent cluster of farm-houses standing on the cross-roads, with one of its stores closed and the other kept by a Negro preacher. They tell great tales of busy times at Gillonsville before all the railroads came to Albany; now it is chiefly a memory. Riding down the street, we stop at the preacher's and seat ourselves before the door. It was one of those scenes one cannot soon forget:—a wide, low, little house, whose motherly roof reached over and sheltered a snug little porch. There we sat, after the long hot drive, drinking cool water,—the talkative little storekeeper who is my daily companion; the silent old black woman patching pantaloons and saying never a word; the ragged picture of helpless misfortune who called in just to see the preacher; and finally the neat matronly preacher's wife, plump, yellow, and intelligent. "Own land?" said the wife; "well, only this house." Then she added quietly, "We did buy seven hundred acres up yonder, and paid for it; but they cheated us out of it. Sells was the

owner." "Sells!" echoed the ragged misfortune, who was leaning against the balustrade and listening, "he's a regular cheat.
I worked for him thirty-seven days this spring, and he paid me
in cardboard checks which were to be cashed at the end of the
month. But he never cashed them,—kept putting me off. Then
the sheriff came and took my mule and corn and furniture—"
"Furniture?" I asked; "but furniture is exempt from seizure by
law." "Well, he took it just the same," said the hard-faced man.

VIII

OF THE QUEST OF THE GOLDEN FLEECE

But the Brute said in his breast, "Till the mills I grind have
  ceased,
The riches shall be dust of dust, dry ashes be the feast!
    "On the strong and cunning few
     Cynic favors I will strew;
I will stuff their maw with overplus until their spirit dies;
    From the patient and the low
    I will take the joys they know;
    They shall hunger after vanities and still an-hungered go.
Madness shall be on the people, ghastly jealousies arise;
Brother's blood shall cry on brother up the dead and empty
  skies."

WILLIAM VAUGHN MOODY

Have you ever seen a cotton-field white with the harvest,—its
golden fleece hovering above the black earth like a silvery cloud
edged with dark green, its bold white signals waving like the

foam of billows from Carolina to Texas across that Black and human Sea? I have sometimes half suspected that here the winged ram Chrysomallus left that Fleece after which Jason and his Argonauts went vaguely wandering into the shadowy East three thousand years ago; and certainly one might frame a pretty and not far-fetched analogy of witchery and dragon's teeth, and blood and armed men, between the ancient and the modern Quest of the Golden Fleece in the Black Sea.

And now the golden fleece is found; not only found, but, in its birthplace, woven. For the hum of the cotton-mills is the newest and most significant thing in the New South to-day. All through the Carolinas and Georgia, away down to Mexico, rise these gaunt red buildings, bare and homely, and yet so busy and noisy withal that they scarce seem to belong to the slow and sleepy land. Perhaps they sprang from dragons' teeth. So the Cotton Kingdom still lives; the world still bows beneath her sceptre. Even the markets that once defied the *parvenu* have crept one by one across the seas, and then slowly and reluctantly, but surely, have started toward the Black Belt.

To be sure, there are those who wag their heads knowingly and tell us that the capital of the Cotton Kingdom has moved from the Black to the White Belt,—that the Negro of to-day raises not more than half of the cotton crop. Such men forget that the cotton crop has doubled, and more than doubled, since the era of slavery, and that, even granting their contention, the Negro is still supreme in a Cotton Kingdom larger than that on which the Confederacy builded its hopes. So the Negro forms to-day one of the chief figures in a great world-industry; and this, for its own sake, and in the light of historic interest, makes the field-hands of the cotton country worth studying.

We seldom study the condition of the Negro to-day honestly and carefully. It is so much easier to assume that we know it all. Or perhaps, having already reached conclusions in our own minds, we are loth to have them disturbed by facts. And yet how little we really know of these millions,—of their daily lives and longings, of their homely joys and sorrows, of their real shortcomings and the meaning of their crimes! All this we can only learn by intimate contact with the masses, and not by wholesale arguments covering millions separate in time and space, and differing widely in training and culture. To-day, then, my reader, let us turn our faces to the Black Belt of Georgia and seek simply to know the condition of the black farm-laborers of one county there.

Here in 1890 lived ten thousand Negroes and two thousand whites. The country is rich, yet the people are poor. The key-note of the Black Belt is debt; not commercial credit, but debt in the sense of continued inability on the part of the mass of the population to make income cover expense. This is the direct heritage of the South from the wasteful economies of the slave *régime*; but it was emphasized and brought to a crisis by the Emancipation of the slaves. In 1860, Dougherty County had six thousand slaves, worth at least two and a half millions of dollars; its farms were estimated at three millions,—making five and a half millions of property, the value of which depended largely on the slave system, and on the speculative demand for land once marvellously rich but already partially devitalized by careless and exhaustive culture. The war then meant a financial crash; in place of the five and a half millions of 1860, there remained in 1870 only farms valued at less than two millions. With this came increased competition in cotton culture from the rich lands of Texas; a steady fall in the normal price of cotton followed, from about fourteen cents a pound in 1860 until it reached four cents in 1898. Such a financial revolution was it that involved the owners of the cotton-belt in debt. And if things went ill with the master, how fared it with the man?

The plantations of Dougherty County in slavery days were not as imposing and aristocratic as those of Virginia. The Big House was smaller and usually one-storied, and sat very near the slave cabins. Sometimes these cabins stretched off on either side like wings; sometimes only on one side, forming a double row, or edging the road that turned into the plantation from the main thoroughfare. The form and disposition of the laborers' cabins throughout the Black Belt is to-day the same as in slavery days. Some live in the self-same cabins, others in cabins rebuilt on the sites of the old. All are sprinkled in little groups over the face of the land, centering about some dilapidated Big

House where the head-tenant or agent lives. The general character and arrangement of these dwellings remains on the whole
unaltered. There were in the county, outside the corporate town
of Albany, about fifteen hundred Negro families in 1898. Out
of all these, only a single family occupied a house with seven
rooms; only fourteen have five rooms or more. The mass live in
one- and two-room homes.

The size and arrangements of a people's homes are no unfair
index of their condition. If, then, we inquire more carefully into
these Negro homes, we find much that is unsatisfactory. All
over the face of the land is the one-room cabin—now standing
in the shadow of the Big House, now staring at the dusty road,
now rising dark and sombre amid the green of the cotton-fields.
It is nearly always old and bare, built of rough boards, and neither plastered nor ceiled. Light and ventilation are supplied by
the single door and by the square hole in the wall with its
wooden shutter. There is no glass, porch, or ornamentation without. Within is a fireplace, black and smoky, and usually unsteady with age. A bed or two, a table, a wooden chest, and a
few chairs compose the furniture; while a stray show-bill or a
newspaper makes up the decorations for the walls. Now and
then one may find such a cabin kept scrupulously neat, with
merry steaming fireplace and hospitable door; but the majority
are dirty and dilapidated, smelling of eating and sleeping, poorly
ventilated, and anything but homes.

Above all, the cabins are crowded. We have come to associate crowding with homes in cities almost exclusively. This is
primarily because we have so little accurate knowledge of country life. Here in Dougherty County one may find families of
eight and ten occupying one or two rooms, and for every ten
rooms of house accommodation for the Negroes there are
twenty-five persons. The worst tenement abominations of New
York do not have above twenty-two persons for every ten rooms.
Of course, one small, close room in a city, without a yard, is in
many respects worse than the larger single country room. In
other respects it is better; it has glass windows, a decent chim-
ney, and a trustworthy floor. The single great advantage of the

Negro peasant is that he may spend most of his life outside his hovel, in the open fields.

There are four chief causes of these wretched homes: First, long custom born of slavery has assigned such homes to Negroes; white laborers would be offered better accommodations, and might, for that and similar reasons, give better work. Secondly, the Negroes, used to such accommodations, do not as a rule demand better; they do not know what better houses mean. Thirdly, the landlords as a class have not yet come to realize that it is a good business investment to raise the standard of living among labor by slow and judicious methods; that a Negro laborer who demands three rooms and fifty cents a day would give more efficient work and leave a larger profit than a discouraged toiler herding his family in one room and working for thirty cents. Lastly, among such conditions of life there are few incentives to make the laborer become a better farmer. If he is ambitious, he moves to town or tries other labor; as a tenant-farmer his outlook is almost hopeless, and following it as a makeshift, he takes the house that is given him without protest.

In such homes, then, these Negro peasants live. The families are both small and large; there are many single tenants,— widows and bachelors, and remnants of broken groups. The system of labor and the size of the houses both tend to the breaking up of family groups: The grown children go away as contract hands or migrate to town, the sister goes into service; and so one finds many families with hosts of babies, and many newly married couples, but comparatively few families with half-grown and grown sons and daughters. The average size of Negro families has undoubtedly decreased since the war, primarily from economic stress. In Russia over a third of the bridegrooms and over half the brides are under twenty; the same was true of the ante-bellum Negroes. To-day, however, very few of the boys and less than a fifth of the Negro girls under twenty are married. The young men marry between the ages of twenty-five and thirty-five; the young women between twenty and thirty. Such postponement is due to the difficulty of earning sufficient to rear and support a family; and it undoubtedly leads, in the

country districts, to sexual immorality. The form of this immorality, however, is very seldom that of prostitution, and less
frequently that of illegitimacy than one would imagine. Rather,
it takes the form of separation and desertion after a family group
has been formed. The number of separated persons is thirty-five
to the thousand,—a very large number. It would of course be
unfair to compare this number with divorce statistics, for many
of these separated women are in reality widowed, were the truth
known, and in other cases the separation is not permanent.
Nevertheless, here lies the seat of greatest moral danger. There
is little or no prostitution among these Negroes, and over three-
fourths of the families, as found by house-to-house investigation, deserve to be classed as decent people with considerable
regard for female chastity. To be sure, the ideas of the mass
would not suit New England, and there are many loose habits
and notions. Yet the rate of illegitimacy is undoubtedly lower
than in Austria or Italy, and the women as a class are modest.
The plague-spot in sexual relations is easy marriage and easy
separation. This is no sudden development, nor the fruit of
Emancipation. It is the plain heritage from slavery. In those days
Sam, with his master's consent, "took up" with Mary. No ceremony was necessary, and in the busy life of the great plantations of the Black Belt it was usually dispensed with. If now the
master needed Sam's work in another plantation or in another
part of the same plantation, or if he took a notion to sell the
slave, Sam's married life with Mary was usually unceremoni-
ously broken, and then it was clearly to the master's interest to
have both of them take new mates. This widespread custom of
two centuries has not been eradicated in thirty years. To-day
Sam's grandson "takes up" with a woman without license or
ceremony; they live together decently and honestly, and are, to
all intents and purposes, man and wife. Sometimes these unions
are never broken until death; but in too many cases family quar-
rels, a roving spirit, a rival suitor, or perhaps more frequently
the hopeless battle to support a family, lead to separation, and
a broken household is the result. The Negro church has done
much to stop this practice, and now most marriage ceremonies
are performed by the pastors. Nevertheless, the evil is still deep

seated, and only a general raising of the standard of living will finally cure it.

Looking now at the county black population as a whole, it is fair to characterize it as poor and ignorant. Perhaps ten per cent compose the well-to-do and the best of the laborers, while at least nine per cent are thoroughly lewd and vicious. The rest, over eighty per cent, are poor and ignorant, fairly honest and well meaning, plodding, and to a degree shiftless, with some but not great sexual looseness. Such class lines are by no means fixed; they vary, one might almost say, with the price of cotton. The degree of ignorance cannot easily be expressed. We may say, for instance, that nearly two-thirds of them cannot read or write. This but partially expresses the fact. They are ignorant of the world about them, of modern economic organization, of the function of government, of individual worth and possibilities,— of nearly all those things which slavery in self-defence had to keep them from learning. Much that the white boy imbibes from his earliest social atmosphere forms the puzzling problems of the black boy's mature years. America is not another word for Opportunity to *all* her sons.

It is easy for us to lose ourselves in details in endeavoring to grasp and comprehend the real condition of a mass of human beings. We often forget that each unit in the mass is a throbbing human soul. Ignorant it may be, and poverty stricken, black and curious in limb and ways and thought; and yet it loves and hates, it toils and tires, it laughs and weeps its bitter tears, and looks in vague and awful longing at the grim horizon of its life,—all this, even as you and I. These black thousands are not in reality lazy; they are improvident and careless; they insist on breaking the monotony of toil with a glimpse at the great town-world on Saturday; they have their loafers and their rascals; but the great mass of them work continuously and faithfully for a return, and under circumstances that would call forth equal voluntary effort from few if any other modern laboring class. Over eighty-eight per cent of them—men, women, and children—are farmers. Indeed, this is almost the only industry. Most of the children get their schooling after the "crops are laid by," and very few there are that stay in school after the spring work has begun. Child-labor is to be found here in some of its worst phases, as fostering ignorance and stunting physical development. With the grown men of the county there is little variety in work: thirteen hundred are farmers, and two hundred are laborers, teamsters, etc., including twenty-four artisans, ten merchants, twenty-one preachers, and four teachers. This narrowness of life reaches its maximum among the women: thirteen hundred and fifty of these are farm laborers, one hundred are servants and washerwomen, leaving sixty-five housewives, eight teachers, and six seamstresses.

Among this people there is no leisure class. We often forget that in the United States over half the young and adults are not in the world earning incomes, but are making homes, learning of the world, or resting after the heat of the strife. But here ninety-six per cent are toiling; no one with leisure to turn the bare and cheerless cabin into a home, no old folks to sit beside the fire and hand down traditions of the past; little of careless happy childhood and dreaming youth. The dull monotony of daily toil is broken only by the gayety of the thoughtless and the Saturday trip to town. The toil, like all farm toil, is monotonous, and here there are little machinery and few tools to relieve its burdensome drudgery. But with all this, it is work in the pure open air, and this is something in a day when fresh air is scarce.

The land on the whole is still fertile, despite long abuse. For nine or ten months in succession the crops will come if asked: garden vegetables in April, grain in May, melons in June and July, hay in August, sweet potatoes in September, and cotton from then to Christmas. And yet on two-thirds of the land there is but one crop, and that leaves the toilers in debt. Why is this?

Away down the Baysan Road, where the broad flat fields are flanked by great oak forests, is a plantation; many thousands of acres it used to run, here and there, and beyond the great wood. Thirteen hundred human beings here obeyed the call of one,—were his in body, and largely in soul. One of them lives there yet,—a short, stocky man, his dull-brown face seamed and drawn, and his tightly curled hair gray-white. The crops? Just tolerable, he said; just tolerable. Getting on? No—he wasn't getting on at all. Smith of Albany "furnishes" him, and his rent is eight hundred pounds of cotton. Can't make anything at that. Why didn't he buy land? *Humph!* Takes money to buy land. And he turns away. Free! The most piteous thing amid all the black ruin of war-time, amid the broken fortunes of the masters, the blighted hopes of mothers and maidens, and the fall of an empire,—the most piteous thing amid all this was the black freedman who threw down his hoe because the world called him free. What did such a mockery of freedom mean? Not a cent of money, not an inch of land, not a mouthful of victuals,—not even ownership of the rags on his back. Free! On Saturday, once or twice a month, the old master, before the war, used to dole out bacon and meal to his Negroes. And after the first flush of freedom wore off, and his true helplessness dawned on the freedman, he came and picked up his hoe, and old master still doled out his bacon and meal. The legal form of service was theoretically far different; in practice, task-work or "cropping" was substituted for daily toil in gangs; and the slave gradually became a metayer, or tenant on shares, in name, but a laborer with indeterminate wages in fact.

Still the price of cotton fell, and gradually the landlords deserted their plantations, and the reign of the merchant began. The merchant of the Black Belt is a curious institution,—part banker, part landlord, part contractor, and part despot. His store, which used most frequently to stand at the cross-roads and become the centre of a weekly village, has now moved to town; and thither the Negro tenant follows him. The merchant keeps everything,—clothes and shoes, coffee and sugar, pork and meal, canned and dried goods, wagons and ploughs, seed and fertilizer,—and what he has not in stock he can give you an order for at the store across the way. Here, then, comes the tenant, Sam Scott, after he has contracted with some absent landlord's agent for hiring forty acres of land; he fingers his hat nervously until the merchant finishes his morning chat with Colonel Sanders, and calls out, "Well, Sam, what do you want?" Sam wants him to "furnish" him,—*i.e.*, to advance him food and clothing for the year, and perhaps seed and tools, until his crop is raised and sold. If Sam seems a favorable subject, he and

the merchant go to a lawyer, and Sam executes a chattel mortgage on his mule and wagon in return for seed and a week's
rations. As soon as the green cotton-leaves appear above the
ground, another mortgage is given on the "crop." Every Saturday, or at longer intervals, Sam calls upon the merchant for his
"rations"; a family of five usually gets about thirty pounds of
fat side-pork and a couple of bushels of corn-meal a month.
Besides this, clothing and shoes must be furnished; if Sam or
his family is sick, there are orders on the druggist and doctor;
if the mule wants shoeing, an order on the blacksmith, etc. If
Sam is a hard worker and crops promise well, he is often encouraged to buy more,—sugar, extra clothes, perhaps a buggy.
But he is seldom encouraged to save. When cotton rose to ten
cents last fall, the shrewd merchants of Dougherty County sold
a thousand buggies in one season, mostly to black men.

The security offered for such transactions—a crop and chattel mortgage—may at first seem slight. And, indeed, the merchants tell many a true tale of shiftlessness and cheating; of
cotton picked at night, mules disappearing, and tenants ab-
sconding. But on the whole the merchant of the Black Belt is
the most prosperous man in the section. So skilfully and so
closely has he drawn the bonds of the law about the tenant, that
the black man has often simply to choose between pauperism
and crime; he "waives" all homestead exemptions in his contract; he cannot touch his own mortgaged crop, which the laws
put almost in the full control of the land-owner and of the merchant. When the crop is growing the merchant watches it like
a hawk; as soon as it is ready for market he takes possession of
it, sells it, pays the land-owner his rent, subtracts his bill for
supplies, and if, as sometimes happens, there is anything left,
he hands it over to the black serf for his Christmas celebration.

The direct result of this system is an all-cotton scheme of agriculture and the continued bankruptcy of the tenant. The currency of the Black Belt is cotton. It is a crop always salable for
ready money, not usually subject to great yearly fluctuations
in price, and one which the Negroes know how to raise. The
landlord therefore demands his rent in cotton, and the merchant will accept mortgages on no other crop. There is no use

asking the black tenant, then, to diversify his crops,—he cannot under this system. Moreover, the system is bound to bankrupt the tenant. I remember once meeting a little one-mule wagon on the River road. A young black fellow sat in it driving listlessly, his elbows on his knees. His dark-faced wife sat beside him, stolid, silent.

"Hello!" cried my driver,—he has a most impudent way of addressing these people, though they seem used to it,—"what have you got there?"

"Meat and meal," answered the man, stopping. The meat lay uncovered in the bottom of the wagon,—a great thin side of fat pork covered with salt; the meal was in a white bushel bag.

"What did you pay for that meat?"

"Ten cents a pound." It could have been bought for six or seven cents cash.

"And the meal?"

"Two dollars." One dollar and ten cents is the cash price in town. Here was a man paying five dollars for goods which he could have bought for three dollars cash, and raised for one dollar or one dollar and a half.

Yet it is not wholly his fault. The Negro farmer started behind,—started in debt. This was not his choosing, but the crime of this happy-go-lucky nation which goes blundering along with its Reconstruction tragedies, its Spanish war interludes and Philippine matinees, just as though God really were dead. Once in debt, it is no easy matter for a whole race to emerge.

In the year of low-priced cotton, 1898, out of three hundred tenant families one hundred and seventy-five ended their year's work in debt to the extent of fourteen thousand dollars; fifty cleared nothing, and the remaining seventy-five made a total profit of sixteen hundred dollars. The net indebtedness of the black tenant families of the whole county must have been at least sixty thousand dollars. In a more prosperous year the situation is far better; but on the average the majority of tenants end the year even, or in debt, which means that they work for board and clothes. Such an economic organization is radically wrong. Whose is the blame?

The underlying causes of this situation are complicated but

discernible. And one of the chief, outside the carelessness of the nation in letting the slave start with nothing, is the widespread opinion among the merchants and employers of the Black Belt that only by the slavery of debt can the Negro be kept at work. Without doubt, some pressure was necessary at the beginning of the free-labor system to keep the listless and lazy at work; and even to-day the mass of the Negro laborers need stricter guardianship than most Northern laborers. Behind this honest and widespread opinion dishonesty and cheating of the ignorant laborers have a good chance to take refuge. And to all this must be added the obvious fact that a slave ancestry and a system of unrequited toil has not improved the efficiency or temper of the mass of black laborers. Nor is this peculiar to Sambo; it has in history been just as true of John and Hans, of Jacques and Pat, of all ground-down peasantries. Such is the situation of the mass of the Negroes in the Black Belt to-day; and they are thinking about it. Crime, and a cheap and dangerous socialism, are the inevitable results of this pondering. I see now that ragged black man sitting on a log, aimlessly whittling a stick. He muttered to me with the murmur of many ages, when he said: "White man sit down whole year; Nigger work day and night and make crop; Nigger hardly gits bread and meat; white man sittin' down gits all. *It's wrong.*" And what do the better classes of Negroes do to improve their situation? One of two things: if any way possible, they buy land; if not, they migrate to town. Just as centuries ago it was no easy thing for the serf to escape into the freedom of town-life, even so to-day there are hindrances laid in the way of county laborers. In considerable parts of all the Gulf States, and especially in Mississippi, Louisiana, and Arkansas, the Negroes on the plantations in the back-country districts are still held at forced labor practically without wages. Especially is this true in districts where the farmers are composed of the more ignorant class of poor whites, and the Negroes are beyond the reach of schools and intercourse with their advancing fellows. If such a peon should run away, the sheriff, elected by white suffrage, can usually be depended on to catch the fugitive, return him, and ask no questions. If he escape to another county, a charge of petty thieving, easily true, can be depended upon to secure his return. Even if some unduly offi-cious person insists upon a trial, neighborly comity will probably make his conviction sure, and then the labor due the county can easily be bought by the master. Such a system is impossible in the more civilized parts of the South, or near the large towns and cities; but in those vast stretches of land beyond the tele-graph and the newspaper the spirit of the Thirteenth Amend-ment is sadly broken. This represents the lowest economic depths of the black American peasant; and in a study of the rise and condition of the Negro freeholder we must trace his eco-nomic progress from this modern serfdom.

Even in the better-ordered country districts of the South the free movement of agricultural laborers is hindered by the migration-agent laws. The Associated Press recently informed the world of the arrest of a young white man in Southern Geor-gia who represented the "Atlantic Naval Supplies Company," and who "was caught in the act of enticing hands from the tur-pentine farm of Mr. John Greer." The crime for which this young man was arrested is taxed five hundred dollars for each county in which the employment agent proposes to gather la-borers for work outside the State. Thus the Negroes' ignorance of the labor-market outside his own vicinity is increased rather than diminished by the laws of nearly every Southern State.

Similar to such measures is the unwritten law of the back districts and small towns of the South, that the character of all Negroes unknown to the mass of the community must be vouched for by some white man. This is really a revival of the old Roman idea of the patron under whose protection the new-made freedman was put. In many instances this system has been of great good to the Negro, and very often under the protection and guidance of the former master's family, or other white friends, the freedman progressed in wealth and morality. But the same system has in other cases resulted in the refusal of whole communities to recognize the right of a Negro to change his habitation and to be master of his own fortunes. A black stranger in Baker County, Georgia, for instance, is liable to be stopped anywhere on the public highway and made to state his business to the satisfaction of any white interrogator. If he fails to give a suitable answer, or seems too independent or "sassy," he may be arrested or summarily driven away.

Thus it is that in the country districts of the South, by written or unwritten law, peonage, hindrances to the migration of labor, and a system of white patronage exists over large areas. Besides this, the chance for lawless oppression and illegal exactions is vastly greater in the country than in the city, and nearly all the more serious race disturbances of the last decade have arisen from disputes in the county between master and man,—as, for instance, the Sam Hose affair. As a result of such a situation, there arose, first, the Black Belt; and, second, the Migration to Town. The Black Belt was not, as many assumed, a movement toward fields of labor under more genial climatic conditions; it was primarily a huddling for self-protection,—a massing of the black population for mutual defence in order to secure the peace and tranquillity necessary to economic advance. This movement took place between Emancipation and 1880, and only partially accomplished the desired results. The rush to town since 1880 is the counter-movement of men disappointed in the economic opportunities of the Black Belt.

In Dougherty County, Georgia, one can see easily the results of this experiment in huddling for protection. Only ten per cent of the adult population was born in the county, and yet the blacks outnumber the whites four or five to one. There is undoubtedly a security to the blacks in their very numbers,—a personal freedom from arbitrary treatment, which makes hundreds of laborers cling to Dougherty in spite of low wages and economic distress. But a change is coming, and slowly but surely even here the agricultural laborers are drifting to town and leaving the broad acres behind. Why is this? Why do not the Negroes become land-owners, and build up the black landed peasantry, which has for a generation and more been the dream of philanthropist and statesman?

To the car-window sociologist, to the man who seeks to understand and know the South by devoting the few leisure hours of a holiday trip to unravelling the snarl of centuries,—to such men very often the whole trouble with the black field-hand may be summed up by Aunt Ophelia's word, "Shiftless!" They have noted repeatedly scenes like one I saw last summer. We were riding along the highroad to town at the close of a long hot day. A couple of young black fellows passed us in a mule-team, with several bushels of loose corn in the ear. One was driving, listlessly bent forward, his elbows on his knees,—a happy-go-lucky, careless picture of irresponsibility. The other was fast asleep in the bottom of the wagon. As we passed we notice an ear of corn fall from the wagon. They never saw it,—not they. A rod farther on we noted another ear on the ground; and between that creeping mule and town we counted twenty-six ears of corn. Shiftless? Yes, the personification of shiftlessness. And yet follow those boys: they are not lazy; to-morrow morning they'll be up with the sun; they work hard when they do work, and they work willingly. They have no sordid, selfish, money-getting ways, but rather a fine disdain for mere cash. They'll loaf before your face and work behind your back with good-natured honesty. They'll steal a watermelon, and hand you back your lost purse intact. Their great defect as laborers lies in their lack of incentive to work beyond the mere pleasure of physical exertion. They are careless because they have not found that it pays to be careful; they are improvident because the improvident ones of their acquaintance get on about as well as the provident. Above all, they cannot see why they should take unusual pains to make the white man's land better, or to fatten his mule, or save his corn. On the other hand, the white land-owner argues that any attempt to improve these laborers by increased responsibility, or higher wages, or better homes, or land of their own, would be sure to result in failure. He shows his Northern visitor the scarred and wretched land; the ruined mansions, the worn-out soil and mortgaged acres, and says, This is Negro freedom!

Now it happens that both master and man have just enough argument on their respective sides to make it difficult for them to understand each other. The Negro dimly personifies in the white man all his ills and misfortunes; if he is poor, it is because the white man seizes the fruit of his toil; if he is ignorant, it is because the white man gives him neither time or facilities to learn; and, indeed, if any misfortune happens to him, it is because of some hidden machinations of "white folks." On the other hand, the masters and the masters' sons have never been able to see why the Negro, instead of settling down to be day-laborers for bread and clothes, are infected with a silly desire to rise in the world, and why they are sulky, dissatisfied, and careless, where their fathers were happy and dumb and faithful. "Why, you niggers have an easier time than I do," said a puzzled Albany merchant to his black customer. "Yes," he replied, "and so does yo' hogs."

Taking, then, the dissatisfied and shiftless field-hand as a starting-point, let us inquire how the black thousands of Dougherty have struggled from him up toward their ideal, and what that ideal is. All social struggle is evidenced by the rise, first of economic, then of social classes, among a homogeneous population. To-day the following economic classes are plainly differentiated among these Negroes.

A "submerged tenth" of croppers, with a few paupers; forty per cent who are metayers and thirty-nine per cent of semi-metayers and wage-laborers. There are left five per cent of money-renters and six per cent of freeholders,—the "Upper Ten" of the land. The croppers are entirely without capital, even in the limited sense of food or money to keep them from seed-time to harvest. All they furnish is their labor; the land-owner furnishes land, stock, tools, seed, and house; and at the end of the year the laborer gets from a third to a half of the crop. Out of his share, however, comes pay and interest for food and clothing advanced him during the year. Thus we have a laborer without capital and without wages, and an employer whose capital is largely his employees' wages. It is an unsatisfactory arrangement, both for hirer and hired, and is usually in vogue on poor land with hard-pressed owners.

Above the croppers come the great mass of the black population who work the land on their own responsibility, paying rent in cotton and supported by the crop-mortgage system. After the war this system was attractive to the freedmen on account of its larger freedom and its possibilities for making a surplus. But with the carrying out of the crop-lien system, the deterioration of the land, and the slavery of debt, the position of the metayers has sunk to a dead level of practically unrewarded toil. Formerly all tenants had some capital, and often consider-able; but absentee landlordism, rising rack-rent, and falling cotton have stripped them well-nigh of all, and probably not over half of them to-day own their mules. The change from cropper to tenant was accomplished by fixing the rent. If, now, the rent fixed was reasonable, this was an incentive to the tenant to strive. On the other hand, if the rent was too high, or if the land deteriorated, the result was to discourage and check the efforts of the black peasantry. There is no doubt that the latter case is true; that in Dougherty County every economic advantage of the price of cotton in market and of the strivings of the tenant has been taken advantage of by the landlords and merchants, and swallowed up in rent and interest. If cotton rose in price, the rent rose even higher; if cotton fell, the rent remained or followed reluctantly. If a tenant worked hard and raised a large crop, his rent was raised the next year; if that year the crop failed, his corn was confiscated and his mule sold for debt. There were, of course, exceptions to this,—cases of personal kindness and forbearance; but in the vast majority of cases the rule was to extract the uttermost farthing from the mass of the black farm laborers.

The average metayer pays from twenty to thirty per cent of his crop in rent. The result of such rack-rent can only be evil,—abuse and neglect of the soil, deterioration in the character of the laborers, and a widespread sense of injustice. "Wherever the country is poor," cried Arthur Young, "it is in the hands of metayers," and "their condition is more wretched than that of day-laborers." He was talking of Italy a century ago; but he might have been talking of Dougherty County to-day. And especially is that true to-day which he declares was true in France before the Revolution: "The metayers are considered as little better than menial servants, removable at pleasure, and obliged to conform in all things to the will of the landlords." On this low plane half the black population of Dougherty County—perhaps more than half the black millions of this land—are to-day struggling.

A degree above these we may place those laborers who receive money wages for their work. Some receive a house with perhaps a garden-spot; then supplies of food and clothing are advanced, and certain fixed wages are given at the end of the year, varying from thirty to sixty dollars, out of which the supplies must be paid for, with interest. About eighteen per cent of the population belong to this class of semi-metayers, while twenty-two per cent are laborers paid by the month or year, and are either "furnished" by their own savings or perhaps more usually by some merchant who takes his chances of payment. Such laborers receive from thirty-five to fifty cents a day during the working season. They are usually young unmarried persons, some being women; and when they marry they sink to the class of metayers, or, more seldom, become renters.

The renters for fixed money rentals are the first of the emerging classes, and form five per cent of the families. The sole advantage of this small class is their freedom to choose their crops, and the increased responsibility which comes through having money transactions. While some of the renters differ little in condition from the metayers, yet on the whole they are more intelligent and responsible persons, and are the ones who eventually become land-owners. Their better character and greater shrewdness enable them to gain, perhaps to demand, better terms in rents; rented farms, varying from forty to a hundred acres, bear an average rental of about fifty-four dollars a year. The men who conduct such farms do not long remain renters; either they sink to metayers, or with a successful series of harvests rise to be land-owners.

In 1870 the tax-books of Dougherty report no Negroes as landholders. If there were any such at that time,—and there may have been a few,—their land was probably held in the name of some white patron,—a method not uncommon during slavery. In 1875 ownership of land had begun with seven hundred and fifty acres; ten years later this had increased to over sixty-five hundred acres, to nine thousand acres in 1890 and ten thousand in 1900. The total assessed property has in this same period risen from eighty thousand dollars in 1875 to two hundred and forty thousand dollars in 1900.

Two circumstances complicate this development and make it in some respects difficult to be sure of the real tendencies; they are the panic of 1893, and the low price of cotton in 1898. Besides this, the system of assessing property in the country districts of Georgia is somewhat antiquated and of uncertain statistical value; there are no assessors, and each man makes a sworn return to a tax-receiver. Thus public opinion plays a large part, and the returns vary strangely from year to year. Certainly these figures show the small amount of accumulated capital among the Negroes, and the consequent large dependence of their property on temporary prosperity. They have little to tide over a few years of economic depression, and are at the mercy of the cotton-market far more than the whites. And thus the land-owners, despite their marvellous efforts, are really a transient class, continually being depleted by those who fall back into the class of renters or metayers, and augmented by newcomers from the masses. Of the one hundred land-owners in 1898, half had bought their land since 1983, a fourth between 1890 and 1893, a fifth between 1884 and 1890, and the rest between 1870 and 1884. In all, one hundred and eighty-five Negroes have owned land in this county since 1875.

If all the black land-owners who had ever held land here had kept it or left it in the hands of black men, the Negroes would have owned nearer thirty thousand acres than the fifteen thousand they now hold. And yet these fifteen thousand acres are a creditable showing,—a proof of no little weight of the worth and ability of the Negro people. If they had been given an economic start at Emancipation, if they had been in an enlightened and rich community which really desired their best good, then we might perhaps call such a result small or even insignificant. But for a few thousand poor ignorant field-hands, in the face of poverty, a falling market, and social stress, to save and capitalize two hundred thousand dollars in a generation has meant a tremendous effort. The rise of a nation, the pressing forward of a social class, means a bitter struggle, a hard and soul-sickening battle with the world such as few of the more favored classes know or appreciate.

Out of the hard economic conditions of this portion of the Black Belt, only six per cent of the population have succeeded in emerging into peasant proprietorship; and these are not all firmly fixed, but grow and shrink in number with the wavering of the cotton-market. Fully ninety-four per cent have struggled for land and failed, and half of them sit in hopeless serfdom. For these there is one other avenue of escape toward which they have turned in increasing numbers, namely, migration to town. A glance at the distribution of land among the black owners curiously reveals this fact. In 1898 the holdings were as follows: Under forty acres, forty-nine families; forty to two hundred and fifty acres, seventeen families; two hundred and fifty to one thousand acres, thirteen families; one thousand or more acres, two families. Now in 1890 there were forty-four holdings, but only nine of these were under forty acres. The great increase of holdings, then, has come in the buying of small homesteads near town, where their owners really share in the town life; this is a part of the rush to town. And for every land-owner who has thus hurried away from the narrow and hard conditions of country life, how many field-hands, how many tenants, how many ruined renters, have joined that long procession? Is it not strange compensation? The sin of the country districts is visited on the town, and the social sores of city life to-day may, here in Dougherty County, and perhaps in many places near and far, look for their final healing without the city walls.

IX

OF THE SONS OF MASTER AND MAN

Life treads on life, and heart on heart;
We press too close in church and mart
To keep a dream or grave apart.
                    MRS. BROWNING

The world-old phenomenon of the contact of diverse races of men is to have new exemplification during the new century. Indeed, the characteristic of our age is the contact of European civilization with the world's undeveloped peoples. Whatever we may say of the results of such contact in the past, it certainly forms a chapter in human action not pleasant to look back upon. War, murder, slavery, extermination, and debauchery,—this has again and again been the result of carrying civilization and the blessed gospel to the isles of the sea and the heathen without the law. Nor does it altogether satisfy the conscience of the modern world to be told complacently that all this has been right and proper, the fated triumph of strength over weakness, of righteousness over evil, of superiors over inferiors. It would certainly be soothing if one could readily believe all this; and yet there are too many ugly facts for everything to be thus easily explained away. We feel and know that there are many delicate differences in race psychology, numberless changes that our crude social measurements are not yet able to follow minutely, which explain much of history and social development. At the same time, too, we know that these considerations have never adequately explained or excused the triumph of brute force and cunning over weakness and innocence.

It is, then, the strife of all honorable men of the twentieth century to see that in the future competition of races the survival of the fittest shall mean the triumph of the good, the beautiful, and the true; that we may be able to preserve for future civilization all that is really fine and noble and strong, and not continue to put a premium on greed and impudence and cruelty. To bring this hope to fruition, we are compelled daily to turn more and more to a conscientious study of the phenomena of race-contact,—to a study frank and fair, and not falsified and colored by our wishes or our fears. And we have in the South as fine a field for such a study as the world affords,—a field, to be sure, which the average American scientist deems somewhat beneath his dignity, and which the average man who is not a scientist knows all about, but nevertheless a line of study which by reason of the enormous race complications with which God seems about to punish this nation must increasingly claim our sober attention, study, and thought, we must ask, what are the actual relations of whites and blacks in the South? and we must be answered, not by apology or fault-finding, but by a plain, unvarnished tale.

In the civilized life of to-day the contact of men and their relations to each other fall in a few main lines of action and communication: there is, first, the physical proximity of homes and dwelling-places, the way in which neighborhoods group themselves, and the contiguity of neighborhoods. Secondly, and in our age chiefest, there are the economic relations,—the methods by which individuals cooperate for earning a living, for the mutual satisfaction of wants, for the production of wealth.

Next, there are the political relations, the cooperation in social control, in group government, in laying and paying the burden of taxation. In the fourth place, there are the less tangible but highly important forms of intellectual contact and commerce, the interchange of ideas through conversation and conference, through periodicals and libraries; and, above all, the gradual formation for each community of that curious *tertium quid* which we call public opinion. Closely allied with this come the various forms of social contact in everyday life, in travel, in theatres, in house gatherings, in marrying and giving in marriage. Finally, there are the varying forms of religious enterprise, of moral teaching and benevolent endeavor. These are the principal ways in which men living in the same communities are brought into contact with each other. It is my present task, therefore, to indicate, from my point of view, how the black race in the South meet and mingle with the whites in these matters of everyday life.

First, as to physical dwelling. It is usually possible to draw in nearly every Southern community a physical color-line on the map, on the one side of which whites dwell and on the other Negroes. The winding and intricacy of the geographical color-line varies, of course, in different communities. I know some towns where a straight line drawn through the middle of the main street separates nine-tenths of the whites from nine-tenths of the blacks. In other towns the older settlement of whites has been encircled by a broad band of blacks; in still other cases little settlements or nuclei of blacks have sprung up amid surrounding whites. Usually in cities each street has its distinctive color, and only now and then do the colors meet in close proximity. Even in the country something of this segregation is manifest in the smaller areas, and of course in the larger phenomena of the Black Belt.

All this segregation by color is largely independent of that natural clustering by social grades common to all communities. A Negro slum may be in dangerous proximity to a white residence quarter, while it is quite common to find a white slum planted in the heart of a respectable Negro district. One thing, however, seldom occurs: the best of the whites and the best of the Negroes almost never live in anything like close proximity. It thus happens that in nearly every Southern town and city, both whites and blacks see commonly the worst of each other. This is a vast change from the situation in the past, when, through the close contact of master and house-servant in the patriarchal big house, one found the best of both races in close contact and sympathy, while at the same time the squalor and dull round of toil among the field-hands was removed from the sight and hearing of the family. One can easily see how a person who saw slavery thus from his father's parlors, and sees freedom on the streets of a great city, fails to grasp or comprehend the whole of the new picture. On the other hand, the settled belief of the mass of the Negroes that the Southern white people do not have the black man's best interests at heart has been intensified in later years by this continual daily contact of the better class of blacks with the worst representatives of the white race.

Coming now to the economic relations of the races, we are on ground made familiar by study, much discussion, and no little philanthropic effort. And yet with all this there are many essential elements in the cooperation of Negroes and whites for work and wealth that are too readily overlooked or not thoroughly understood. The average American can easily conceive of a rich land awaiting development and filled with black laborers. To him the Southern problem is simply that of making efficient workingmen out of this material, by giving them the requisite technical skill and the help of invested capital. The problem, however, is by no means as simple as this, from the obvious fact that these workingmen have been trained for centuries as slaves. They exhibit, therefore, all the advantages and defects of such training; they are willing and good-natured, but not self-reliant, provident, or careful. If now the economic development of the South is to be pushed to the verge of exploitation, as seems probable, then we have a mass of workingmen thrown into relentless competition with the workingmen of the world, but handicapped by a training the very opposite to that of the modern self-reliant democratic laborer. What the black laborer needs is careful personal guidance, group leadership of men with hearts in their bosoms, to train them to foresight, carefulness, and honesty. Nor does it require any fine-spun theories of racial differences to prove the necessity of such group training after the brains of the race have been knocked out by two hundred and fifty years of assiduous education in submission, carelessness, and stealing. After Emancipation, it was the plain duty of some one to assume this group leadership and training of the Negro laborer. I will not stop here to inquire whose duty it was,—whether that of the white ex-master who had profited by unpaid toil, or the Northern philanthropist whose persistence brought on the crisis, or the National Government whose edict freed the bondmen; I will not stop to ask whose duty it was, but I insist it was the duty of some one to see that these workingmen were not left along and unguided, without capital, without land, without skill, without economic organization, without even the bald protection of law, order, and decency,—left in a great land, not to settle down to slow and careful internal development, but destined to be thrown almost immediately into relentless and sharp competition with the best of modern workingmen under an economic system where every participant is fighting for himself, and too often utterly regardless of the rights or welfare of his neighbor.

For we must never forget that the economic system of the South to-day which has succeeded the old *régime* is not the same system as that of the old industrial North, of England, or of France, with their trades-unions, their restrictive laws, their written and unwritten commercial customs, and their long experience. It is, rather, a copy of that England of the early nineteenth century, before the factory acts,—the England that wrung pity from thinkers and fired the wrath of Carlyle. The rod of empire that passed from the hands of Southern gentlemen in 1865, partly by force, partly by their own petulance, has never returned to them. Rather it has passed to those men who have come to take charge of the industrial exploitation of the New South,—the sons of poor whites fired with a new thirst for wealth and power, thrifty and avaricious Yankees, shrewd and unscrupulous Jews. Into the hands of these men the Southern laborers, white and black, have fallen; and this to their sorrow. For the laborers as such there is in these new captains of industry neither love nor hate, neither sympathy nor romance; it is a cold question of dollars and dividends. Under such a system all labor is bound to suffer. Even the white laborers are not yet intelligent, thrifty, and well trained enough to maintain themselves against the powerful inroads of organized capital. The results among them, even, are long hours of toil, low wages, child labor, lack of protection against usury and cheating. But among the black laborers all this is aggravated, first, by a race prejudice which varies from a doubt and distrust among the best element of whites to a frenzied hatred among the worst; and, secondly, it is aggravated, as I have said before, by the wretched economic heritage of the freedmen from slavery. With this training it is difficult for the freedman to learn to grasp the opportunities already opened to him, and the new opportunities are seldom given him, but go by favor to the whites.

Left by the best elements of the South with little protection or oversight, he has been made in law and custom the victim of the worst and most unscrupulous men in each community. The crop-lien system which is depopulating the fields of the South is not simply the result of shiftlessness on the part of Negroes, but is also the result of cunningly devised laws as to mortgages, liens, and misdemeanors, which can be made by conscienceless men to entrap and snare the unwary until escape is impossible, further toil a farce, and protest a crime. I have seen, in the Black Belt of Georgia, an ignorant, honest Negro buy and pay for a farm in installments three separate times, and then in the face of law and decency the enterprising Russian Jew who sold it to him pocketed money and deed and left the black man landless, to labor on his own land at thirty cents a day. I have seen a black farmer fall in debt to a white storekeeper, and that storekeeper go to his farm and strip it of every single marketable article,—mules, ploughs, stored crops, tools, furniture, bedding, clocks, looking-glass,—and all this without a warrant, without process of law, without a sheriff or officer, in the face of the law for homestead exemptions, and without rendering to a single responsible person any account or reckoning. And such proceedings can happen, and will happen, in any community where a class of ignorant toilers are placed by custom and race-prejudice beyond the pale of sympathy and race-brotherhood. So long as the best elements of a community do not feel in duty bound to protect and train and care for the weaker members of their group, they leave them to be preyed upon by these swindlers and rascals.

This unfortunate economic situation does not mean the hindrance of all advance in the black South, or the absence of a class of black landlords and mechanics, who, in spite of disadvantages, are accumulating property and making good citizens. But it does mean that this class is not nearly so large as a fairer economic system might easily make it, that those who survive in the competition are handicapped so as to accomplish much less than they deserve to, and that, above all, the *personnel* of the successful class is left to chance and accident, and not to any intelligent culling or reasonable methods of selection. As a remedy for this, there is but one possible procedure. We must accept some of the race prejudice in the South as a fact,— deplorable in its intensity, unfortunate in results, and dangerous for the future, but nevertheless a hard fact which only time can efface. We cannot hope, then, in this generation, or for several generations, that the mass of the whites can be brought to assume that close sympathetic and self-sacrificing leadership of the blacks which their present situation so eloquently demands. Such leadership, such social teaching and example, must come from the blacks themselves. For some time men doubted as to whether the Negro could develop such leaders; but to-day no one seriously disputes the capability of individual Negroes to assimilate the culture and common sense of modern civilization, and to pass it on, to some extent at least, to their fellows. If this is true, then here is the path out of the economic situation, and here is the imperative demand for trained Negro leaders of character and intelligence,—men of skill, men of light and leading, college-bred men, black captains of industry, and missionaries of culture; men who thoroughly comprehend and know modern civilization, and can take hold of Negro communities and raise and train them by force of precept and example, deep sympathy, and the inspiration of common blood and ideals. But if such men are to be effective they must have some power,—they must be backed by the best public opinion of these communities, and able to wield for their objects and aims such weapons as the experience of the world has taught are indispensable to human progress.

Of such weapons the greatest, perhaps, in the modern world is the power of the ballot; and this brings me to a consideration of the third form of contact between whites and blacks in the South,—political activity.

In the attitude of the American mind toward Negro suffrage can be traced with unusual accuracy the prevalent conceptions of government. In the fifties we were near enough the echoes of the French Revolution to believe pretty thoroughly in universal suffrage. We argued, as we thought then rather logically, that no social class was so good, so true, and so disinterested as to be trusted wholly with the political destiny of its neighbors; that in every state the best arbiters of their own welfare are the persons directly affected; consequently that it is only by arming every hand with a ballot,—with the right to have a voice in the policy of the state,—that the greatest good to the greatest number could be attained. To be sure, there were objections to these arguments, but we thought we had answered them tersely and convincingly; if some one complained of the ignorance of voters, we answered, "Educate them." If another complained of their venality, we replied, "Disfranchise them or put them in jail." And, finally, to the men who feared demagogues and the natural perversity of some human beings we insisted that time and bitter experience would teach the most hardheaded. It was at this time that the question of Negro suffrage in the South was raised. Here was a defenceless people suddenly made free. How were they to be protected from those who did not believe in their freedom and were determined to thwart it? Not by force, said the North; not by government guardianship, said the South; then by the ballot, the sole and legitimate defence of a free people, said the Common Sense of the Nation. No one thought, at the time, that the ex-slaves could use the ballot intelligently or very effectively; but they did think that the possession of so great power by a great class in the nation would compel their fellows to educate this class to its intelligent use.

Meantime, new thoughts came to the nation: the inevitable period of moral retrogression and political trickery that ever follows in the wake of war overtook us. So flagrant became the political scandals that reputable men began to leave politics alone, and politics consequently became disreputable. Men began to pride themselves on having nothing to do with their own government, and to agree tacitly with those who regarded public office as a private perquisite. In this state of mind it became easy to wink at the suppression of the Negro vote in the South, and to advise self-respecting Negroes to leave politics entirely alone. The decent and reputable citizens of the North who neglected their own civic duties grew hilarious over the exaggerated importance with which the Negro regarded the franchise. Thus it easily happened that more and more the better class of Negroes followed the advice from abroad and the pressure from home, and took no further interest in politics, leaving to the careless and the venal of their race the exercise of their rights as voters. The black vote that still remained was not trained and educated, but further debauched by open and unblushing bribery, or force and fraud; until the Negro voter was thoroughly inoculated with the idea that politics was a method of private gain by disreputable means.

And finally, now, to-day, when we are awakening to the fact that the perpetuity of republican institutions on this continent depends on the purification of the ballot, the civic training of voters, and the raising of voting to the plane of a solemn duty which a patriotic citizen neglects to his peril and to the peril of his children's children,—in this day, when we are striving for a renaissance of civic virtue, what are we going to say to the black voter of the South? Are we going to tell him still that politics is a disreputable and useless form of human activity? Are we going to induce the best class of Negroes to take less and less interest in government, and to give up their right to take such an interest, without a protest? I am not saying a word against all legitimate efforts to purge the ballot of ignorance, pauperism, and crime. But few have pretended that the present movement for disfranchisement in the South is for such a purpose; it has been plainly and frankly declared in nearly every case that the object of the disfranchising laws is the elimination of the black man from politics.

Now, is this a minor matter which has no influence on the main question of the industrial and intellectual development of the Negro? Can we establish a mass of black laborers and artisans and landholders in the South who, by law and public opinion, have absolutely no voice in shaping the laws under which they live and work? Can the modern organization of industry, assuming as it does free democratic government and the power and ability of the laboring classes to compel respect for their welfare,—can this system be carried out in the South when half its laboring force is voiceless in the public councils and powerless in its own defense? To-day the black man of the South has almost nothing to say as to how much he shall be taxed, or how those taxes shall be expended; as to who shall execute the laws, and how they shall do it; as to who shall make the laws, and how they shall be made. It is pitiable that frantic efforts must be made at critical times to get lawmakers in some States even to listen to the respectful presentation of the black man's side of a current controversy. Daily the Negro is coming more and more to look upon law and justice, not as protecting safeguards, but as sources of humiliation and oppression. The laws are made by men who have little interest in him; they are executed by men who have absolutely no motive for treating the black people with courtesy or consideration; and, finally, the accused law-breaker is tried, not by his peers, but too often by men who would rather punish ten innocent Negroes than let one guilty one escape.

I should be the last one to deny the patent weaknesses and shortcomings of the Negro people; I should be the last to withhold sympathy from the white South in its efforts to solve its intricate social problems. I freely acknowledge that it is possible, and sometimes best, that a partially undeveloped people should be ruled by the best of their stronger and better neighbors for their own good, until such time as they can start and fight the world's battles alone. I have already pointed out how sorely in need of such economic and spiritual guidance the emancipated Negro was, and I am quite willing to admit that if the representatives of the best white Southern public opinion were the ruling and guiding powers in the South to-day the conditions indicated would be fairly well fulfilled. But the point I have insisted upon, and now emphasize again, is that the best opinion of the South to-day is not the ruling opinion. That to leave the Negro helpless and without a ballot to-day is to leave him, not to the guidance of the best, but rather to the exploitation and debauchment of the worst; that this is no truer of the South than of the North,—of the North than of Europe: in any land, in any country under modern free competition, to lay any class of weak and despised people, be they white, black, or blue, at the political mercy of their stronger, richer, and more resourceful fellows, is a temptation which human nature seldom has withstood and seldom will withstand.

Moreover, the political status of the Negro in the South is closely connected with the question of Negro crime. There can be no doubt that crime among Negroes has sensibly increased in the last thirty years, and that there has appeared in the slums of great cities a distinct criminal class among the blacks. In explaining this unfortunate development, we must note two things: (1) that the inevitable result of Emancipation was to increase crime and criminals, and (2) that the police system of the South was primarily designed to control slaves. As to the first point, we must not forget that under a strict slave system there can scarcely be such a thing as crime. But when these variously constituted human particles are suddenly thrown broadcast on the sea of life, some swim, some sink, and some hang suspended, to be forced up or down by the chance currents of a busy hurrying world. So great an economic and social revolution as swept the South in '63 meant a weeding out among the Negroes of the incompetents and vicious, the beginning of a differentiation of social grades. Now a rising group of people are not lifted bodily from the ground like an inert solid mass, but rather stretch upward like a living plant with its roots still clinging in the mould. The appearance, therefore, of the Negro criminal was a phenomenon to be awaited; and while it causes anxiety, it should not occasion surprise.

Here again the hope for the future depended peculiarly on

careful and delicate dealing with these criminals. Their offences
at first were those of laziness, carelessness, and impulse, rather
than of malignity or ungoverned viciousness. Such misdemeanors needed discriminating treatment, firm but reformatory, with
no hint of injustice, and full proof of guilt. For such dealing
with criminals, white or black, the South had no machinery, no
adequate jails or reformatories; its police system was arranged
to deal with blacks alone, and tacitly assumed that every white
man was *ipso facto* a member of that police. Thus grew up a
double system of justice, which erred on the white side by undue
leniency and the practical immunity of red-handed criminals,
and erred on the black side by undue severity, injustice, and lack
of discrimination. For, as I have said, the police system of the
South was originally designed to keep track of all Negroes, not
simply of criminals; and when the Negroes were freed and the
whole South was convinced of the impossibility of free Negro
labor, the first and almost universal device was to use the courts
as a means of reënslaving the blacks. It was not then a question
of crime, but rather one of color, that settled a man's conviction
on almost any charge. Thus Negroes came to look upon courts
as instruments of injustice and oppression, and upon those con-
victed in them as martyrs and victims.

When, now, the real Negro criminal appeared, and instead
of petty stealing and vagrancy we began to have highway robbery, burglary, murder, and rape, there was a curious effect on
both sides of the color-line: the Negroes refused to believe the
evidence of white witnesses or the fairness of white juries, so
that the greatest deterrent to crime, the public opinion of one's
own social caste, was lost, and the criminal was looked upon
as crucified rather than hanged. On the other hand, the whites,
used to being careless as to the guilt or innocence of accused
Negroes, were swept in moments of passion beyond law, reason,
and decency. Such a situation is bound to increase crime, and
has increased it. To natural viciousness and vagrancy are being
daily added motives of revolt and revenge which stir up all the
latent savagery of both races and made peaceful attention to
economic development often impossible.

But the chief problem in any community cursed with crime

is not the punishment of the criminals, but the preventing of the young from being trained to crime. And here again the peculiar conditions of the South have prevented proper precautions. I have seen twelve-year-old boys working in chains on the public streets of Atlanta, directly in front of the schools, in company with old and hardened criminals; and this indiscriminate mingling of men and women and children makes the chain-gangs perfect schools of crime and debauchery. The struggle for reformatories, which has gone on in Virginia, Georgia, and other States, is the one encouraging sign of the awakening of some communities to the suicidal results of this policy.

It is the public schools, however, which can be made, outside the homes, the greatest means of training decent self-respecting citizens. We have been so hotly engaged recently in discussing trade-schools and the higher education that the pitiable plight of the public-school system in the South has almost dropped from view. Of every five dollars spent for public education in the State of Georgia, the white schools get four dollars and the Negro one dollar; and even then the white public-school system, save in the cities, is bad and cries for reform. If this is true of the whites, what of the blacks? I am becoming more and more convinced, as I look upon the system of common-school training in the South, that the national government must soon step in and aid popular education in some way. To-day it has been only by the most strenuous efforts on the part of the thinking men of the South that the Negro's share of the school fund has not been cut down to a pittance in some half-dozen States; and that movement not only is not dead, but in many communities is gaining strength. What in the name of reason does this nation expect of a people, poorly trained and hard pressed in severe economic competition, without political rights, and with ludicrously inadequate common-school facilities? What can it expect but crime and listlessness, offset here and there by the dogged struggles of the fortunate and more determined who are themselves buoyed by the hope that in due time the country will come to its senses?

I have thus far sought to make clear the physical, economic, and political relations of the Negroes and whites in the South, as I have conceived them, including, for the reasons set forth, crime and education. But after all that has been said on these more tangible matters of human contact, there still remains a part essential to a proper description of the South which it is difficult to describe or fix in terms easily understood by strangers. It is, in fine, the atmosphere of the land, the thought and feeling, the thousand and one little actions which go to make up life. In any community or nation it is these little things which are most elusive to the grasp and yet most essential to any clear conception of the group life taken as a whole. What is thus true of all communities is peculiarly true of the South, where, outside of written history and outside of printed law, there has been going on for a generation as deep a storm and stress of human souls, as intense a ferment of feeling, as intricate a writhing of spirit, as ever a people experienced. Within and without the sombre veil of color vast social forces have been at work,— efforts for human betterment, movements toward disintegration and despair, tragedies and comedies in social and economic life, and a swaying and lifting and sinking of human hearts which have made this land a land of mingled sorrow and joy, of change and excitement and unrest.

The centre of this spiritual turmoil has ever been the millions of black freedmen and their sons, whose destiny is so fatefully bound up with that of the nation. And yet the casual observer visiting the South sees at first little of this. He notes the growing frequency of dark faces as he rides along,—but otherwise the days slip lazily on, the sun shines, and this little world seems as happy and contented as other worlds he has visited. Indeed, on the question of questions—the Negro problem—he hears so little that there almost seems to be a conspiracy of silence; the morning papers seldom mention it, and then usually in a far-fetched academic way, and indeed almost every one seems to forget and ignore the darker half of the land, until the astonished visitor is inclined to ask if after all there is any problem here. But if he lingers long enough there comes the awakening: perhaps in a sudden whirl of passion which leaves him gasping at its bitter intensity; more likely in a gradually dawning sense of things he had not at first noticed. Slowly but surely his eyes begin to catch the shadows of the color-line: here he meets crowds of Negroes and whites; then he is suddenly aware that he cannot discover a single dark face; or again at the close of a day's wandering he may find himself in some strange assembly, where all faces are tinged brown or black, and where he has the vague, uncomfortable feeling of the stranger. He realizes at last that silently, resistlessly, the world about flows by him in two great streams: they ripple on in the same sunshine, they approach and mingle their waters in seeming carelessness,—then they divide and flow wide apart. It is done quietly; no mistakes are made, or if one occurs, the swift arm of the law and of public opinion swings down for a moment, as when the other day a black man and a white woman were arrested for talking together on Whitehall Street in Atlanta.

Now if one notices carefully one will see that between these two worlds, despite much physical contact and daily intermingling, there is almost no community of intellectual life or point of transference where the thoughts and feelings of one race can come into direct contact and sympathy with thoughts and feelings of the other. Before and directly after the war, when all the best of the Negroes were domestic servants in the best of the white families, there were bonds of intimacy, affection, and sometimes blood relationship, between the races. They lived in the same home, shared in the family life, often attended the same church, and talked and conversed with each other. But the increasing civilization of the Negro since then has naturally meant the development of higher classes: there are increasing numbers of ministers, teachers, physicians, merchants, mechanics, and independent farmers, who by nature and training are the aristocracy and leaders of the blacks. Between them, however, and the best element of the whites, there is little or no intellectual commerce. They go to separate churches, they live in separate sections, they are strictly separated in all public gatherings, they travel separately, and they are beginning to read different papers and books. To most libraries, lectures, concerts, and museums, Negroes are either not admitted at all, or on terms peculiarly galling to the pride of the very classes who might otherwise be attracted. The daily paper chronicles the doings of the black world from afar with no great regard for accuracy; and so on, throughout the category of means for intellectual communication,—schools, conferences, efforts, for social betterment, and the like,—it is usually true that the very representatives of the two races, who for mutual benefit and the welfare of the land ought to be in complete understanding and sympathy, are so far strangers that one side thinks all whites are narrow and prejudiced, and the other thinks educated Negroes dangerous and insolent. Moreover, in a land where the tyranny of public opinion and the intolerance of criticism is for obvious historical reasons so strong as in the South, such a situation is extremely difficult to correct. The white man, as well as the Negro, is bound and barred by the color-line, and many a scheme of friendliness and philanthropy, of broad-minded sympathy and generous fellowship between the two has dropped still-born because some busybody has forced the color-question to the front and brought the tremendous force of unwritten law against the innovators.

It is hardly necessary for me to add very much in regard to the social contact between the races. Nothing has come to replace that finer sympathy and love between some masters and house servants which the radical and more uncompromising drawing of the color-line in recent years has caused almost completely to disappear. In a world where it means so much to take a man by the hand and sit beside him, to look frankly into his eyes and feel his heart beating with red blood; in a world where a social cigar or a cup of tea together means more than legislative halls and magazine articles and speeches,—one can imagine the consequences of the almost utter absence of such social amenities between estranged races, whose separation extends even to parks and street-cars.

Here there can be none of that social going down to the people,—the opening of heart and hand of the best to the worst, in generous acknowledgment of a common humanity and a common destiny. On the other hand, in matters of simple almsgiving, where there can be no question of social contact, and in the succor of the aged and sick, the South, as if stirred by a feeling of its unfortunate limitations, is generous to a fault. The black beggar is never turned away without a good deal more than a crust, and a call for help for the unfortunate meets quick response. I remember, one cold winter, in Atlanta, when I refrained from contributing to a public relief fund lest Negroes should be discriminated against, I afterward inquired of a friend: "Were any black people receiving aid?" "Why," said he, "they were *all* black."

And yet this does not touch the kernel of the problem. Human advancement is not a mere question of almsgiving, but rather of sympathy and cooperation among classes who would scorn charity. And here is a land where, in the higher walks of life, in all the higher striving for the good and noble and true, the color-line comes to separate natural friends and coworkers; while at the bottom of the social group, in the saloon, the gambling-hell, and the brothel, that same line wavers and disappears.

I have sought to paint an average picture of real relations between the sons and master and man in the South. I have not glossed over matters for policy's sake, for I fear we have already gone too far in that sort of thing. On the other hand, I have sincerely sought to let no unfair exaggerations creep in. I do not doubt that in some Southern communities conditions are better than those I have indicated; while I am no less certain that in other communities they are far worse.

Nor does the paradox and danger of this situation fail to interest and perplex the best conscience of the South. Deeply religious and intensely democratic as are the mass of the whites, they feel acutely the false position in which the Negro problems place them. Such an essentially honest-hearted and generous people cannot cite the caste-levelling precepts of Christianity, or believe in equality of opportunity for all men, without coming to feel more and more with each generation that the present drawing of the color-line is a flat contradiction to their beliefs and professions. But just as often as they come to this point, the present social condition of the Negro stands as a menace and a portent before even the most open-minded: if there were nothing to charge against the Negro but his blackness or other physical peculiarities, they argue, the problem would be comparatively simple; but what can we say to his ignorance, shiftlessness, poverty, and crime? can a self-respecting group hold anything but the least possible fellowship with such persons and survive? and shall we let a mawkish sentiment sweep away the culture of our fathers or the hope of our children? The argument so put is of great strength but it is not a whit stronger than the argument of thinking Negroes: granted, they reply, that the condition of our masses is bad; there is certainly on the one hand adequate historical cause for this, and unmistakable evidence that no small number have, in spite of tremendous disadvantages, risen to the level of American civilization. And when, by proscription and prejudice, these same Negroes are classed with and treated like the lowest of their people, simply *because* they are Negroes, such a policy not only discourages thrift and intelligence among black men, but puts a direct premium on the very things you complain of,—inefficiency and crime. Draw lines of crime, of incompetency, of vice, as tightly and uncompromisingly as you will, for these things must be proscribed; but a color-line not only does not accomplish this purpose, but thwarts it.

In the face of two such arguments, the future of the South depends on the ability of the representatives of these opposing views to see and appreciate and sympathize with each other's position,—for the Negro to realize more deeply than he does at present the need of uplifting the masses of his people, for the white people to realize more vividly than they have yet done the deadening and disastrous effect of a color-prejudice that classes Phillis Wheatley and Sam Hose in the same despised class.

It is not enough for the Negroes to declare that color-prejudice is the sole cause of their social condition, nor for the white South to reply that their social condition is the main cause of prejudice. They both act as reciprocal cause and effect, and a change in neither alone will bring the desired effect. Both must change, or neither can improve to any great extent. The Negro cannot stand the present reactionary tendencies and unreasoning drawing of the color-line indefinitely without discouragement and retrogression. And the condition of the Negro is ever the excuse for further discrimination. Only by a union of intelligence and sympathy across the color-line in this critical period of the Republic shall justice and right triumph,—

> "That mind and soul according well,
> May make one music as before,
> But vaster."

X

OF THE FAITH OF
THE FATHERS

Dim face of Beauty haunting all the world,
　Fair face of Beauty all too fair to see,
Where the lost stars adown the heavens are hurled,—
　　There, there alone for thee
　　May white peace be.

Beauty, sad face of Beauty, Mystery, Wonder,
　What are these dreams to foolish babbling men
Who cry with little noises 'neath the thunder
　　Of Ages ground to sand,
　　To a little sand.

FIONA MACLEOD

It was out in the country, far from home, far from my foster
home, on a dark Sunday night. The road wandered from our
rambling log-house up the stony bed of a creek, past wheat and
corn, until we could hear dimly across the fields a rhythmic cadence of song,—soft, thrilling, powerful, that swelled and died
sorrowfully in our ears. I was a country schoolteacher then,
fresh from the East, and had never seen a Southern Negro revival. To be sure, we in Berkshire were not perhaps as stiff and

formal as they in Suffolk of olden time; yet we were very quiet and subdued, and I know not what would have happened those clear Sabbath mornings had some one punctuated the sermon with a wild scream, or interrupted the long prayer with a loud Amen! And so most striking to me, as I approached the village and the little plain church perched aloft, was the air of intense excitement that possessed that mass of black folk. A sort of suppressed terror hung in the air and seemed to seize us,—a pythian madness, a demoniac possession, that lent terrible reality to song and word. The black and massive form of the preacher swayed and quivered as the words crowded to his lips and flew at us in singular eloquence. The people moaned and fluttered, and then the gaunt-checked brown woman beside me suddenly leaped straight into the air and shrieked like a lost soul, while round about came wail and groan and outcry, and a scene of human passion such as I had never conceived before.

Those who have not thus witnessed the frenzy of a Negro revival in the untouched backwoods of the South can but dimly realize the religious feeling of the slave; as described, such scenes appear grotesque and funny, but as seen they are awful. Three things characterized this religion of the slave,—the Preacher, the Music and the Frenzy. The Preacher is the most unique personality developed by the Negro on American soil. A leader, a politician, an orator, a "boss," an intriguer, an idealist,—all these he is, and ever, too, the centre of a group of men, now twenty, now a thousand in number. The combination of a certain adroitness with deep-seated earnestness, of tact with consummate ability, gave him his preëminence, and helps him maintain it. The type, of course, varies according to time and place, from the West Indies in the sixteenth century to New England in the nineteenth, and from the Mississippi bottoms to cities like New Orleans or New York.

The Music of Negro religion is that plaintive rhythmic melody, with its touching minor cadences, which, despite caricature and defilement, still remains the most original and beautiful expression of human life and longing yet born on American soil. Sprung from the African forests, where its counterpart can still be heard, it was adapted, changed, and intensified by the tragic soul-life of the slave, until, under the stress of law and whip, it became the one true expression of a people's sorrow, despair, and hope.

Finally the Frenzy or "Shouting," when the Spirit of the Lord passed by, and, seizing the devotee, made him mad with super-natural joy, was the last essential of Negro religion and the one more devoutly believed in than all the rest. It varied in expression from the silent rapt countenance or the low murmur and moan to the mad abandon of physical fervor,—the stamping, shrieking, and shouting, the rushing to and fro and wild waving of arms, the weeping and laughing, the vision and the trance. All this is nothing new in the world, but old as religion, as Delphi and Endor. And so firm a hold did it have on the Negro, that many generations firmly believed that without this visible manifestation of the God there could be no true communion with the Invisible.

These were the characteristics of Negro religious life as developed up by the time of Emancipation. Since under the peculiar circumstances of the black man's environment they were the one expression of his higher life, they are of deep interest to the student of his development, both socially and psychologically. Numerous are the attractive lines of inquiry that here group themselves. What did slavery mean to the African savage? What was his attitude toward the World and Life? What seemed to him good and evil,—God and Devil? Whither went his longings and strivings, and wherefore were his heart-burnings and disappointments? Answers to such questions can come only from a study of Negro religion as a development, through its gradual changes from the heathenism of the Gold Coast to the institutional Negro church of Chicago.

Moreover, the religious growth of millions of men, even though they be slaves, cannot be without potent influence upon their contemporaries. The Methodists and Baptists of America owe much of their condition to the silent but potent influence of their millions of Negro converts. Especially is this noticeable in the South, where theology and religious philosophy are on this account a long way behind the North, and where the religion of the poor whites is a plain copy of Negro thought and methods. The mass of "gospel" hymns which has swept through American churches and well-nigh ruined our sense of song consists largely of debased imitations of Negro melodies made by ears that caught the jingle but not the music, the body but not the soul, of the Jubilee songs. It is thus clear that the study of Negro religion is not only a vital part of the history of the Negro in America, but no uninteresting part of American history.

The Negro church of to-day is the social centre of Negro life in the United States, and the most characteristic expression of African character. Take a typical church in a small Virginian town: it is the "First Baptist"—a roomy brick edifice seating five hundred or more persons, tastefully finished in Georgia pine, with a carpet, a small organ, and stained-glass windows. Underneath is a large assembly room with benches. This building is the central club-house of a community of a thousand or more Negroes. Various organizations meet here,—the church proper, the Sunday-school, two or three insurance societies, women's societies, secret societies, and mass meetings of various kinds. Entertainments, suppers, and lectures are held beside the five or six regular weekly religious services. Considerable sums of money are collected and expended here, employment is found for the idle, strangers are introduced, news is disseminated and charity distributed. At the same time this social, intellectual, and economic centre is a religious centre of great power. Depravity, Sin, Redemption, Heaven, Hell, and Damnation are preached twice a Sunday with much fervor, and revivals take place every year after the crops are laid by; and few indeed of the community have the hardihood to withstand conversion. Back of this more formal religion, the Church often stands as a real conserver of morals, a strengthener of family life, and the final authority on what is Good and Right.

Thus one can see in the Negro church to-day, reproduced in microcosm, all that great world from which the Negro is cut off by color-prejudice and social condition. In the great city churches the same tendency is noticeable and in many respects emphasized. A great church like the Bethel of Philadelphia has over eleven hundred members, an edifice seating fifteen hundred persons and valued at one hundred thousand dollars, an annual

budget of five thousand dollars, and a government consisting
of a pastor with several assisting local preachers, an executive
and legislative board, financial boards and tax collectors ; general church meetings for making laws; subdivided groups led
by class leaders, a company of militia, and twenty-four auxiliary
societies. The activity of a church like this is immense and far-
reaching, and the bishops who preside over these organizations
throughout the land are among the most powerful Negro rulers
in the world.

Such churches are really governments of men, and consequently a little investigation reveals the curious fact that, in the
South, at least, practically every American Negro is a church
member. Some, to be sure, are not regularly enrolled, and a few
do not habitually attend services; but practically, a proscribed
people must have a social centre, and that centre for this people
is the Negro church. The census of 1890 shows nearly twenty-
four thousand Negro churches in the country, with a total enrolled membership of over two and a half millions, or ten actual
church members to every twenty-eight persons, and in some
Southern States one in every two persons. Besides these there
is the large number who, while not enrolled as members, attend
and take part in many of the activities of the church. There is
an organized Negro church for every sixty black families in the
nation, and in some States for every forty families, owning, on
an average, a thousand dollars' worth of property each, or
nearly twenty-six million dollars in all.

Such, then, is the large development of the Negro church since
Emancipation. The question now is, What have been the successive steps of this social history and what are the present tendencies? First, we must realize that no such institution as the Negro
church could rear itself without definite historical foundations.
These foundations we can find if we remember that the social
history of the Negro did not start in America. He was brought
from a definite social environment,—the polygamous clan life
under the headship of the chief and the potent influence of the
priest. His religion was nature-worship, with profound belief in
invisible surrounding influences, good and bad, and his worship
was through incantation and sacrifice. The first rude change in

this life was the slave ship and the West Indian sugar-fields. The plantation organization replaced the clan and tribe, and the white master replaced the chief with far greater and more despotic powers. Forced and long-continued toil became the rule of life, the old ties of blood relationship and kinship disappeared, and instead of the family appeared a new polygamy and polyandry, which, in some cases, almost reached promiscuity. It was a terrific social revolution, and yet some traces were retained of the former group life, and the chief remaining institution was the Priest or Medicine-man. He early appeared on the plantation and found his function as the healer of the sick, the interpreter of the Unknown, the comforter of the sorrowing, the supernatural avenger of wrong, and the one who rudely but picturesquely expressed the longing, disappointment, and resentment of a stolen and oppressed people. Thus, as bard, physician, judge, and priest, within the narrow limits allowed by the slave system, rose the Negro preacher, and under him the first Afro-American institution, the Negro church. This church was not at first by any means Christian nor definitely organized; rather it was an adaption and mingling of heathen rites among the members of each plantation, and roughly designated as Voodoo-ism. Association with the masters, missionary effort and motives of expediency gave these rites an early veneer of Christianity, and after the lapse of many generations the Negro church became Christian.

Two characteristic things must be noticed in regard to this church. First, it became almost entirely Baptist and Methodist in faith; secondly, as a social institution it antedated by many decades the monogamic Negro home. From the very circumstances of its beginning, the church was confined to the plantation, and consisted primarily of a series of disconnected units; although, later on, some freedom of movement was allowed, still this geographical limitation was always important and was one cause of the spread of the decentralized and democratic Baptist faith among the slaves. At the same time, the visible rite of baptism appealed strongly to their mystic temperament. To-day the Baptist Church is still largest in membership among Negroes, and has a million and a half communicants. Next in popularity came the churches organized in connection with the white neighboring churches, chiefly Baptist and Methodist, with a few Episcopalian and others. The Methodists still form the second greatest denomination, with nearly a million members. The faith of these two leading denominations was more suited to the slave church from the prominence they gave to religious feeling and fervor. The Negro membership in other denominations has always been small and relatively unimportant, although the Episcopalians and Presbyterians are gaining among the more intelligent classes to-day, and the Catholic Church is making headway in certain sections. After Emancipation, and still earlier in the North, the Negro churches largely severed such affiliations as they had had with the white churches, either by choice or by compulsion. The Baptist churches became independent, but the Methodists were compelled early to unite for purposes of episcopal government. This gave rise to the great African Methodist Church, the greatest Negro organization in the world, to the Zion Church and the Colored Methodist, and to the black conferences and churches in this and other denominations.

The second fact noted, namely, that the Negro church antedates the Negro home, leads to an explanation of much that is paradoxical in this communistic institution and in the morals of its members. But especially it leads us to regard this institution as peculiarly the expression of the inner ethical life of a people in a sense seldom true elsewhere. Let us turn, then, from the outer physical development of the church to the more important inner ethical life of the people who compose it. The Negro has already been pointed out many times as a religious animal,—a being of that deep emotional nature which turns instinctively toward the supernatural. Endowed with a rich tropical imagination and a keen, delicate appreciation of Nature, the transplanted African lived in a world animate with gods and devils, elves and witches; full of strange influences,—of Good to be implored, of Evil to be propitiated. Slavery, then, was to him the dark triumph of Evil over him. All the hateful powers of the Under-world were striving against him, and a spirit of revolt and revenge filled his heart. He called up all the resources of heathenism to aid,—exorcism and witchcraft, the mysterious Obi worship with its barbarous rites, spells, and blood-sacrifice even, now and then, of human victims. Weird midnight orgies and mystic conjurations were in-voked, the witch-woman and the voodoo-priest became the cen-tre of Negro group life, and that vein of vague superstition which characterizes the unlettered Negro even to-day was deepened and strengthened.

In spite, however, of such success as that of the fierce Maroons, the Danish blacks, and others, the spirit of revolt gradually died away under the untiring energy and superior strength of the slave masters. By the middle of the eighteenth century the black slave had sunk, with hushed murmurs, to his place at the bottom of a new economic system, and was unconsciously ripe for a new phi-losophy of life. Nothing suited his condition then better than the doctrines of passive submission embodied in the newly learned Christianity. Slave masters early realized this, and cheerfully aided religious propaganda within certain bounds. The long sys-tem of repression and degradation of the Negro tended to em-phasize the elements in his character which made him a valuable chattel: courtesy became humility, moral strength degenerated into submission, and the exquisite native appreciation of the beau-tiful became an infinite capacity for dumb suffering. The Negro, losing the joy of this world, eagerly seized upon the offered con-ceptions of the next; the avenging Spirit of the Lord enjoining patience in this world, under sorrow and tribulation until the Great Day when He should lead His dark children home,—this became his comforting dream. His preacher repeated the proph-ecy, and his bards sang,—

"Children, we all shall be free
    When the Lord shall appear!"

This deep religious fatalism, painted so beautifully in "Uncle Tom," came soon to breed, as all fatalistic faiths will, the sen-sualist side by side with the martyr. Under the lax moral life of the plantation, where marriage was a farce, laziness a virtue, and property a theft, a religion of resignation and submission degenerated easily, in less strenuous minds, into a philosophy of indulgence and crime. Many of the worst characteristics of the Negro masses of to-day had their seed in this period of the slave's ethical growth. Here it was that the Home was ruined under the very shadow of the Church, white and black; here habits of shiftlessness took root, and sullen hopelessness replaced hopeful strife.

With the beginning of the abolition movement and the gradual growth of a class of free Negroes came a change. We often neglect the influence of the freedman before the war, because of the paucity of his numbers and the small weight he had in the history of the nation. But we must not forget that his chief influence was internal,—was exerted on the black world; and that there he was the ethical and social leader. Huddled as he was in a few centres like Philadelphia, New York, and New Orleans, the masses of the freedmen sank into poverty and listlessness; but not all of them. The free Negro leader early arose and his chief characteristic was intense earnestness and deep feeling on the slavery question. Freedom became to him a real thing and not a dream. His religion became darker and more intense, and into his ethics crept a note of revenge, into his songs a day of reckoning close at hand. The "Coming of the Lord" swept this side of Death, and came to be a thing to be hoped for in this day. Through fugitive slaves and irrepressible discussion this desire for freedom seized the black millions still in bondage, and became their one ideal of life. The black bards caught new notes, and sometimes even dared to sing,—

> "O Freedom, O Freedom, O Freedom over me!
> Before I'll be a slave
> I'll be buried in my grave,
> And go home to my Lord
> And be free."

For fifty years Negro religion thus transformed itself and identified itself with the dream of Abolition, until that which was a radical fad in the white North and an anarchistic plot in the white South had become a religion to the black world. Thus, when Emancipation finally came, it seemed to the freedman a literal Coming of the Lord. His fervid imagination was stirred as never before, by the tramp of armies, the blood and dust of battle, and the wail and whirl of social upheaval. He stood dumb and motionless before the whirl-wind: what had he to do with it? Was it not the Lord's doing, and marvellous in his eyes? Joyed and bewildered with what came, he stood awaiting new wonders till the inevitable Age of Reaction swept over the nation and brought the crisis of to-day.

It is difficult to explain clearly the present critical stage of Negro religion. First, we must remember that living as the blacks do in close contact with a great modern nation, and sharing, although imperfectly, the soul-life of that nation, they must necessarily be affected more or less directly by all the religious and ethical forces that are to-day moving the United States. These questions and movements are, however, overshadowed and dwarfed by the (to them) all-important question of their civil, political, and economic status. They must perpetually discuss the "Negro problem,"—must live, move, and have their being in it, and interpret all else in its light or darkness. With this come, too, peculiar problems of their inner life,—of the status of women, the maintenance of Home, the training of children, the accumulation of wealth, and the prevention of crime. All this must mean a time of intense ethical ferment, of religious heart-searching and intellectual unrest. From the double life every American Negro must live, as a Negro and as an American, as swept on by the current of the nineteenth while yet struggling in the eddies of the fifteenth century,—from this must arise a painful self-consciousness, an almost morbid sense of personality and a moral hesitancy which is fatal to self-confidence. The worlds within and without the Veil of Color are changing, and changing rapidly, but not at the same rate, not in the same way; and this must produce a peculiar wrenching of the soul, a peculiar sense of doubt and bewilderment. Such a double life, with double thoughts, double duties, and double social classes, must give rise to double words and double ideals, and tempt the mind to pretence or to revolt, to hypocrisy or to radicalism.

In some such doubtful words and phrases can one perhaps most clearly picture the peculiar ethical paradox that faces the Negro of to-day and is tingeing and changing his religious life.

Feeling that his rights and his dearest ideals are being trampled upon, that the public conscience is ever more deaf to his righteous appeal, and that all the reactionary forces of prejudice, greed, and revenge are daily gaining new strength and fresh allies, the Negro faces no enviable dilemma. Conscious of his impotence, and pessimistic, he often becomes bitter and vindictive; and his religion, instead of a worship, is a complaint and a curse, a wail rather than a hope, a sneer rather than a faith. On the other hand, another type of mind, shrewder and keener and more tortuous too, sees in the very strength of the anti-Negro movement its patent weaknesses, and with Jesuitic casuistry is deterred by no ethical considerations in the endeavor to turn this weakness to the black man's strength. Thus we have two great and hardly reconcilable streams of thought and ethical strivings; the danger of the one lies in anarchy, that of the other in hypocrisy. The one type of Negro stands almost ready to curse God and die, and the other is too often found a traitor to right and a coward before force; the one is wedded to ideals remote, whimsical, perhaps impossible of realization; the other forgets that life is more than meat and the body more than raiment. But, after all, is not this simply the writhing of the age translated into black,—the triumph of the Lie which to-day, with its false culture, faces the hideousness of the anarchist assassin?

To-day the two groups of Negroes, the one in the North, the other in the South, represent these divergent ethical tendencies, the first tending toward radicalism, the other toward hypocritical compromise. It is no idle regret with which the white South mourns the loss of the old-time Negro,—the frank, honest, simple old servant who stood for the earlier religious age of submission and humility. With all his laziness and lack of many elements of true manhood, he was at least open-hearted, faithful, and sincere. To-day he is gone, but who is to blame for his going? Is it not those very persons who mourn for him? Is it not the tendency, born of Reconstruction and Reaction, to found a society on lawlessness and deception, to tamper with the moral fibre of a naturally honest and straightforward people until the whites threaten to become ungovernable tyrants and the blacks criminals and hypocrites? Deception is the natural defence of the weak against the strong, and the South used it for many years against its conquerors; to-day it must be prepared to see its black proletariat turn that same two-edged weapon against itself. And how natural this is! The death of Denmark Vesey and Nat Turner proved long since to the Negro the present hopelessness of physical defence. Political defence is becoming less and less available, and economic defence is still only partially effective. But there is a patent defence at hand,—the defence of deception and flattery, of cajoling and lying. It is the same defence which the Jews of the Middle Age used and which left its stamp on their character for centuries. To-day the young Negro of the South who would succeed cannot be frank and outspoken, honest and self-assertive, but rather he is daily tempted to be silent and wary, politic and sly; he must flatter and be pleasant, endure petty insults with a smile, shut his eyes to wrong; in too many cases he sees positive personal advantage in deception and lying. His real thoughts, his real aspirations, must be guarded in whispers; he must not criticise, he must not complain. Patience, humility, and adroitness must, in these growing black youth, replace impulse, manliness, and courage. With this sacrifice there is an economic opening, and perhaps peace and some prosperity. Without this there is riot, migration, or crime. Nor is this situation peculiar to the Southern United States,—is it not rather the only method by which undeveloped races have gained the right to share modern culture? The price of culture is a Lie.

On the other hand, in the North the tendency is to emphasize the radicalism of the Negro. Driven from his birthright in the South by a situation at which every fibre of his more outspoken and assertive nature revolts, he finds himself in a land where he can scarcely earn a decent living amid the harsh competition and the color discrimination. At the same time, through schools and periodicals, discussions and lectures, he is intellectually quickened and awakened. The soul, long pent up and dwarfed, suddenly expands in new-found freedom. What wonder that every tendency is to excess,—radical complaint, radical remedies, bitter denunciation or angry silence. Some sink, some rise. The criminal and the sensualist leave the church for the gambling-hell and the brothel, and fill the slums of Chicago and Baltimore; the better classes segregate themselves from the group-life of both white and black, and form an aristocracy, cultured but pessimistic, whose bitter criticism stings while it points out no way of escape. They despise the submission and subserviency of the Southern Negroes, but offer no other means by which a poor and oppressed minority can exist side by side with its masters. Feeling deeply and keenly the tendencies and opportunities of the age in which they live, their souls are bitter at the fate which drops the Veil between; and the very fact that this bitterness is natural and justifiable only serves to intensify it and make it more maddening.

Between the two extreme types of ethical attitude which I have thus sought to make clear wavers the mass of the millions of Negroes, North and South; and their religious life and activity partake of this social conflict within their ranks. Their churches are differentiating,—now into groups of cold, fashionable devotees, in no way distinguishable from similar white groups save in color of skin; now into large social and business institutions catering to the desire for information and amusement of their members, warily avoiding unpleasant questions both within and without the black world, and preaching in effect if not in word: *Dum vivimus, vivamus.*

But back of this still broods silently the deep religious feeling of the real Negro heart, the stirring, unguided might of powerful human souls who have lost the guiding star of the past and are seeking in the great night a new religious ideal. Some day the Awakening will come, when the pent-up vigor of ten million souls shall sweep irresistibly toward the Goal, out of the Valley of the Shadow of Death, where all that makes life worth living—Liberty, Justice, and Right—is marked "For White People Only."

XI

OF THE PASSING OF
THE FIRST-BORN

O sister, sister, thy first-begotten,
The hands that cling and the feet that follow,
The voice of the child's blood crying yet,
Who hath remembered me? who hath forgotten?
Thou has forgotten, O summer swallow,
But the world shall end when I forget.

SWINBURNE

"Unto you a child is born," sang the bit of yellow paper that fluttered into my room one brown October morning. Then the fear of fatherhood mingled wildly with the job of creation; I wondered how it looked and how it felt,—what were its eyes, and how its hair curled and crumpled itself. And I thought in awe of her,—she who had slept with Death to tear a man-child from underneath her heart, while I was unconsciously wandering. I fled to my wife and child, repeating the while to myself half wonderingly, "Wife and child? Wife and child?"—fled fast and faster than boat and steam-car, and yet must ever impatiently await them; away from the hard-voiced city, away from the flickering sea into my own Berkshire Hills that sit all sadly guarding the gates of Massachusetts.

Up the stairs I ran to the wan mother and whimpering babe, to the sanctuary on whose altar a life at my bidding had offered itself to win a life, and won. What is this tiny formless thing, this newborn wail from an unknown world,—all head and voice? I handle it curiously, and watch perplexed its winking, breathing, and sneezing. I did not love it then; it seemed a ludicrous thing to love; but her I loved, my girl-mother, she whom now I saw unfolding like the glory of the morning—the transfigured woman.

Through her I came to love the wee thing, as it grew and waxed strong; as its little soul unfolded itself in twitter and cry and half-formed word, and as its eyes caught the gleam and flash of life. How beautiful he was, with his olive-tinted flesh and dark gold ringlets, his eyes of mingled blue and brown, his perfect little limbs, and the soft voluptuous roll which the blood of Africa had moulded into his features! I held him in my arms, after we had sped far away to our Southern home,—held him, and glanced at the hot red soil of Georgia and the breathless city of a hundred hills, and felt a vague unrest. Why was his hair tinted with gold? An evil omen was golden hair in my life. Why had not the brown of his eyes crushed out and killed the blue?—for brown were his father's eyes, and his father's father's. And thus in the Land of the Color-line I saw, as it fell across my baby, the shadow of the Veil.

Within the Veil was he born, said I; and there within shall he live,—a Negro and a Negro's son. Holding in that little head— ah, bitterly!—the unbowed pride of a hunted race, clinging with that tiny dimpled hand—ah, wearily!—to a hope not hopeless but unhopeful, and seeing with those bright wondering eyes that peer into my soul a land whose freedom is to us a mockery and whose liberty a lie. I saw the shadow of the Veil as it passed over my baby, I saw the cold city towering above the blood-red land. I held my face beside his little cheek, showed him the star-children and the twinkling lights as they began to flash, and stilled with an even-song the unvoiced terror of my life.

So sturdy and masterful he grew, so filled with bubbling life, so tremulous with the unspoken wisdom of a life but eighteen months distant from the All-life,—we were not far from worshipping this revelation of the divine, my wife and I. Her own life builded and moulded itself upon the child; he tinged her every dream and idealized her every effort. No hands but hers must touch and garnish those little limbs; no dress or frill must touch them that had not wearied her fingers; no voice but hers could coax him off to Dreamland, and she and he together spoke some soft and unknown tongue and in it held communion. I too mused above his little white bed; saw the strength of my own arm stretched onward through the ages through the newer strength of his; saw the dream of my black fathers stagger a step onward in the wild phantasm of the world; heard in his baby voice the voice of the Prophet that was to rise within the Veil.

And so we dreamed and loved and planned by fall and winter, and the full flush of the long Southern spring, till the hot winds rolled from the fetid Gulf, till the roses shivered and the still stern sun quivered its awful light over the hills of Atlanta. And then one night the little feet pattered wearily to the wee white bed, and the tiny hands trembled; and a warm flushed face tossed on the pillow, and we knew baby was sick. Ten days he lay there,—a swift week and three endless days, wasting, wasting away. Cheerily the mother nursed him the first days, and laughed into the little eyes that smiled again. Tenderly then she hovered round him, till the smile fled away and Fear crouched beside the little bed.

Then the day ended not, and night was a dreamless terror, and joy and sleep slipped away. I hear now that Voice at midnight calling me from dull and dreamless trance,—crying, "The Shadow of Death! The Shadow of Death!" Out into the starlight I crept, to rouse the gray physician,—the Shadow of Death, the Shadow of Death. The hours trembled on; the night listened; the ghastly dawn glided like a tired thing across the lamplight. Then we two alone looked upon the child as he turned toward us with great eyes, and stretched his string-like hands,—the Shadow of Death! And we spoke no word, and turned away.

He died at eventide, when the sun lay like a brooding sorrow above the western hills, veiling its face; when the winds spoke not, and the trees, the great green trees he loved, stood motionless. I saw his breath beat quicker and quicker, pause, and then his little soul leapt like a star that travels in the night and left a world of darkness in its train. The day changed not; the same tall trees peeped in at the windows, the same green grass glinted in the setting sun. Only in the chamber of death writhed the world's most piteous thing—a childless mother.

I shirk not. I long for work. I pant for a life full of striving. I am no coward, to shrink before the rugged rush of the storm, nor even quail before the awful shadow of the Veil. But hearken, O Death! Is not this my life hard enough,—is not that dull land that stretches its sneering web about me cold enough,—is not all the world beyond these four little walls pitiless enough, but that thou must needs enter here,—thou, O Death? About my head the thundering storm beat like a heartless voice, and the crazy forest pulsed with the curses of the weak; but what cared I, within my home beside my wife and baby boy? Was thou so jealous of one little coign of happiness that thou must needs enter there,—thou, O Death?

A perfect life was his, all joy and love, with tears to make it brighter,—sweet as a summer's day beside the Housatonic. The world loved him; the women kissed his curls, the men looked gravely into his wonderful eyes, and the children hovered and fluttered about him. I can see him now, changing like the sky from sparkling laughter to darkening frowns, and then to wondering thoughtfulness as he watched the world. He knew no color-line, poor dear,—and the Veil, though it shadowed him, had not yet darkened half his sun. He loved the white matron, he loved his black nurse; and in his little world walked souls alone, uncolored and unclothed. I—yea, all men—are larger and purer by the infinite breath of that one little life. She who in simple clearness of vision sees beyond the stars said when he had flown, "He will be happy There; he ever loved beautiful things." And I, far more ignorant, and blind by the web of mine own weaving, sit alone winding words and muttering, "If still he be, and he be There, and there be a There, let him be happy, O Fate!"

Blithe was the morning of his burial, with bird and song and sweet-smelling flowers. The trees whispered to the grass, but the children sat with hushed faces. And yet it seemed a ghostly unreal day,—the wraith of Life. We seemed to rumble down an unknown street behind a little white bundle of posies, with the shadow of a song in our ears. The busy city dinned about us; they did not say much, those pale-faced hurrying men and women; they did not say much,—they only glanced and said, "Niggers!"

We could not lay him in the ground there in Georgia, for the earth there is strangely red; so we bore him away to the northward, with his flowers and his little folded hands. In vain, in vain!—for where, O God! beneath thy broad blue sky shall my dark baby rest in peace,—where Reverence dwells, and Goodness, and a Freedom that is free?

All that day and all that night there sat an awful gladness in my heart,—nay, blame me not if I see the world thus darkly through the Veil,—and my soul whispers ever to me, saying, "Not dead, not dead, but escaped; not bond, but free." No bitter meanness now shall sicken his baby heart till it die a living death, no taunt shall madden his happy boyhood. Fool that I was to think or wish that this little soul should grow choked and deformed within the Veil! I might have known that yonder deep unworldly look that ever and anon floated past his eyes was peering far beyond this narrow Now. In the poise of his little curl-crowned head did there not sit all that wild pride of being which his father had hardly crushed in his own heart? For what, forsooth, shall a Negro want with pride amid the studied humiliations of fifty million fellows? Well sped, my boy, before the world had dubbed your ambition insolence, had held your ideals unattainable, and taught you to cringe and bow. Better far this nameless void that stops my life than a sea of sorrow for you.

Idle words; he might have borne his burden more bravely than we,—aye, and found it lighter too, some day; for surely, surely this is not the end. Surely there shall yet dawn some mighty morning to lift the Veil and set the prisoned free. Not for me,—I shall die in my bonds,—but for fresh young souls who have not known the night and waken to the morning; a morning when men ask of the workman, not "Is he white?" but "Can he work?" When men ask artists, not "Are they black?" but "Do they know?" Some morning this may be, long, long years to come. But now there wails, on that dark shore within the Veil, the same deep voice, Thou *shalt forego!* And all have I foregone at that command, and with small complaint,—all save that fair young form that lies so coldly wed with death in the nest I had builded.

If one must have gone, why not I? Why may I not rest me from this restlessness and sleep from this wide waking? Was not the world's alembic, Time, in his young hands, and is not my time waning? Are there so many workers in the vineyard that the fair promise of this little body could lightly be tossed away? The wretched of my race that line the alleys of the nation sit fatherless and unmothered; but Love sat beside his cradle, and in his ear Wisdom waited to speak. Perhaps now he knows the All-love, and needs not to be wise. Sleep, then, child,—sleep till I sleep and waken to a baby voice and the ceaseless patter of little feet—above the Veil.

XII

OF ALEXANDER CRUMMELL

Then from the Dawn it seemed there came, but faint
As from beyond the limit of the world,
Like the last echo born of a great cry,
Sounds, as if some fair city were one voice
Around a king returning from his wars.

TENNYSON

This is the history of a human heart,—the tale of a black boy who many long years ago began to struggle with life that he might know the world and know himself. Three temptations he met on those dark dunes that lay gray and dismal before the wonder-eyes of the child: the temptation of Hate, that stood out against the red dawn; the temptation of Despair, that darkened noonday; and the temptation of Doubt, that ever steals along with twilight. Above all, you must hear of the vales he crossed,—the Valley of Humiliation and the Valley of the Shadow of Death.

I saw Alexander Crummell first at a Wilberforce commencement season, amid its bustle and crush. Tall, frail, and black he stood, with simple dignity and an unmistakable air of good breeding. I talked with him apart, where the storming of the lusty young orators could not harm us. I spoke to him politely, then curiously, then eagerly, as I began to feel the fineness of his character;—his calm courtesy, the sweetness of his strength, and his fair blending of the hope and truth of life. Instinctively I bowed before this man, as one bows before the prophets of the world. Some seer he seemed, that came not from the crimson Past or the gray To-come, but from the pulsing Now,—that mocking world which seemed to me at once so light and dark, so splendid and sordid. Four-score years had he wandered in this same world of mine, within the Veil.

He was born with the Missouri Compromise and lay a-dying amid the echoes of Manila and El Caney: stirring times for living, times dark to look back upon, darker to look forward to. The black-faced lad that paused over his mud and marbles seventy years ago saw puzzling vistas as he looked down the world. The slave-ship still groaned across the Atlantic, faint cries burdened the Southern breeze, and the great black father whispered mad tales of cruelty into those young ears. From the low doorway the mother silently watched her boy at play, and at nightfall sought him eagerly lest the shadows bear him away to the land of slaves.

So his young mind worked and winced and shaped curiously a vision of Life; and in the midst of that vision ever stood one dark figure alone,—ever with the hard, thick countenance of that bitter father, and a form that fell in vast and shapeless folds. Thus the temptation of Hate grew and shadowed the growing child,—gliding stealthily into his laughter, fading into his play, and seizing his dreams by day and night with rough, rude turbulence. So the black boy asked of sky and sun and flower the never-answered Why? and loved, as he grew, neither the world nor the world's rough ways.

Strange temptation for a child, you may think; and yet in this wide land to-day a thousand thousand dark children brood before this same temptation, and feel its cold and shuddering arms.

For them, perhaps, some one will some day lift the Veil,—will come tenderly and cheerily into those sad little lives and brush the brooding hate away, just as Beriah Green strode in upon the life of Alexander Crummell. And before the bluff, kind-hearted man the shadow seemed less dark. Beriah Green had a school in Oneida County, New York, with a score of mischievous boys. "I'm going to bring a black boy here to educate," said Beriah Green, as only a crank and an abolitionist would have dared to say. "Ohio!" laughed the boys. "Ye-es," said his wife; and Alexander came. Once before, the black had sought a school, had travelled, cold and hungry, four hundred miles up into free New Hampshire, to Canaan. But the godly farmers hitched ninety yoke of oxen to the abolition schoolhouse and dragged it into the middle of the swamp. The black boy trudged away.

The nineteenth was the first century of human sympathy,— the age when half wonderingly we began to descry in others that transfigured spark of divinity which we call Myself; when clodhopper and peasants, and tramps and thieves, and millionaires and—sometimes—Negroes, became throbbing souls whose warm pulsing life touched us so nearly that we half gasped with surprise, crying, "Thou too! Hast Thou seen Sorrow and the dull waters of Hopelessness? Hast Thou known Life?" And then all helplessly we peered into those Other-worlds, and wailed, "O World of Worlds, how shall man make you one?"

So in that little Oneida school there came to those school-boys a revelation of thought and longing beneath one black skin, of which they had not dreamed before. And to the lonely boy came a new dawn of sympathy and inspiration. The shadowy, formless thing—the temptation of Hate, that hovered between him and the world—grew fainter and less sinister. It did not wholly fade away, but diffused itself and lingered thick at the edges. Through it the child now first saw the blue and gold of life,—the sun-swept road that ran 'twixt heaven and earth until in one far-off wan wavering line they met and kissed. A vision of life came to the growing boy,—mystic, wonderful. He raised his head, stretched himself, breathed deep of the fresh new air. Yonder, behind the forests, he heard strange sounds; then glinting through the trees he saw, far, far away, the bronzed hosts of a nation calling,—calling faintly, calling loudly. He heard the fateful clank of their chains, he felt them cringe and grovel, and there rose within him a protest and a prophecy. And he girded himself to walk down the world.

A voice and vision called him to be a priest,—a seer to lead the uncalled out of the house of bondage. He saw the headless host turn toward him like the whirling of mad waters,—he stretched forth his hands eagerly, and then, even as he stretched them, suddenly there swept across the vision the temptation of Despair.

They were not wicked men,—the problem of life is not the problem of the wicked,—they were calm, good men, Bishops of the Apostolic Church of God, and strove toward righteousness. They said slowly, "It is all very natural—it is even commendable; but the General Theological Seminary of the Episcopal Church cannot admit a Negro." And when that thin, half-grotesque figure still haunted their doors, they put their hands kindly, half sorrowfully, on his shoulders, and said, "Now,—of course, we—we know how *you* feel about it; but you see it is impossible,—that is—well—it is premature. Sometime, we trust—sincerely trust—all such distinctions will fade away; but now the world is as it is."

This was the temptation of Despair; and the young man fought it doggedly. Like some grave shadow he flitted by those halls, pleading, arguing, half angrily demanding admittance, until there came the final *No*; until men hustled the disturber away, marked him as foolish, unreasonable, and injudicious, a vain rebel against God's law. And then from that Vision Splendid all the glory faded slowly away, and left an earth gray and stern rolling on beneath a dark despair. Even the kind hands that stretched themselves toward him from out the depths of that dull morning seemed but parts of the purple shadows. He saw them coldly, and asked, "Why should I strive by special grace when the way of the world is closed to me?" All gently yet, the hands urged him on,—the hand of young John Jay, that daring father's daring son; the hands of the good folk of

Boston, that free city. And yet, with a way to the priesthood of the Church open at last before him, the cloud lingered there; and even when in old St. Paul's the venerable Bishop raised his white arms above the Negro deacon—even then the burden had not lifted from that heart, for there had passed a glory from the earth.

And yet the fire through which Alexander Crummell went did not burn in vain. Slowly and more soberly he took up again his plan of life. More critically he studied the situation. Deep down below the slavery and servitude of the Negro people he saw their fatal weaknesses, which long years of mistreatment had emphasized. The dearth of strong moral character, of unbending righteousness, he felt, was their great shortcoming, and here he would begin. He would gather the best of his people into some little Episcopal chapel and there lead, teach, and inspire them, till the leaven spread, till the children grew, till the world hearkened, till—till—and then across his dream gleamed some faint after-glow of that first fair vision of youth—only an after-glow, for there had passed a glory from the earth.

One day—it was in 1842, and the springtide was struggling merrily with the May winds of New England—he stood at the last in his own chapel in Providence, a priest of the Church. The days sped by, and the dark young clergyman labored; he wrote his sermons carefully; he intoned his prayers with a soft, earnest voice; he haunted the streets and accosted the wayfarers; he visited the sick, and knelt beside the dying. He worked and toiled, week by week, day by day, month by month. And yet month by month the congregation dwindled, week by week the hollow walls echoed more sharply, day by day the calls came fewer and fewer, and day by day the third temptation sat clearer and still more clearly within the Veil; a temptation, as it were, bland and smiling, with just a shade of mockery in its smooth tones. First it came casually, in the cadence of a voice: "Oh, colored folks? Yes." Or perhaps more definitely: "What do you *expect?*" In voice and gesture lay the doubt—the temptation of Doubt. How he hated it, and stormed at it furiously! "Of course they are capable," he cried; "of course they can learn and strive and achieve—" and "Of course," added the temptation softly, "they do nothing of the sort." Of all the three temptations, this one struck the deepest. Hate? He had outgrown so childish a thing. Despair? He had steeled his right arm against it, and fought it with the vigor of determination. But to doubt the worth of his life-work,—to doubt the destiny and capability of the race his soul loved because it was his; to find listless squalor instead of eager endeavor; to hear his own lips whispering, "They do not care; they cannot know; they are dumb driven cattle,—why cast your pearls before swine?"—this, this seemed more than man could bear; and he closed the door, and sank upon the steps of the chancel, and cast his robe upon the floor and writhed.

The evening sunbeams had set the dust to dancing in the gloomy chapel when he arose. He folded his vestments, put away the hymn-books, and closed the great Bible. He stepped out into the twilight, looked back upon the narrow little pulpit with a weary smile, and locked the door. Then he walked briskly to the Bishop, and told the Bishop what the Bishop already knew. "I have failed," he said simply. And gaining courage by the confession, he added: "What I need is a larger constituency. There are comparatively few Negroes here, and perhaps they are not of the best. I must go where the field is wider, and try again." So the Bishop sent him to Philadelphia, with a letter to Bishop Onderdonk.

Bishop Onderdonk lived at the head of six white steps,— corpulent, red-faced, and the author of several thrilling tracts on Apostolic Succession. It was after dinner, and the Bishop had settled himself for a pleasant season of contemplation, when the bell must needs ring, and there must burst in upon the Bishop a letter and a thin, ungainly Negro. Bishop Onderdonk read the letter hastily and frowned. Fortunately, his mind was already clear on this point; and he cleared his brow and looked at Crummell. Then he said, slowly and impressively: "I will receive you into this diocese on one condition: no Negro priest can sit in my church convention, and no Negro church must ask for representation there."

I sometimes fancy I can see that tableau: the frail black figure, nervously twitching his hat before the massive abdomen of Bishop Onderdonk; his threadbare coat thrown against the dark woodwork of the book-cases, where Fox's "Lives of the Martyrs" nestled happily beside "The Whole Duty of Man." I seem to see the wide eyes of the Negro wander past the Bishop's broadcloth to where the swinging glass doors of the cabinet glow in the sunlight. A little blue fly is trying to cross the yawning keyhole. He marches briskly up to it, peers into the chasm in a surprised sort of way, and rubs his feelers reflectively; then he essays its depths, and, finding it bottomless, draws back again. The dark-faced priest finds himself wondering if the fly too has faced its Valley of Humiliation, and if it will plunge into it,—when lo! it spreads its tiny wings and buzzes merrily across, leaving the watcher wingless and alone.

Then the full weight of his burden fell upon him. The rich walls wheeled away, and before him lay the cold rough moor winding on through life, cut in twain by one thick granite ridge,—here, the Valley of Humiliation; yonder, the Valley of the Shadow of Death. And I know not which be darker,—no, not I. But this I know: in yonder Vale of the Humble stand to-day a million swarthy men, who willingly would

> ". . . bear the whips and scorns of time,
> The oppressor's wrong, the proud man's contumely,
> The pangs of despised love, the law's delay,
> The insolence of office, and the spurns
> That patient merit of the unworthy takes,"

all this and more would they bear did they but know that this were sacrifice and not a meaner thing. So surged the thought within that lone black breast. The Bishop cleared his throat suggestively; then, recollecting that there was really nothing to say, considerately said nothing, only sat tapping his foot impatiently. But Alexander Crummell said, slowly and heavily: "I will never enter your diocese on such terms." And saying this, he turned and passed into the Valley of the Shadow of Death.

You might have noted only the physical dying, the shattered frame and hacking cough; but in that soul lay deeper death than that. He found a chapel in New York,—the church of his father; he labored for it in poverty and starvation, scorned by his fellow priests. Half in despair, he wandered across the sea, a beggar with outstretched hands. Englishmen clasped them,— Wilberforce and Stanley, Thirwell and Ingles, and even Froude and Macaulay; Sir Benjamin Brodie bade him rest awhile at Queen's College in Cambridge, and there he lingered, struggling for health of body and mind, until he took his degree in '53. Restless still and unsatisfied, he turned toward Africa, and for long years, amid the spawn of the slave-smugglers, sought a new heaven and a new earth.

So the man groped for light; all this was not Life,—it was the world-wandering of a soul in search of itself, the striving of one who vainly sought his place in the world, ever haunted by the shadow of a death that is more than death,—the passing of a soul that has missed its duty. Twenty years he wandered,— twenty years and more; and yet the hard rasping question kept gnawing within him, "What, in God's name, am I on earth for?" In the narrow New York parish his soul seemed cramped and smothered. In the fine old air of the English University he heard the millions wailing over the sea. In the wild fever-cursed swamps of West Africa he stood helpless and alone.

You will not wonder at his weird pilgrimage,—you who in the swift whirl of living, amid its cold paradox and marvellous vision, have fronted life and asked its riddle face to face. And if you find that riddle hard to read, remember that yonder black boy finds it just a little harder; if it is difficult for you to find and face your duty, it is a shade more difficult for him; if your heart sickens in the blood and dust of battle, remember that to him the dust is thicker and the battle fiercer. No wonder the wanderers fall! No wonder we point to thief and murderer, and haunting prostitute, and the never-ending throng of unhearsed dead! The Valley of the Shadow of Death gives few of its pilgrims back to the world.

But Alexander Crummell it gave back. Out of the temptation of Hate, and burned by the fire of Despair, triumphant over

Doubt, and steeled by Sacrifice against Humiliation, he turned at last home across the waters, humble and strong, gentle and determined. He bent to all the gibes and prejudices, to all hatred and discrimination, with that rare courtesy which is the armor of pure souls. He fought among his own, the low, the grasping, and the wicked, with that unbending righteousness which is the sword of the just. He never faltered, he seldom complained; he simply worked, inspiring the young, rebuking the old, helping the weak, guiding the strong.

So he grew, and brought within his wide influence all that was best of those who walk within the Veil. They who live without knew not nor dreamed of that full power within, that mighty inspiration which the dull gauze of caste decreed that most men should not know. And now that he is gone, I sweep the Veil away and cry, Lo! the soul to whose dear memory I bring this little tribute. I can see his face still, dark and heavy-lined beneath his snowy hair; lighting and shading, now with inspiration for the future, now in innocent pain at some human wickedness, now with sorrow at some hard memory from the past. The more I met Alexander Crummell, the more I felt how much that world was losing which knew so little of him. In another age he might have sat among the elders of the land in purple-bordered toga; in another country mothers might have sung him to the cradles.

He did his work,—he did it nobly and well; and yet I sorrow that here he worked alone, with so little human sympathy. His name to-day, in this broad land, means little, and comes to fifty million ears laden with no incense of memory or emulation. And herein lies the tragedy of the age: not that men are poor,— all men know something of poverty; not that men are wicked,— who is good? not that men are ignorant,—what is Truth? Nay, but that men know so little of men.

He sat one morning gazing toward the sea. He smiled and said, "The gate is rusty on the hinges." That night at star-rise a wind came moaning out of the west to blow the gate ajar, and then the soul I loved fled like a flame across the Seas, and in its seat sat Death.

I wonder where he is to-day? I wonder if in that dim world beyond, as he came gliding in, there rose on some wan throne a King,—a dark and pierced Jew, who knows the writhings of the earthly damned, saying, as he laid those heart-wrung talents down, "Well done!" while round about the morning stars sat singing.

XIII

OF THE COMING OF JOHN

What bring they 'neath the midnight,
　Beside the River-sea?
They bring the human heart wherein
　No nightly calm can be;
That droppeth never with the wind,
　Nor drieth with the dew;
O calm it, God; thy calm is broad
　To cover spirits too.
　　The river floweth on.

MRS. BROWNING

Carlisle Street runs westward from the centre of Johnstown, across a great black bridge, down a hill and up again, by little shops and meat-markets, past single-storied homes, until suddenly it stops against a wide green lawn. It is a broad, restful place, with two large buildings outlined against the west. When at evening the winds come swelling from the east, and the great pall of the city's smoke hangs wearily above the valley, then the red west glows like a dream-land down Carlisle Street, and, at the tolling of the supper-bell, throws the passing forms of students in dark silhouette against the sky. Tall and black, they move slowly by, and seem in the sinister light to flit before the city like dim warning ghosts. Perhaps they are; for this is Wells Institute, and these black students have few dealings with the white city below.

And if you will notice, night after night, there is one dark form that ever hurries last and late toward the twinkling lights of Swain Hall,—for Jones is never on time. A long, straggling fellow he is, brown and hard-haired, who seems to be growing straight out of his clothes, and walks with a half-apologetic roll. He used perpetually to set the quiet dining-room into waves of merriment, as he stole to his place after the bell had tapped for prayers; he seemed so perfectly awkward. And yet one glance at his face made one forgive him much,—that broad, good-natured smile in which lay no bit of art or artifice, but seemed just bubbling good-nature and genuine satisfaction with the world.

He came to us from Altamaha, away down there beneath the gnarled oaks of Southeastern Georgia, where the sea croons to the sands and the sands listen till they sink half drowned beneath the waters, rising only here and there in long, low islands. The white folk of Altamaha voted John a good boy,—fine plough-hand, good in the rice-fields, handy everywhere, and always good-natured and respectful. But they shook their heads when his mother wanted to send him off to school. "It'll spoil him,—ruin him," they said; and they talked as though they knew. But full half the black folk followed him proudly to the station, and carried his queer little trunk and many bundles. And there they shook and shook hands, and the girls kissed him shyly and the boys clapped him on the back. So the train came, and he pinched his little sister lovingly, and put his great arms about his mother's neck, and then was away with a puff and a roar into the great yellow world that flamed and flared about the doubtful pilgrim. Up the coast they hurried, past the squares and palmettos of Savannah, through the cotton-fields and through the weary night, to Millville, and came with the morning to the noise and bustle of Johnstown.

And they that stood behind, that morning in Altamaha, and watched the train as it noisily bore playmate and brother and son away to the world, had thereafter one ever-recurring word,—"When John comes." Then what parties were to be, and what speakings in the churches; what new furniture in the front room,—perhaps even a new front room; and there would be a new schoolhouse, with John as teacher; and then perhaps a big wedding; all this and more—when John comes. But the white people shook their heads.

At first he was coming at Christmas-time,—but the vacation proved too short; and then, the next summer,—but times were hard and schooling costly, and so, instead, he worked in Johnstown. And so it drifted to the next summer, and the next,—till playmates scattered, and mother grew gray, and sister went up to the Judge's kitchen to work. And still the legend lingered,— "When John comes."

Up at the Judge's they rather liked this refrain; for they too had a John—a fair-haired, smooth-faced boy, who had played many a long summer's day to its close with his darker namesake. "Yes, sir! John is at Princeton, sir," said the broad-shouldered gray-haired Judge every morning as he marched down to the post-office. "Showing the Yankees what a Southern gentleman can do," he added; and strode home again with his letters and papers. Up at the great pillared house they lingered long over the Princeton letter,—the Judge and his frail wife, his sister and growing daughters. "It'll make a man of him," said the Judge, "college is the place." And then he asked the shy little waitress, "Well, Jennie, how's your John?" and added reflectively, "Too bad, too bad your mother sent him off,—it will spoil him." And the waitress wondered.

Thus in the far-away Southern village the world lay waiting, half consciously, the coming of two young men, and dreamed in an inarticulate way of new things that would be done and new thoughts that all would think. And yet it was singular that few thought of two Johns,—for the black folk thought of one John, and he was black; and the white folk thought of another John, and he was white. And neither world thought the other world's thought, save with a vague unrest.

Up in Johnstown, at the Institute, we were long puzzled at the case of John Jones. For a long time the clay seemed unfit for any sort of moulding. He was loud and boisterous, always laughing and singing, and never able to work consecutively at anything. He did not know how to study; he had no idea of thoroughness; and with his tardiness, carelessness, and appalling good-humor, we were sore perplexed. One night we sat in faculty-meeting, worried and serious; for Jones was in trouble again. This last escapade was too much, and so we solemnly voted "that Jones, on account of repeated disorder and inattention to work, be suspended for the rest of the term."

It seemed to us that the first time life ever struck Jones as a really serious thing was when the Dean told him he must leave school. He stared at the gray-haired man blankly, with great eyes. "Why,—why," he faltered, "but—I haven't graduated!" Then the Dean slowly and clearly explained, reminding him of the tardiness and the carelessness, of the poor lessons and neglected work, of the noise and disorder, until the fellow hung his head in confusion. Then he said quickly, "But you won't tell mammy and sister,—you won't write mammy, now will you? For if you won't I'll go out into the city and work, and come back next term and show you something." So the Dean promised faithfully, and John shouldered his little trunk, giving neither word nor look to the giggling boys, and walked down Carlisle Street to the great city, with sober eyes and a set and serious face.

Perhaps we imagined it, but someway it seemed to us that the serious look that crept over his boyish face that afternoon never left it again. When he came back to us he went to work with all his rugged strength. It was a hard struggle, for things did not come easily to him,—few crowding memories of early life and teaching came to help him on his new way; but all the world toward which he strove was of his own building, and he builded slow and hard. As the light dawned lingeringly on his new creations, he sat rapt and silent before the vision, or wandered alone over the green campus peering through and beyond the world of men into a world of thought. And the thoughts at times puzzled him sorely; he could not see just why the circle was not square, and carried it out fifty-six decimal places one midnight,— would have gone further, indeed, had not the matron rapped for lights out. He caught terrible colds lying on his back in the meadows of nights, trying to think out the solar system; he had grave doubts as to the ethics of the Fall of Rome, and strongly suspected the Germans of being thieves and rascals, despite his text-books; he pondered long over every new Greek word, and wondered why this meant that and why it couldn't mean something else, and how it must have felt to think all things in Greek. So he thought and puzzled along for himself,— pausing perplexed where others skipped merrily, and walking steadily through the difficulties where the rest stopped and surrendered.

Thus he grew in body and soul, and with him his clothes seemed to grow and arrange themselves; coat sleeves got longer, cuffs appeared, and collars got less soiled. Now and then his boots shone, and a new dignity crept into his walk. And we who saw daily a new thoughtfulness growing in his eyes began to expect something of this plodding boy. Thus he passed out of the preparatory school into college, and we who watched him felt four more years of change, which almost transformed the tall, grave man who bowed to us commencement morning. He had left his queer thought-world and come back to a world of motion and of men. He looked now for the first time sharply about him, and wondered he had seen so little before. He grew slowly to feel almost for the first time the Veil that lay between him and the white world; he first noticed now the oppression that had not seemed oppression before, differences that erstwhile seemed natural, restraints and slights that in his boyhood days had gone unnoticed or been greeted with a laugh. He felt angry now when men did not call him "Mister," he clenched his hands at the "Jim Crow" cars, and chafed at the color-line that hemmed in him and his. A tinge of sarcasm crept into his speech, and a vague bitterness into his life; and he sat long hours wondering and planning a way around these crooked things. Daily he found himself shrinking from the choked and narrow life of his native town. And yet he always planned to go back to Altamaha,—always planned to work there. Still, more and more as the day approached he hesitated with a nameless dread; and even the day after graduation he seized with eagerness the offer of the Dean to send him North with the quartette during the summer vacation, to sing for the Institute. A breath of air before the plunge, he said to himself in half apology.

It was a bright September afternoon, and the streets of New York were brilliant with moving men. They reminded John of the sea, as he sat in the square and watched them, so changelessly changing, so bright and dark, so grave and gay. He scanned their rich and faultless clothes, the way they carried their hands, the shape of their hats; he peered into the hurrying carriages. Then, leaning back with a sigh, he said, "This is the World." The notion suddenly seized him to see where the world was going; since many of the richer and brighter seemed hurrying all one way. So when a tall, light-haired young man and a little talkative lady came by, he rose half hesitatingly and followed them. Up the street they went, past stores and gay shops, across a broad square, until with a hundred others they entered the high portal of a great building.

He was pushed toward the ticket-office with the others, and felt in his pocket for the new five-dollar bill he had hoarded. There seemed really no time for hesitation, so he drew it bravely out, passed it to the busy clerk, and received simply a ticket but no change. When at last he realized that he had paid five dollars to enter he knew not what, he stood stock-still amazed. "Be careful," said a low voice behind him; "you must not lynch the colored gentlemen simply because he's in your way," and a girl looked up roguishly into the eyes of her fair-haired escort. A shade of annoyance passed over the escort's face. "You will not understand us at the South," he said half impatiently as if continuing an argument. "With all your professions, one never sees in the North so cordial and intimate relations between white and black as are everyday occurrences with us. Why, I remember my closest playfellow in boyhood was a little Negro named after me, and surely no two,—*well!*" The man stopped short and flushed to the roots of his hair, for there directly beside his reserved orchestra chairs sat the Negro he had stumbled over in the hallway. He hesitated and grew pale with anger, called the usher and gave him his card, with a few peremptory words, and slowly sat down. The lady deftly changed the subject.

All this John did not see, for he sat in a half-maze minding the scene about him; the delicate beauty of the hall, the faint perfume, the moving myriad of men, the rich clothing and low hum of talking seemed all a part of a world so different from his, so strangely more beautiful than anything he had known, that he sat in dreamland, and started when, after a hush, rose high and clear the music of Lohengrin's swan. The infinite beauty of the wail lingered and swept through every muscle of his frame, and put it all a-tune. He closed his eyes and grasped the elbows of the chair, touching unwittingly the lady's arm. And the lady drew away. A deep longing swelled in all his heart to rise with that clear music out of the dirt and dust of that low life that held him prisoned and befouled. If he would only live up in the free air where birds sang and setting suns had no touch of blood! Who had called him to be the slave and butt of all? And if he had called, what right had he to call when a world like this lay open before men?

Then the movement changed, and fuller, mightier harmony swelled away. He looked thoughtfully across the hall, and wondered why the beautiful gray-haired woman looked so listless, and what the little man could be whispering about. He would not like to be listless and idle, he thought, for he felt with the music the movement of power within him. If he but had some master-work, some life-service, hard,—aye, bitter hard, but without the cringing and sickening servility, without the cruel hurt that hardened his heart and soul. When at last a soft sorrow crept across the violins, there came to him the vision of a far-off home,—the great eyes of his sister, and the dark drawn face of his mother. And his heart sank below the waters, even as the sea-sand sinks by the shores of Altamaha, only to be lifted aloft again with that last ethereal wail of the swan that quivered and faded away into the sky.

It left John sitting so silent and rapt that he did not for some time notice the usher tapping him lightly on the shoulder and saying politely, "Will you step this way, please, sir?" A little surprised, he arose quickly at the last tap, and, turning to leave his seat, looked full into the face of the fair-haired young man. For the first time the young man recognized his dark boyhood playmate, and John knew that it was the Judge's son. The white John started, lifted his hand, and then froze into his chair; the black John smiled lightly, then grimly, and followed the usher down the aisle. The manager was sorry, very, very sorry,—but he explained that some mistake had been made in selling the gentleman a seat already disposed of; he would refund the money, of course,—and indeed felt the matter keenly, and so forth, and—before he had finished John was gone, walking hurriedly across the square and down the broad streets, and as he passed the park he buttoned his coat and said, "John Jones, you're a natural-born fool." Then he went to his lodgings and wrote a letter, and tore it up; he wrote another, and threw it in the fire. Then he seized a scrap of paper and wrote: "Dear Mother and Sister—I am coming—John."

"Perhaps," said John, as he settled himself on the train, "perhaps I am to blame myself in struggling against my manifest destiny simply because it looks hard and unpleasant. Here is my duty to Altamaha plain before me; perhaps they'll let me help settle the Negro problems there,—perhaps they won't. 'I will go in to the King, which is not according to the law; and if I perish, I perish.'" And then he mused and dreamed, and planned a life-work; and the train flew south.

Down in Altamaha, after seven long years, all the world knew John was coming. The homes were scrubbed and scoured,— above all, one; the gardens and yards had an unwonted trimness, and Jennie bought a new gingham. With some finesse and negotiation, all the dark Methodists and Presbyterians were induced to join in a monster welcome at the Baptist Church; and as the day drew near, warm discussions arose on every corner as to the exact extent and nature of John's accomplishments.

It was noontide on a gray and cloudy day when he came. The black town flocked to the depot, with a little of the white at the edges,—a happy throng, with "Good-mawnings" and "Howdys" and laughing and joking and jostling. Mother sat yonder in the window watching; but sister Jennie stood on the platform, nervously fingering her dress,—tall and lithe, with soft brown skin and loving eyes peering from out a tangled wilderness of hair. John rose gloomily as the train stopped, for he was thinking of the "Jim Crow" car; he stepped to the platform, and paused: a little dingy station, a black crowd gaudy and dirty, a half-mile of dilapidated shanties along a straggling ditch of mud. An overwhelming sense of the sordidness and narrowness of it all seized him; he looked in vain for his mother, kissed coldly the tall, strange girl who called him brother, spoke a short, dry word here and there; then, lingering neither for hand-shaking nor gossip, started silently up the street, raising his hat merely to the least eager old aunty, to her open-mouthed astonishment. The people were distinctly bewildered. This silent, cold man,—was this John? Where was his smile and hearty hand-grasp? "'Peared kind o' down in the mouf," said the Methodist preacher thoughtfully. "Seemed monstus stuck up," complained a Baptist sister. But the white postmaster from the edge of the crowd expressed the opinion of his folks plainly. "That damn Nigger," said he, as he shouldered the mail and arranged his tobacco, "has gone North and got plum full o' fool notions; but they won't work in Altamaha." And the crowd melted away.

The meeting of welcome at the Baptist Church was a failure. Rain spoiled the barbecue, and thunder turned the milk in the ice-cream. When the speaking came at night, the house was crowded to overflowing. The three preachers had especially prepared themselves, but somehow John's manner seemed to throw a blanket over everything,—he seemed so cold and pre-occupied, and had so strange an air of restraint that the Methodist brother could not warm up to his theme and elicited not a single "Amen"; the Presbyterian prayer was but feebly responded to, and even the Baptist preacher, though he wakened faint enthusiasm, got so mixed up in his favorite sentence that he had to close it by stopping fully fifteen minutes sooner than

he meant. The people moved uneasily in their seats as John rose
to reply. He spoke slowly and methodically. The age, he said,
demanded new ideas; we were far different from those men of
the seventeenth and eighteenth centuries,—with broader ideas
of human brotherhood and destiny. Then he spoke of the rise of
charity and popular education, and particularly of the spread
of wealth and work. The question was, then, he added reflectively, looking at the low discolored ceiling, what part the
Negroes of this land would take in the striving of the new century. He sketched in vague outline the new Industrial School
that might rise among these pines, he spoke in detail of the
charitable and philanthropic work that might be organized, of
money that might be saved for banks and business. Finally he
urged unity, and deprecated especially religious and denomina-
tional bickering. "To-day," he said, with a smile, "the world
cares little whether a man be Baptist or Methodist, or indeed a
churchman at all, so long as he is good and true. What difference does it make whether a man be baptized in river or wash-
bowl, or not at all? Let's leave all that littleness, and look
higher." Then, thinking of nothing else, he slowly sat down. A
painful hush seized that crowded mass. Little had they understood of what he said, for he spoke an unknown tongue, save
the last word about baptism; that they knew, and they sat very
still while the clock ticked. Then at last a low suppressed snarl
came from the Amen corner, and an old bent man arose, walked
over the seats, and climbed straight up into the pulpit. He was
wrinkled and black, with scant gray and tufted hair; his voice
and hands shook as with palsy; but on his face lay the intense
rapt look of the religious fanatic. He seized the Bible with his
rough, huge hands; twice he raised it inarticulate, and then
fairly burst into the words, with rude and awful eloquence. He
quivered, swayed, and bent; then rose aloft in perfect majesty,
till the people moaned and wept, wailed and shouted, and a
wild shrieking arose from the corners where all the pent-up feeling of the hour gathered itself and rushed into the air. John
never knew clearly what the old man said; he only felt himself
held up to scorn and scathing denunciation for trampling on
the true Religion, and he realized with amazement that all

unknowingly he had put rough, rude hands on something this little world held sacred. He arose silently, and passed out into the right. Down toward the sea he went, in the fitful starlight, half conscious of the girl who followed timidly after him. When at last he stood upon the bluff, he turned to his little sister and looked upon her sorrowfully, remembering with sudden pain how little thought he had given her. He put his arm about her and let her passion of tears spend itself on his shoulder.

Long they stood together, peering over the gray unresting water.

"John," she said, "does it make every one—unhappy when they study and learn lots of things?"

He paused and smiled. "I am afraid it does," he said.

"And, John, are you glad you studied?"

"Yes," came the answer, slowly but positively.

She watched the flickering lights upon the sea, and said thoughtfully, "I wish I was unhappy,—and—and," putting both arms about his neck, "I think I am, a little, John."

It was several days later that John walked up to the Judge's house to ask for the privilege of teaching the Negro school. The Judge himself met him at the front door, stared a little hard at him, and said brusquely, "Go round to the kitchen door, John, and wait." Sitting on the kitchen steps, John stared at the corn, thoroughly perplexed. What on earth had come over him? Every step he made offended some one. He had come to save his people, and before he left the depot he had hurt them. He sought to teach them at the church, and had outraged their deepest feelings. He had schooled himself to be respectful to the Judge, and then blundered into his front door. And all the time he had meant right,—and yet, and yet, somehow he found it so hard and strange to fit his old surroundings again, to find his place in the world about him. He could not remember that he used to have any difficulty in the past, when life was glad and gay. The world seemed smooth and easy then. Perhaps,—but his sister came to the kitchen door just then and said the Judge awaited him.

The Judge sat in the dining-room amid his morning's mail, and he did not ask John to sit down. He plunged squarely into the business. "You've come for the school, I suppose. Well, John, I want to speak to you plainly. You know I'm a friend to your people. I've helped you and your family, and would have done more if you hadn't got the notion of going off. Now I like the colored people, and sympathize with all their reasonable aspirations; but you and I both know, John, that in this country the Negro must remain subordinate, and can never expect to be the equal of white men. In their place, your people can be honest and respectful; and God knows, I'll do what I can to help them. But when they want to reverse nature, and rule white men, and marry white women, and sit in my parlor, then, by God! we'll hold them under if we have to lynch every Nigger in the land. Now, John, the question is, are you, with your education and Northern notions, going to accept the situation and teach the darkies to be faithful servants and laborers as your fathers were,—I knew your father, John, he belonged to my brother, and he was a good Nigger. Well—well, are you going to be like him, or are you going to try to put fool ideas of rising and equality into these folks' heads, and make them discontented and unhappy?"

"I am going to accept the situation, Judge Henderson," answered John, with a brevity that did not escape the keen old man. He hesitated a moment, and then said shortly, "Very well,—we'll try you awhile. Good-morning."

It was a full month after the opening of the Negro school that the other John came home, tall, gay, and headstrong. The mother wept, the sisters sang. The whole white town was glad. A proud man was the Judge, and it was a goodly sight to see the two swinging down Main Street together. And yet all did not go smoothly between them, for the younger man could not and did not veil his contempt for the little town, and plainly had his heart set on New York. Now the one cherished ambition of the Judge was to see his son mayor of Altamaha, representative to the legislature, and—who could say?—governor of Georgia. So the argument often waxed hot between them. "Good heavens, father," the younger man would say after dinner, as he lighted a cigar and stood by the fireplace, "you surely don't expect a young fellow like me to settle down permanently in this—this God-forgotten town with nothing but mud and Negroes?" "*I* did," the Judge would answer laconically; and on this particular day it seemed from the gathering scowl that he was about to add something more emphatic, but neighbors had already begun to drop in to admire his son, and the conversation drifted.

"Heah that John is livenin' things up at the darky school," volunteered the postmaster, after a pause.

"What now?" asked the Judge, sharply.

"Oh, nothin' in particulah,—just his almighty air and uppish ways. B'lieve I did heah somethin' about his givin' talks on the French Revolution, equality, and such like. He's what I call a dangerous Nigger."

"Have you heard him say anything out of the way?"

"Why, no,—but Sally, our girl, told my wife a lot of rot. Then, too, I don't need to heah: a Nigger what won't say 'sir' to a white man, or—"

"Who is this John?" interrupted the son.

"Why, it's little black John, Peggy's son,—your old play-fellow."

The young man's face flushed angrily, and then he laughed.

"Oh," said he, "it's the darky that tried to force himself into a seat beside the lady I was escorting—"

But Judge Henderson waited to hear no more. He had been nettled all day, and now at this he rose with a half-smothered oath, took his hat and cane, and walked straight to the schoolhouse.

For John, it had been a long, hard pull to get things started in the rickety old shanty that sheltered his school. The Negroes were rent into factions for and against him, the parents were careless, the children irregular and dirty, and books, pencils, and slates largely missing. Nevertheless, he struggled hopefully on, and seemed to see at last some glimmering of dawn. The attendance was larger and the children were a shade cleaner this week. Even the booby class in reading showed a little comforting progress. So John settled himself with renewed patience this afternoon.

"Now, Mandy," he said cheerfully, "that's better; but you

mustn't chop your words up so: 'If—the—man—goes.' Why, your little brother even wouldn't tell a story that way, now would he?"

"Naw, suh, he cain't talk."

"All right; now let's try again: 'If the man—'"

"John!"

The whole school started in surprise, and the teacher half arose, as the red, angry face of the Judge appeared in the open doorway.

"John, this school is closed. You children can go home and get to work. The white people of Altamaha are not spending their money on black folks to have their heads crammed with impudence and lies. Clear out! I'll lock the door myself."

Up at the great pillared house the tall young son wandered aimlessly about after his father's abrupt departure. In the house there was little to interest him; the books were old and stale, the local newspaper flat, and the women had retired with headaches and sewing. He tried a nap, but it was too warm. So he sauntered out into the fields, complaining disconsolately, "Good Lord! how long will this imprisonment last!" He was not a bad fellow,—just a little spoiled and self-indulgent, and as headstrong as his proud father. He seemed a young man pleasant to look upon, as he sat on the great black stump at the edge of the pines idly swinging his legs and smoking. "Why, there isn't even a girl worth getting up a respectable flirtation with," he growled. Just then his eye caught a tall, willowy figure hurrying toward him on the narrow path. He looked with interest at first, and then burst into a laugh as he said, "Well, I declare, if it isn't Jennie, the little brown kitchen-maid! Why, I never noticed before what a trim little body she is. Hello, Jennie! Why, you haven't kissed me since I came home," he said gaily. The young girl stared at him in surprise and confusion,—faltered something inarticulate, and attempted to pass. But a wilful mood had seized the young idler, and he caught at her arm. Frightened, she slipped by; and half mischievously he turned and ran after her through the tall pines.

Yonder, toward the sea, at the end of the path, came John slowly, with his head down. He had turned wearily homeward from the schoolhouse; then, thinking to shield his mother from the blow, started to meet his sister as she came from work and break the news of his dismissal to her. "I'll go away," he said slowly; "I'll go away and find work, and send for them. I cannot live here longer." And then the fierce, buried anger surged up into his throat. He waved his arms and hurried wildly up the path.

The great brown sea lay silent. The air scarce breathed. The dying day bathed the twisted oaks and mighty pines in black and gold. There came from the wind no warning, not a whisper from the cloudless sky. There was only a black man hurrying on with an ache in his heart, seeing neither sun nor sea, but starting as from a dream at the frightened cry that woke the pines, to see his dark sister struggling in the arms of a tall and fair-haired man.

He said not a word, but, seizing a fallen limb, struck him with all the pent-up hatred of his great black arm; and the body lay white and still beneath the pines, all bathed in sunshine and in blood. John looked at it dreamily, then walked back to the house briskly, and said in a soft voice, "Mammy, I'm going away,—I'm going to be free."

She gazed at him dimly and faltered, "No'th, honey, is yo' gwine No'th agin?"

He looked out where the North Star glistened pale above the waters, and said, "Yes, mammy, I'm going—North."

Then, without another word, he went out into the narrow lane, up by the straight pines, to the same winding path, and seated himself on the great black stump, looking at the blood where the body had lain. Yonder in the gray past he had played with that dead boy, romping together under the solemn trees. The night deepened; he thought of the boys at Johnstown. He wondered how Brown had turned out, and Carey? And Jones,—Jones? Why, he was Jones, and he wondered what they would all say when they knew, when they knew, in that great long dining-room with its hundreds of merry eyes. Then as the sheen of the starlight stole over him, he thought of the gilded ceiling of that vast concert hall, and heard stealing toward him the faint sweet music of the swan. Hark! was it music, or the hurry and shouting of men? Yes, surely! Clear and high the faint sweet melody rose and fluttered like a living thing, so that the very earth trembled as with the tramp of horses and murmur of angry men.

He leaned back and smiled toward the sea, whence rose the strange melody, away from the dark shadows where lay the noise of horses galloping, galloping on. With an effort he roused himself, bent forward, and looked steadily down the pathway, softly humming the "Song of the Bride,"—

"Freudig geführt, ziehet dahin."

Amid the trees in the dim morning twilight he watched their shadows dancing and heard their horses thundering toward him, until at last they came sweeping like a storm, and he saw in front that haggard white-haired man, whose eyes flashed red with fury. Oh, how he pitied him,—pitied him,—and wondered if he had the coiling twisted rope. Then, as the storm burst round him, he rose slowly to his feet and turned his closed eyes toward the Sea.

And the world whistled in his ears.

XIV

THE SORROW SONGS

> I walk through the churchyard
>   To lay this body down;
> I know moon-rise, I know star-rise;
> I walk in the moonlight, I walk in the starlight;
> I'll lie in the grave and stretch out my arms,
> I'll go to judgment in the evening of the day,
> And my soul and thy soul shall meet that day,
>   When I lay this body down.
>
> Negro Song

They that walked in darkness sang songs in the olden days—
Sorrow Songs—for they were weary at heart. And so before
each thought that I have written in this book I have set a phrase,
a haunting echo of these weird old songs in which the soul of
the black slave spoke to men. Ever since I was a child these songs
have stirred me strangely. They came out of the South unknown
to me, one by one, and yet at once I knew them as of me and
of mine. Then in after years when I came to Nashville I saw the

great temple builded of these songs towering over the pale city. To me Jubilee Hall seemed ever made of the songs themselves, and its bricks were red with the blood and dust of toil. Out of them rose for me morning, noon, and night, bursts of wonderful melody, full of the voices of my brothers and sisters, full of the voices of the past.

Little of beauty has America given the world save the rude grandeur God himself stamped on her bosom; the human spirit in this new world has expressed itself in vigor and ingenuity rather than in beauty. And so by fateful chance the Negro folk-song— the rhythmic cry of the slave—stands to-day not simply as the sole American music, but as the most beautiful expression of human experience born this side the seas. It has been neglected, it has been, and is, half despised, and above all it has been persistently mistaken and misunderstood; but notwithstanding, it still remains as the singular spiritual heritage of the nation and the greatest gift of the Negro people.

Away back in the thirties the melody of these slave songs stirred the nation, but the songs were soon half forgotten. Some, like "Near the lake where drooped the willow," passed into current airs and their source was forgotten; others were caricatured on the "minstrel" stage and their memory died away. Then in wartime came the singular Port Royal experiment after the capture of Hilton Head, and perhaps for the first time the North met the Southern slave face to face and heart to heart with no third witness. The Sea Islands of the Carolinas, where they met, were filled with a black folk of primitive type, touched and moulded less by the world about them than any others outside the Black Belt. Their appearance was uncouth, their language funny, but their hearts were human and their singing stirred men with a mighty power. Thomas Wentworth Higginson hastened to tell of these songs, and Miss McKim and others urged upon the world their rare beauty. But the world listened only half credulously until the Fisk Jubilee Singers sang the slave songs so deeply into the world's heart that it can never wholly forget them again.

There was once a blacksmith's son born at Cadiz, New York, who in the changes of time taught school in Ohio and helped defend Cincinnati from Kirby Smith. Then he fought at

Chancellorsville and Gettysburg and finally served in the Freed-men's Bureau at Nashville. Here he formed a Sunday school class of black children in 1866, and sang with them and taught them to sing. And then they taught him to sing, and when once the glory of the Jubilee songs passed into the soul of George L. White, he knew his life-work was to let those Negroes sing to the world as they had sung to him. So in 1871 the pilgrimage of the Fisk Jubilee Singers began. North to Cincinnati they rode,—four half-clothed black boys and five girl-women,—led by a man with a cause and a purpose. They stopped at Wilber-force, the oldest of Negro schools, where a black bishop blessed them. Then they went, fighting cold and starvation, shut out of hotels, and cheerfully sneered at, ever northward; and ever the magic of their song kept thrilling hearts, until a burst of ap-plause in the Congregational Council at Oberlin revealed them to the world. They came to New York and Henry Ward Beecher dared to welcome them, even though the metropolitan dailies sneered at his "Nigger Minstrels." So their songs conquered till they sang across the land and across the sea, before Queen and Kaiser, in Scotland and Ireland, Holland and Switzerland. Seven years they sang, and brought back a hundred and fifty thousand dollars to found Fisk University.

Since their day they have been imitated—sometimes well, by the singers of Hampton and Atlanta, sometimes ill, by strag-gling quartettes. Caricature has sought again to spoil the quaint beauty of the music, and has filled the air with many debased melodies which vulgar ears scarce know from the real. But the true Negro folk-song still lives in the hearts of those who have heard them truly sung and in the hearts of the Negro people.

What are these songs, and what do they mean? I know little of music and can say nothing in technical phrase, but I know something of men, and knowing them, I know that these songs are the articulate message of the slave to the world. They tell us in these eager days that life was joyous to the black slave, care-less and happy. I can easily believe this of some, of many. But not all the past South, though it rose from the dead, can gainsay the heart-touching witness of these songs. They are the music of an unhappy people, of the children of disappointment; they tell of death and suffering and unvoiced longing toward a truer world, of misty wanderings and hidden ways.

The songs are indeed the siftings of centuries; the music is far more ancient than the words, and in it we can trace here and there signs of development. My grandfather's grandmother was seized by an evil Dutch trader two centuries ago; and coming to the valleys of the Hudson and Housatonic, black, little, and lithe, she shivered and shrank in the harsh north winds, looking longingly at the hills, and often crooned a heathen melody to the child between her knees, thus:

The child sang it to his children and they to their children's children, and so two hundred years it has travelled down to us and we sing it to our children, knowing as little as our fathers what its words may mean, but knowing well the meaning of its music.

This was primitive African music; it may be seen in larger form in the strange chant which heralds "The Coming of John":

> "You may bury me in the East,
>   You may bury me in the West,
>   But I'll hear the trumpet sound in that morning,"

—the voice of exile.

Ten master songs, more or less, one may pluck from this forest of melody—songs of undoubted Negro origin and wide popular currency, and songs peculiarly characteristic of the slave. One of these I have just mentioned. Another whose strains begin this book is "Nobody knows the trouble I've seen." When, struck with a sudden poverty, the United States refused to fulfill its promises of land to the freedmen, a brigadier-general went down to the Sea Islands to carry the news. An old woman on the outskirts of the throng began singing this song; all the mass joined with her, swaying. And the soldier wept.

The third song is the cradle-song of death which all men know,—"Swing low, sweet chariot,"—whose bars begin the life story of "Alexander Crummell." Then there is the song of many waters, "Roll, Jordan, roll," a mighty chorus with minor cadences. There were many songs of the fugitive like that which opens "The Wings of Atalanta," and the more familiar "Been a-listening." The seventh is the song of the End and the Beginning—"My Lord, what a mourning! when the stars begin to fall"; a strain of this is placed before "The Dawn of Freedom." The song of groping—"My way's cloudy"—begins "The Meaning of Progress"; the ninth is the song of this chapter—"Wrestlin' Jacob, the day is a-breaking,"—a paean of hopeful strife. The last master song is the song of songs—"Steal away,"—sprung from "The Faith of the Fathers."

There are many others of the Negro folk-songs as striking and characteristic as these, as, for instance, the three strains in the third, eighth, and ninth chapters; and others I am sure could easily make a selection on more scientific principles. There are, too, songs that seem to me a step removed from the more primitive types: there is the maze-like medley, "Bright sparkles," one phrase of which heads "The Black Belt"; the Easter carol, "Dust, dust and ashes"; the dirge, "My mother's took her flight and gone home"; and that burst of melody hovering over "The Passing of the First-Born"—"I hope my mother will be there in that beautiful world on high."

These represent a third step in the development of the slave song, of which "You may bury me in the East" is the first, and songs like "March on" (chapter six) and "Steal away" are the second. The first is African music, the second Afro-American, while the third is a blending of Negro music with the music heard in the foster land. The result is still distinctively Negro and the method of blending original, but the elements are both Negro and Caucasian. One might go further and find a fourth step in this development, where the songs of white America have been distinctively influenced by the slave songs or have incorporated whole phrases of Negro melody, as "Swanee River" and "Old Black Joe." Side by side, too, with the growth has gone the debasements and imitations—the Negro "minstrel" songs, many of the "gospel" hymns, and some of the contemporary "coon" songs,—a mass of music in which the novice may easily lose himself and never find the real Negro melodies.

In these songs, I have said, the slave spoke to the world. Such a message is naturally veiled and half articulate. Words and music have lost each other and new and cant phrases of a dimly understood theology have displaced the older sentiment. Once in a while we catch a strange world of an unknown tongue, as the "Mighty Myo," which figures as a river of death; more often slight words or mere doggerel are joined to music of singular sweetness. Purely secular songs are few in number, partly because many of them were turned into hymns by a change of words, partly because the frolics were seldom heard by the stranger, and the music less often caught. Of nearly all the songs, however, the music is distinctly sorrowful. The ten master songs I have mentioned tell in word and music of trouble and exile, of strife and hiding; they grope toward some unseen power and sigh for rest in the End.

The world that are left to us are not without interest, and, cleared of evident dross, they conceal much of real poetry and meaning beneath conventional theology and unmeaning rhapsody. Like all primitive folk, the slave stood near to Nature's heart. Life was a "rough and rolling sea" like the brown Atlantic of the Sea Islands; the "Wilderness" was the home of God, and the "lonesome valley" led to the way of life. "Winter'll soon be over," was the picture of life and death to a tropical imagination. The sudden wild thunderstorms of the South awed and impressed the Negroes,—at times the rumbling seemed to them "mournful," at times imperious:

"My Lord calls me,
  He calls me by the thunder,
  The trumpet sounds it in my soul."

The monotonous toil and exposure is painted in many words.
One sees the plough-men in the hot, moist furrow, singing:

"Dere's no rain to wet you,
  Dere's no sun to burn you,
  Oh, push along, believer,
  I want to go home."

The bowed and bent old man cries, with thrice-repeated wail:

"O Lord, keep me from sinking down,"

and he rebukes the devil of doubt who can whisper:

"Jesus is dead and God 's gone away."

Yet the soul-hunger is there, the restlessness of the savage, the
wail of the wanderer, and the plaint is put in one little phrase:

My   soul   wants some thing that's new, that's new

Over the inner thoughts of the slaves and their relations one
with another the shadow of fear ever hung, so that we get but
glimpses here and there, and also with them, eloquent omissions
and silences. Mother and child are sung, but seldom father; fugitive and weary wanderer call for pity and affection, but there
is little of wooing and wedding; the rocks and the mountains
are well known, but home is unknown. Strange blending of love
and helplessness sings through the refrain:

"Yonder's my ole mudder,
Been waggin' at de hill so long;
'Bout time she cross over,
Git home bime-by."

Elsewhere comes the cry of the "motherless" and the "Farewell, farewell, my only child."

Love-songs are scarce and fall into two categories—the frivolous and light, and the sad. Of deep successful love there is ominous silence, and in one of the oldest of these songs there is a depth of history and meaning:

Poor Ro - sy, poor gal; Poor Ro - sy, poor gal; Ro - sy break my poor heart. Heav'n shall - a - be my home.

A black woman said of the song, "It can't be sung without a full heart and a troubled sperrit." The same voice sings here that sings in the German folk-song:

"Jetz Geh i' an's brunele, trink' aber net."

Of death the Negro showed little fear, but talked of it familiarly and even fondly as simply a crossing of the waters, perhaps—who knows?—back to his ancient forests again. Later days transfigured his fatalism, and amid the dust and dirt the toiler sang:

"Dust, dust and ashes, fly over my grave,
But the Lord shall bear my spirit home."

The things evidently borrowed from the surrounding world undergo characteristic change when they enter the mouth of the slave. Especially is this true of Bible phrases. "Weep, O captive daughter of Zion," is quaintly turned into "Zion, weep-a-low," and the wheels of Ezekiel are turned every way in the mystic dreaming of the slave, till he says:

> "There's a little wheel a-turnin' in-a-my heart."

As in olden time, the words of these hymns were improvised by some leading minstrel of the religious band. The circumstances of the gathering, however, the rhythm of the songs, and the limitations of allowable thought, confined the poetry for the most part to single or double lines, and they seldom were expanded to quatrains or longer tales, although there are some few examples of sustained efforts, chiefly paraphrases of the Bible. Three short series of verses have always attracted me,— the one that heads this chapter, of one line of which Thomas Wentworth Higginson has fittingly said, "Never, it seems to me, since man first lived and suffered was his infinite longing for peace uttered more plaintively." The second and third are descriptions of the Last Judgment,—the one a late improvisation, with some traces of outside influence:

> "Oh, the stars in the elements are falling,
> And the moon drips away into blood,
> And the ransomed of the Lord are returning unto God,
> Blessed be the name of the Lord."

And the other earlier and homelier picture from the low coast lands:

> "Michael, haul the boat ashore,
> Then you'll hear the horn they blow,
> Then you'll hear the trumpet sound,
> Trumpet sound the world around,
> Trumpet sound for rich and poor,
> Trumpet sound the Jubilee,
> Trumpet sound for you and me."

Through all the sorrow of the Sorrow Songs there breathes a hope—a faith in the ultimate justice of things. The minor cadences of despair change often to triumph and calm confidence. Sometimes it is faith in life, sometimes a faith in death, sometimes assurance of boundless justice in some fair world beyond. But whichever it is, the meaning is always clear: that sometime, somewhere, men will judge men by their souls and not by their skins. Is such a hope justified? Do the Sorrow Songs sing true?

The silently growing assumption of this age is that the probation of races is past, and that the backward races of to-day are of proven inefficiency and not worth the saving. Such an assumption is the arrogance of peoples irreverent toward Time and ignorant of the deeds of men. A thousand years ago such an assumption, easily possible, would have made it difficult for the Teuton to prove his right to life. Two thousand years ago such dogmatism, readily welcome, would have scouted the idea of blond races ever leading civilization. So wofully unorganized is sociological knowledge that the meaning of progress, the meaning of "swift" and "slow" in human doing, and the limits of human perfectability, are veiled, unanswered sphinxes on the shores of science. Why should Æschylus have sung two thousand years before Shakespeare was born? Why has civilization flourished in Europe, and flickered, flamed, and died in Africa? So long as the world stands meekly dumb before such questions, shall this nation proclaim its ignorance and unhallowed prejudices by denying freedom of opportunity to those who brought the Sorrow Songs to the Seats of the Mighty?

Your country? How came it yours? Before the Pilgrims landed we were here. Here we have brought our three gifts and mingled them with yours: a gift of story and song—soft, stirring melody in an ill-harmonized and unmelodious land; the gift of sweat and brawn to beat back the wilderness, conquer the soil, and lay the foundations of this vast economic empire two hundred years earlier than your weak hands could have done it; the third, a gift of the Spirit. Around us the history of the land has centered for thrice a hundred years; out of the nation's heart we have called all that was best to throttle and subdue all that was

worst; fire and blood, prayer and sacrifice, have billowed over
this people, and they have found peace only in the altars of the
God of Right. Nor has our gift of the Spirit been merely passive. Actively we have woven ourselves with the very warp and
woof of this nation,—we fought their battles, shared their sorrow, mingled our blood with theirs, and generation after generation have pleaded with a headstrong, careless people to
despise not Justice, Mercy, and Truth, lest the nation be smitten
with a curse. Our song, our toil, our cheer, and warning have
been given to this nation in blood-brotherhood. Are not these
gifts worth the giving? Is not this work and striving? Would
America have been America without her Negro people?

Even so is the hope that sang in the songs of my father well
sung. If somewhere in this whirl and chaos of things there dwells
Eternal Good, pitiful yet masterful, then anon in His good time
America shall rend the Veil and the prisoned shall go free. Free,
free as the sunshine trickling down the morning into these high
windows of mine, free as yonder fresh young voices welling up
to me from the caverns of brick and mortar below—swelling
with song, instinct with life, tremulous treble and darkening
bass. My children, my little children, are singing to the sunshine,
and thus they sing:

And the traveller girds himself, and sets his face toward the Morning, and goes his way.

THE AFTERTHOUGHT

Hear my cry, O God the Reader; vouchsafe that this my book fall not still-born into the world-wilderness. Let there spring, Gentle One, from out its leaves vigor of thought and thoughtful deed to reap the harvest wonderful. (Let the ears of a guilty people tingle with truth, and seventy millions sigh for the righteousness which exalteth nations, in this drear day when human brotherhood is mockery and a snare.) Thus in Thy good time may infinite reason turn the tangle straight, and these crooked marks on a fragile leaf be not indeed

THE END

THE TALENTED
TENTH

The Negro race, like all races, is going to be saved by its exceptional men. The problem of education, then, among Negroes must first of all deal with the Talented Tenth; it is the problem of developing the Best of this race that they may guide the Mass away from the contamination and death of the Worst, in their own and other races. Now the training of men is a difficult and intricate task. Its technique is a matter for educational experts, but its object is for the vision of seers. If we make money the object of man-training, we shall develop money-makers but not necessarily men; if we make technical skill the object of education, we may possess artisans but not, in nature, men. Men we shall have only as we make manhood the object of the work of the schools—intelligence, broad sympathy, knowledge of the world that was and is, and of the relation of men to it—this is the curriculum of that Higher Education which must underlie true life. On this foundation we may build bread winning, skill of hand and quickness of brain, with never a fear lest the child and man mistake the means of living for the object of life.

If this be true—and who can deny it—three tasks lay before me; first to show from the past that the Talented Tenth as they have risen among American Negroes have been worthy of leadership; secondly to show how these men may be educated and developed; and thirdly to show their relation to the Negro problem.

You misjudge us because you do not know us. From the very first it has been the educated and intelligent of the Negro people that have led and elevated the mass, and the sole obstacles that nullified and retarded their efforts were slavery and race-prejudice; for what is slavery but the legalized survival of the unfit and the nullification of the work of natural internal leadership? Negro leadership therefore sought from the first to rid the race of this awful incubus that it might make way for natural selection and the survival of the fittest. In colonial days came Phillis Wheatley and Paul Cuffe striving against the bars of prejudice; and Benjamin Banneker, the almanac maker, voiced their longings when he said to Thomas Jefferson, "I freely and cheerfully acknowledge that I am of the African race and in colour which is natural to them, of the deepest dye; and it is under a sense of the most profound gratitude to the Supreme Ruler of the Universe, that I now confess to you that I am not under that state of tyrannical thraldom and inhuman captivity to which too many of my brethren are doomed, but that I have abundantly tasted of the fruition of those blessings which proceed from that free and unequalled liberty with which you are favored, and which I hope you will willingly allow, you have mercifully received from the immediate hand of that Being from whom proceedeth every good and perfect gift.

"Suffer me to recall to your mind that time, in which the arms of the British crown were exerted with every powerful effort, in order to reduce you to a state of servitude; look back, I entreat you, on the variety of dangers to which you were exposed; reflect on that period in which every human aid appeared unavailable, and in which even hope and fortitude wore the aspect of inability to the conflict, and you cannot but be led to a serious and grateful sense of your miraculous and providential preservation, you cannot but acknowledge, that the present freedom and tranquility which you enjoy, you have mercifully received, and that a peculiar blessing of heaven.

"This, sir, was a time when you clearly saw into the injustice of a state of Slavery, and in which you had just apprehensions of the horrors of its condition. It was then that your abhorrence thereof was so excited, that you publicly held forth this true and invaluable doctrine, which is worthy to be recorded and remembered in all succeeding ages: "'We hold these truths to be self evident, that all men are created equal; that they are endowed with certain inalienable rights, and that among these are life, liberty and the pursuit of happiness.'"

Then came Dr. James Derham, who could tell even the learned Dr. Rush something of medicine, and Lemuel Haynes, to whom Middlebury College gave an honorary A.M. in 1804. These and others we may call the Revolutionary group of distinguished Negroes—they were persons of marked ability, leaders of a Talented Tenth, standing conspicuously among the best of their time. They strove by word and deed to save the color-line from becoming the line between the bond and free, but all they could do was nullified by Eli Whitney and the Curse of Gold. So they passed into forgetfulness.

But their spirit did not wholly die; here and there in the early part of the century came other exceptional men. Some were natural sons of unnatural fathers and were given often a liberal training and thus a race of educated mulattoes sprang up to plead for black men's rights. There was Ira Aldridge, whom all Europe loved to honor; there was that Voice crying in the Wilderness, David Walker, and saying:

"I declare it does appear to me as though some nations think God is asleep, or that he made the Africans for nothing else but to dig their mines and work their farms, or they cannot believe history sacred or profane. I ask every man who has a heart, and is blessed with the privilege of believing—Is not God a God of justice to all his creatures? Do you say he is? Then if he gives peace and tranquility to tyrants and permits them to keep our fathers, our mothers, ourselves and our children in eternal ignorance and wretchedness to support them and their families, would he be to us a God of Justice? I ask, O, ye Christians, who hold us and our children in the most abject ignorance and degradation that ever a people were afflicted with since the world began—I say if God gives you peace and tranquility, and suffers you thus to go on afflicting us, and our children, who have never given you the least provocation—would He be to us a God of Justice? If you will allow that we are men, who feel for each other, does not the blood of our fathers and of us, their children, cry aloud to the Lord of Sabaoth against you for the cruelties and murders with which you have and do continue to afflict us?"

This was the wild voice that first aroused Southern legislators in 1829 to the terrors of abolitionism.

In 1831 there met that first Negro convention in Philadelphia, at which the world gaped curiously but which bravely attacked the problems of race and slavery, crying out against persecution and declaring that "Laws as cruel in themselves as they were unconstitutional and unjust, have in many places been enacted against our poor, unfriended and unoffending brethren (without a shadow of provocation on our part), at whose bare recital the very savage draws himself up for fear of contagion—looks noble and prides himself because he bears not the name of Christian." Side by side this free Negro movement, and the movement for abolition, strove until they merged into one strong stream. Too little notice has been taken of the work which the Talented Tenth among Negroes took in the great abolition crusade. From the very day that a Philadelphia colored man became the first subscriber to Garrison's "Liberator," to the day when Negro soldiers made the Emancipation Proclamation possible, black leaders worked shoulder to shoulder with white men in a movement, the success of which would have been impossible without them. There was Purvis and Remond, Pennington and Highland Garnett, Sojourner Truth and Alexander Crummel, and above, Frederick Douglass—what would the abolition movement have been without them? They stood as living examples of the possibilities of the Negro race, their own hard experiences and well wrought culture said silently more than all the drawn periods of orators—they were the men who made American slavery impossible. As Maria Weston Chapman said, from the school of anti-slavery agitation "a throng of authors, editors, lawyers, orators and accomplished gentlemen of color have taken their degree! It has equally implanted hopes and aspirations, noble thoughts, and sublime purposes, in the hearts of both races. It has prepared the white man for the freedom of the black man, and it has made the black man scorn the thought of enslavement, as does a white man, as far as its influence has extended. Strengthen that noble influence! Before its organization, the country only saw here and there in slavery some faithful

Cudjoe or Dinah, whose strong natures blossomed even in bond-age, like a fine plant beneath a heavy stone. Now, under the elevating and cherishing influence of the American Anti-slavery Society, the colored race, like the white, furnishes Corinthian capitals for the noblest temples."

Where were these black abolitionists trained? Some, like Fred-erick Douglass, were self-trained, but yet trained liberally; oth-ers, like Alexander Crummell and McCune Smith, graduated from famous foreign universities. Most of them rose up through the colored schools of New York and Philadelphia and Boston, taught by college-bred men like Russworm, of Dartmouth, and college-bred white men like Neau and Benezet.

After emancipation came a new group of educated and gifted leaders: Langston, Bruce and Elliot, Greener, Williams and Payne. Through political organization, historical and polemic writing and moral regeneration, these men strove to uplift their people. It is the fashion of to-day to sneer at them and to say that with freedom Negro leadership should have begun at the plow and not in the Senate—a foolish and mischievous lie; two hundred and fifty years that black serf toiled at the plow and yet that toiling was in vain till the Senate passed the war amendments; and two hundred and fifty years more the half-free serf of to-day may toil at his plow, but unless he have po-litical rights and righteously guarded civic status, he will still remain the poverty-stricken and ignorant plaything of rascals, that he now is. This all sane men know even if they dare not say it.

And so we come to the present—a day of cowardice and vac-illation, of strident wide-voiced wrong and faint hearted com-promise; of double-faced dallying with Truth and Right. Who are to-day guiding the work of the Negro people? The "excep-tions" of course. And yet so sure as this Talented Tenth is pointed out, the blind worshippers of the Average cry out in alarm: "These are exceptions, look here at death, disease and crime—these are the happy rule." Of course they are the rule, because a silly nation made them the rule: Because for three long centuries this people lynched Negroes who dared to be brave, raped black women who dared to be virtuous, crushed dark-hued youth who dared to be ambitious, and encouraged and made to flourish servility and lewdness and apathy. But not even this was able to crush all manhood and chastity and aspiration from black folk. A saving remnant continually survives and persists, continually aspires, continually shows itself in thrift and ability and character. Exceptional it is to be sure, but this is its chiefest promise; it shows the capability of Negro blood, the promise of black men. Do Americans ever stop to reflect that there are in this land a million men of Negro blood, well-educated, owners of homes, against the honor of whose womanhood no breath was ever raised, whose men occupy positions of trust and usefulness, and who, judged by any standard, have reached the full measure of the best type of modern European culture? Is it fair, is it decent, is it Christian to ignore these facts of the Negro problem, to belittle such aspiration, to nullify such leadership and seek to crush these people back into the mass out of which by toil and travail, they and their fathers have raised themselves?

Can the masses of the Negro people be in any possible way more quickly raised than by the effort and example of this aristocracy of talent and character? Was there ever a nation on God's fair earth civilized from the bottom upward? Never; it is, ever was and ever will be from the top downward that culture filters. The Talented Tenth rises and pulls all that are worth the saving up to their vantage ground. This is the history of human progress; and the two historic mistakes which have hindered that progress were the thinking first that no more could ever rise save the few already risen; or second, that it would better the unrisen to pull the risen down.

How then shall the leaders of a struggling people be trained and the hands of the risen few strengthened? There can be but one answer: The best and most capable of their youth must be schooled in the colleges and universities of the land. We will not quarrel as to just what the university of the Negro should teach or how it should teach it—I willingly admit that each soul and each race-soul needs its own peculiar curriculum. But this is true: A university is a human invention for the transmission of knowledge and culture from generation to generation, through the training of quick minds and pure hearts, and for this work no other human invention will suffice, not even trade and industrial schools.

All men cannot go to college but some men must; every isolated group or nation must have its yeast, must have for the talented few centers of training where men are not so mystified and befuddled by the hard and necessary toil of earning a living, as to have no aims higher than their bellies, and no God greater than Gold. This is true training, and thus in the beginning were the favored sons of the freedmen trained. Out of the colleges of the North came, after the blood of war, Ware, Cravath, Chase, Andrews, Bumstead and Spence to build the foundations of knowledge and civilization in the black South. Where ought they to have begun to build? At the bottom, of course, quibbles the mole with his eyes in the earth. Aye! truly at the bottom, at the very bottom; at the bottom of knowledge, down in the very depths of knowledge there where the roots of justice strike into the lowest soil of Truth. And so they did begin; they founded colleges, and up from the colleges shot normal schools, and out from the normal schools went teachers, and around the normal teachers clustered other teachers to teach the public schools; the college trained in Greek and Latin and mathematics, 2,000 men; and these men trained full 50,000 others in morals and manners, and they in turn taught thrift and the alphabet to nine millions of men, who to-day hold $300,000,000 of property. It was a miracle—the most wonderful peace-battle of the 19th century, and yet to-day men smile at it, and in fine superiority tell us that it was all a strange mistake; that a proper way to found a system of education is first to gather the children and buy them spelling books and hoes; afterward men may look about for teachers, if haply they may find them; or again they would teach men Work, but as for Life—why, what has Work to do with Life, they ask vacantly.

Was the work of these college founders successful; did it stand the test of time? Did the college graduates, with all their fine theories of life, really live? Are they useful men helping to civilize and elevate their less fortunate fellows? Let us see. Omitting all institutions which have not actually graduated students from a college course, there are to-day in the United States thirty-four institutions giving something above high school training to Negroes and designed especially for this race.

Three of these were established in border States before the War; thirteen were planted by the Freedmen's Bureau in the years 1864–1869; nine were established between 1870 and 1880 by various church bodies; five were established after 1881 by Negro churches, and four are state institutions supported by United States' agricultural funds. In most cases the college departments are small adjuncts to high and common school-work. As a matter of fact six institutions—Atlanta, Fisk, Howard, Shaw, Wilberforce and Leland—are the important Negro colleges so far as actual work and number of students are concerned. In all these institutions, seven hundred and fifty Negro college students are enrolled. In grade the best of these colleges are about a year behind the smaller New England colleges and a typical curriculum is that of Atlanta University. Here students from the grammar grades, after a three years' high school course, take a college course of 136 weeks. One-fourth of this time is given to Latin and Greek; one-fifth, to English and modern languages; one-sixth, to history and social science; one-seventh, to natural science; one-eighth to mathematics, and one-eighth to philosophy and pedagogy.

In addition to these students in the South, Negroes have attended Northern colleges for many years. As early as 1826 one was graduated from Bowdoin College, and from that time till to-day nearly every year has seen elsewhere, other such graduates. They have, of course, met much color-prejudice. Fifty years ago very few colleges would admit them at all. Even to-day no Negro has ever been admitted to Princeton, and at some other leading institutions they are rather endured than encouraged. Oberlin was the great pioneer in the work of blotting out the color-line in colleges, and has more Negro graduates by far than any other Northern college.

The total number of Negro college graduates up to 1899,

(several of the graduates of that year not being reported), was
as follows:

	NEGRO COLLEGES.	WHITE COLLEGES.
Before '76...............	............137.............	 75
'75–'80.......	.... 143.............	 22
'80–'85	.... 250.............	 31
'85–'90.......	.... 413.............	 43
'90–'95.......	.... 465.............	 66
'96–'99.......	............475.............	 88
Class Unknown	.... 57.............	 64
Total	.... 1,914.............	 390

Of these graduates 2,079 were men and 252 were women; 50
per cent of Northern-born college men come South to work
among the masses of their people, at a sacrifice which few people realize; nearly 90 per cent of the Southern-born graduates
instead of seeking that personal freedom and broader intellectual atmosphere which their training has led them, in some degree, to conceive, stay and labor and wait in the midst of their
black neighbors and relatives.

The most interesting question, and in many respects the crucial question, to be asked concerning college-bred Negroes, is:
Do they earn a living? It has been intimated more than once
that the higher training of Negroes has resulted in sending into
the world of work, men who could find nothing to do suitable
to their talents. Now and then there comes a rumor of a colored
college man working at menial service, etc. Fortunately, returns
as to occupations of college-bred Negroes, gathered by the Atlanta conference, are quite full—nearly sixty per cent of the total
number of graduates.

This enables us to reach fairly certain conclusions as to the
occupations of all college-bred Negroes. Of 1,312 persons reported, there were:

	PERCENT	
Teachers	53.4	████████
Clergymen	16.8	███
Physicians, etc.	6.3	■
Students	5.6	■
Lawyers	4.7	■
In Govt. Service	4.0	■
In Business	3.6	■
Farmers and Artisans	2.7	▮
Editors, Secretaries and Clerks	2.4	▮
Miscellaneous	5	▏

Over half are teachers, a sixth are preachers, another sixth are students and professional men; over 6 per cent are farmers, artisans and merchants, and 4 per cent are in government service. In detail the occupations are as follows:

Occupations of College-Bred Men.

TEACHERS:

     Presidents and Deans.......................... 19

     Teacher of Music 7

     Professors, Principals and Teachers... 675   TOTAL 701

CLERGYMEN:

     Bishop.. 1

     Chaplains U.S. Army........................ 2

     Missionaries 9

     Presiding Elders 12

     Preachers 197   TOTAL 221

PHYSICIANS:

     Doctors of Medicine.......................... 76

     Druggists 4

     Dentists... 3   TOTAL 83

STUDENTS: TOTAL 74

LAWYERS:..   TOTAL 62

CIVIL SERVICE:

U.S. Minister Plenipotentiary............	1	
U.S. Consul...	1	
U.S. Deputy Collector	1	
U.S. Gauger	1	
U.S. Postmasters................................	2	
U.S. Clerks...	44	
State Civil Service.............................	2	
City Civil Service...............................	1	TOTAL 53

BUSINESS MEN:

Merchants, etc.....................................	30	
Managers...	13	
Real Estate Dealers.............................	4	TOTAL 47

FARMERS:		TOTAL 26

CLERKS AND SECRETARIES:

Secretary of National Societies..........	7	
Clerks, etc...	15	TOTAL 22

ARTISANS:		TOTAL 9
EDITORS:..		TOTAL 9
MISCELLANEOUS:		TOTAL 5

These figures illustrate vividly the function of the college-bred Negro. He is, as he ought to be, the group leader, the man who sets the ideals of the community where he lives, directs its thoughts and heads its social movements. It need hardly be argued that the Negro people need social leadership more than most groups; that they have no traditions to fall back upon, no long established customs, no strong family ties, no well defined social classes. All these things must be slowly and painfully evolved. The preacher was, even before the war, the group leader of the Negroes, and the church their greatest social institution. Naturally this preacher was ignorant and often immoral, and the problem of replacing the older type by better educated men has been a difficult one. Both by direct work and by direct influence on other preachers, and on congregations, the college-bred preacher has an opportunity for reformatory work and moral inspiration, the value of which cannot be over-estimated.

It has, however, been in the furnishing of teachers that the Negro college has found its peculiar function. Few persons realize how vast a work, how mighty a revolution has been thus accomplished. To furnish five millions and more of ignorant people with teachers of their own race and blood, in one generation, was not only a very difficult undertaking, but a very important one, in that, it placed before the eyes of almost every Negro child an attainable ideal. It brought the masses of the blacks in contact with modern civilization, made black men the leaders of their communities and trainers of the new generation. In this work college-bred Negroes were first teachers, and then teachers of teachers. And here it is that the broad culture of college work has been of peculiar value. Knowledge of life and its wider meaning, has been the point of the Negro's deepest ignorance, and the sending out of teachers whose training has not been simply for bread winning, but also for human culture, has been of inestimable value in the training of these men.

In earlier years the two occupations of preacher and teacher were practically the only ones open to the black college graduate. Of later years a larger diversity of life among his people, has opened new avenues of employment. Nor have these college men been paupers and spendthrifts; 557 college-bred Negroes owned in 1899, $1,342,862.50 worth of real estate (assessed value), or $2,411 per family. The real value of the total accumulations of the whole group is perhaps about $10,000,000, or $5,000 a piece. Pitiful is it not beside the fortunes of oil kings and steel trusts, but after all is the fortune of the millionaire the only stamp of true and successful living? Alas! it is, with many and there's the rub.

The problem of training the Negro is to-day immensely complicated by the fact that the whole question of the efficiency and appropriateness of our present systems of education, for any kind of child, is a matter of active debate, in which final settlement seems still afar off. Consequently it often happens that persons arguing for or against certain systems of education for Negroes, have these controversies in mind and miss the real question at issue. The main question, so far as the Southern Negro is concerned, is: What under the present circumstance, must a system of education do in order to raise the Negro as quickly as possible in the scale of civilization? The answer to this question seems to me clear: It must strengthen the Negro's character, increase his knowledge and teach him to earn a living. Now it goes without saying that it is hard to do all these things simultaneously or suddenly and that at the same time it will not do to give all the attention to one and neglect the others; we could give black boys trades, but that alone will not civilize a race of ex-slaves; we might simply increase their knowledge of the world, but this would not necessarily make them wish to use this knowledge honestly; we might seek to strengthen character and purpose, but to what end if this people have nothing to eat or to wear? A system of education is not one thing, nor does it have a single definite object, nor is it a mere matter of schools. Education is that whole system of human training within and without the schoolhouse walls, which moulds and develops men. If then we start out to train an ignorant and unskilled people with a heritage of bad habits, our system of training must set before itself two great aims—the one dealing with knowledge and character, the other part seeking to give the child the technical knowledge necessary for him to earn a living under the present circumstances. These objects are accomplished in part by the opening of the common schools on the one, and of the industrial schools on the other. But only in part, for there must also be trained those who are to teach these schools—men and women of knowledge and culture and technical skill who understand modern civilization, and have the training and aptitude to impart it to the children under them. There must be teachers, and teachers of teachers, and to attempt to establish any sort of a system of common and industrial school training, without *first* (and I say *first* advisedly), without *first* providing for the higher training of the very best teachers, is simply throwing your money to the winds. Schoolhouses do not teach themselves—piles of brick and mortar and machinery do not send out *men*. It is the trained, living human soul, cultivated and strengthened by long study and thought, that breathes the real breath of life into boys and girls and makes them human, whether they be black or white, Greek, Russian or American. Nothing, in these latter days, has so dampened the faith of thinking Negroes in recent educational movements, as the fact that such movements have been accompanied by ridicule and denouncement and decrying of those very institutions of higher training which made the Negro public school possible, and make Negro industrial schools thinkable. It was: Fisk, Atlanta, Howard and Straight, those colleges born of the faith and sacrifice of the abolitionists, that placed in the black schools of the South the 30,000 teachers and more, which some, who depreciate the work of these higher schools, are using to teach their own new experiments. If Hampton, Tuskegee and the hundred other industrial schools prove in the future to be as successful as they deserve to be, then their success in training black artisans for the South, will be due primarily to the white colleges of the North and the black colleges of the South, which trained the teachers who to-day conduct these institutions. There was a time when the American people believed pretty devoutly that a log of wood with a boy at one end and Mark Hopkins at the other, represented the highest ideal of human training. But in these eager days it would seem that we have changed all that and think it necessary to add a couple of saw-mills and a hammer to this outfit, and, at a pinch, to dispense with the services of Mark Hopkins.

I would not deny, or for a moment seem to deny, the paramount necessity of teaching the Negro to work, and to work steadily and skilfully; or seem to depreciate in the slightest degree the important part industrial schools must play in the accomplishment of these ends, but I *do* say, and insist upon it, that it is industrialism drunk with its vision of success, to imagine that its own work can be accomplished without providing for the training of broadly cultured men and women to teach its own teachers, and to teach the teachers of the public schools.

But I have already said that human education is not simply a matter of schools; it is much more a matter of family and group life—the training of one's home, of one's daily companions, of one's social class. Now the black boy of the South moves in a black world—a world with its own leaders, its own thoughts, its own ideals. In this world he gets by far the larger part of his life training, and through the eyes of this dark world he peers into the veiled world beyond. Who guides and determines the education which he receives in his world? His teachers here are the group-leaders of the Negro people—the physicians and clergymen, the trained fathers and mothers, the influential and forceful men about him of all kinds; here it is, if at all, that the culture of the surrounding world trickles through and is handed on by the graduates of the higher schools. Can such culture training of group leaders be neglected? Can we afford to ignore it? Do you think that if the leaders of thought among Negroes are not trained and educated thinkers, that they will have no leaders? On the contrary a hundred half-trained demagogues will still hold the places they so largely occupy now, and hundreds of vociferous busy-bodies will multiply. You have no choice; either you must help furnish this race from within its own ranks with thoughtful men of trained leadership, or you must suffer the evil consequences of a headless misguided rabble.

I am an earnest advocate of manual training and trade teaching for black boys, and for white boys, too. I believe that next to the founding of Negro colleges the most valuable addition to Negro education since the war, has been industrial training for black boys. Nevertheless, I insist that the object of all true education is not to make men carpenters, it is to make carpenters men; there are two means of making the carpenter a man, each equally important: the first is to give the group and community in which he works, liberally trained teachers and leaders to teach him and his family what life means; the second is to give him sufficient intelligence and technical skill to make him an efficient workman; the first object demands the Negro college and college-bred men—not a quantity of such colleges, but a few of excellent quality; not too many college-bred men, but enough to leaven the lump—to inspire the masses, to raise the Talented Tenth to leadership; the second object demands a good system of common schools, well-taught, conveniently located and properly equipped.

The Sixth Atlanta Conference truly said in 1901:

"We call the attention of the Nation to the fact that less than one million of the three million Negro children of school age, are at present regularly attending school, and these attend a session which lasts only a few months.

"We are to-day deliberately rearing millions of our citizens in ignorance, and at the same time limiting the rights of citizenship by educational qualifications. This is unjust. Half the black youth of the land have no opportunities open to them for learning to read, write and cipher. In the discussion as to the proper training of Negro children after they leave the public schools, we have forgotten that they are not yet decently provided with public schools.

"Propositions are beginning to be made in the South to reduce the already meagre school facilities of Negroes. We congratulate the South on resisting, as much as it has, this pressure, and on the many millions it has spent on Negro education. But it is only fair to point out that Negro taxes and the Negroes' share of the income from indirect taxes and endowments have fully repaid this expenditure, so that the Negro public school system has not in all probability cost the white taxpayers a single cent since the war.

"This is not fair. Negro schools should be a public burden, since they are a public benefit. The Negro has a right to demand good common school training at the hands of the States and the Nation since by their fault he is not in position to pay for this himself."

What is the chief need for the building up of the Negro public school in the South? The Negro race in the South needs teachers to-day above all else. This is the concurrent testimony of all who know the situation. For the supply of this great demand two things are needed—institutions of higher education and money for schoolhouses and salaries. It is usually assumed that a hundred or more institutions for Negro training are to-day turning out so many teachers and college-bred men that the race is threatened with an over-supply. This is sheer nonsense. There are to-day less than 3,000 living Negro college graduates in the United States, and less than 1,000 Negroes in college.

Moreover, in the 164 schools for Negroes, 95 per cent of their students are doing elementary and secondary work, work which should be done in the public schools. Over half the remaining 2,157 students are taking high school studies. The mass of so-called "normal" schools for the Negro, are simply doing elementary common-school work, or, at most, high school work, with a little instruction in methods. The Negro colleges and the post-graduate courses at other institutions are the only agencies for the broader and more careful training of teachers. The work of these institutions is hampered for lack of funds. It is getting increasingly difficult to get funds for training teachers in the best modern methods, and yet all over the South, from State Superintendents, county officials, city boards and school principals comes the wail, "We need TEACHERS!" and teachers must be trained. As the fairest minded of all white Southerners, Atticus G. Haygood, once said: "The defects of colored teachers are so great as to create an urgent necessity for training better ones. Their excellencies and their successes are sufficient to justify the best hopes of success in the effort, and to vindicate the judgment of those who make large investments of money and service, to give to colored students opportunity for thoroughly preparing themselves for the work of teaching children of their people."

The truth of this has been strikingly shown in the marked improvement of white teachers in the South. Twenty years ago the rank and file of white public school teachers were not as good as the Negro teachers. But they, by scholarships and good salaries, have been encouraged to thorough normal and collegiate preparation, while the Negro teachers have been discouraged by starvation wages and the idea that any training will do for a black teacher. If carpenters are needed it is well and good to train men as carpenters. But to train men as carpenters, and then set them to teaching is wasteful and criminal; and to train men as teachers and then refuse them living wages, unless they become carpenters, is rank nonsense.

The United States Commissioner of Education says in his report for 1900: "For comparison between the white and colored enrollment in secondary and higher education, I have added together the enrollment in high schools and secondary schools, with the attendance on colleges and universities, not being sure of the actual grade of work done in the colleges and universities. The work done in the secondary schools is reported in such detail in this office, that there can be no doubt of its grade."

He then makes the following comparisons of persons in every million enrolled in secondary and higher education:

	WHOLE COUNTRY.	NEGROES.
1880	4,362	1,289
1900	10,743	2,061

And he concludes: "While the number in colored high schools and colleges had increased somewhat faster than the population, it had not kept pace with the average of the whole country, for it had fallen from 30 per cent to 24 per cent of the average quota. Of all colored pupils, one (1) in one hundred was engaged in secondary and higher work, and that ratio has continued substantially for the past twenty years. If the ratio of colored population in secondary and higher education is to be equal to the average for the whole country, it must be increased to five times its present average." And if this be true of the secondary and higher education, it is safe to say that the Negro has not one-tenth his quota in college studies. How baseless, therefore, is the charge of too much training! We need Negro teachers for the Negro common schools, and we need first-class normal schools and colleges to train them. This is the work of higher Negro education and it must be done.

Further than this, after being provided with group leaders of civilization, and a foundation of intelligence in the public schools, the carpenter, in order to be a man, needs technical skill. This calls for trade schools. Now trade schools are not nearly such simple things as people once thought. The original idea was that the "Industrial" school was to furnish education, practically free, to those willing to work for it; it was to "do" things—i.e.: become a center of productive industry, it was to be partially, if not wholly, self-supporting, and it was to teach trades. Admirable as were some of the ideas underlying this scheme, the whole thing simply would not work in practice; it was found that if you were to use time and material to teach trades thoroughly, you could not at the same time keep the industries on a commercial basis and make them pay. Many schools started out to do this on a large scale and went into virtual bankruptcy. Moreover, it was found also that it was possible to teach a boy a trade mechanically, without giving him the full educative benefit of the process, and, vice versa, that there was a distinctive educative value in teaching a boy to use his hands and eyes in carrying out certain physical processes, even though he did not actually learn a trade. It has happened, therefore, in the last decade, that a noticeable change has come over the industrial schools. In the first place the idea of commercially remunerative industry in a school is being pushed rapidly to the background. There are still schools with shops and farms that bring an income, and schools that use student labor partially for the erection of their buildings and the furnishing of equipment. It is coming to be seen, however, in the education of the Negro, as clearly as it has been seen in the education of the youths the world over, that it is the *boy* and not the material product, that is the true object of education. Consequently the object of the industrial school came to be the thorough training of boys regardless of the cost of the training, so long as it was thoroughly well done.

Even at this point, however, the difficulties were not surmounted. In the first place modern industry has taken great strides since the war, and the teaching of trades is no longer a simple matter. Machinery and long processes of work have greatly changed the work of the carpenter, the ironworker and the shoemaker. A really efficient workman must be to-day an intelligent man who has had good technical training in addition to thorough common-school, and perhaps even higher training. To meet this situation the industrial schools began a further development; they established distinct Trade Schools for the thorough training of better class artisans, and at the same time they sought to preserve for the purposes of general education, such of the simpler processes of elementary trade learning as were best suited therefore. In this differentiation of the Trade School and manual training, the best of the industrial schools simply followed the plain trend of the present educational epoch. A prominent educator tells us that, in Sweden, "In the beginning the economic conception was generally adopted, and everywhere manual training was looked upon as a means of preparing the children of the common people to earn their living. But gradually it came to be recognized that manual training has a more elevated purpose, and one, indeed, more useful in the deeper meaning of the term. It came to be considered as an educative process for the complete moral, physical and intellectual development of the child."

Thus, again, in the manning of trade schools and manual training schools we are thrown back upon the higher training as its source and chief support. There was a time when any aged and worn-out carpenter could teach in a trade school. But not so to-day. Indeed the demand for college-bred men by a school like Tuskegee, ought to make Mr. Booker T. Washington the firmest friend of higher training. Here he has as helpers the son of a Negro senator, trained in Greek and the humanities, and graduated at Harvard; the son of a Negro congressman and lawyer, trained in Latin and mathematics, and graduated at Oberlin; he has as his wife, a woman who read Virgil and Homer in the same class room with me; he has as college chaplain, a classical graduate of Atlanta University; as teacher of science, a graduate of Fisk; as teacher of history, a graduate of Smith,—indeed some thirty of his chief teachers are college graduates, and instead of studying French grammars in the midst of weeds, or buying pianos for dirty cabins, they are at Mr. Washington's right hand helping him in a noble work. And yet one of the effects of Mr. Washington's propaganda has been to throw doubt upon the expediency of such training for Negroes, as these persons have had.

Men of America, the problem is plain before you. Here is a race transplanted through the criminal foolishness of your fathers. Whether you like it or not the millions are here, and here they will remain. If you do not lift them up, they will pull you down.

Education and work are the levers to uplift a people. Work alone will not do it unless inspired by the right ideals and guided by intelligence. Education must not simply teach work—it must teach Life. The Talented Tenth of the Negro race must be made leaders of thought and missionaries of culture among their people. No others can do this work and Negro colleges must train men for it. The Negro race, like all other races, is going to be saved by its exceptional men.

THE SOULS OF
WHITE FOLK

High in the tower, where I sit above the loud complaining of the human sea, I know many souls that toss and whirl and pass, but none there are that intrigue me more than the Souls of White Folk.

Of them I am singularly clairvoyant. I see in and through them. I view them from unusual points of vantage. Not as a foreigner do I come, for I am native, not foreign, bone of their thought and flesh of their language. Mine is not the knowledge of the traveller or the colonial composite of dear memories, words and wonder. Nor yet is my knowledge that which servants have of masters, or mass of class, or capitalist of artisan. Rather I see these souls undressed and from the back and side. I see the working of their entrails. I know their thoughts and they know that I know. This knowledge makes them now embarrassed, now furious. They deny my right to live and be and call me misbirth! My word is to them mere bitterness and my soul, pessimism. And yet as they preach and strut and shout and threaten, crouching as they clutch at rags of facts and fancies to hide their nakedness, they go twisting, flying by my tired eyes and I see them ever stripped,—ugly, human.

The discovery of personal whiteness among the world's peoples is a very modern thing,—a nineteenth and twentieth century matter, indeed. The ancient world would have laughed at such a distinction. The Middle Age regarded skin color with mild curiosity; and even up into the eighteenth century we were hammering our national manikins into one, great, Universal Man, with fine frenzy which ignored color and race even more than birth. Today we have changed all that, and the world in a sudden, emotional conversion has discovered that it is white and by that token, wonderful!

This assumption that of all the hues of God whiteness alone is inherently and obviously better than brownness or tan leads to curious acts; even the sweeter souls of the dominant world as they discourse with me on weather, weal, and woe are continually playing above their actual words an obligato of tune and tone, saying:

"My poor, un-white thing! Weep not nor rage. I know, too well, that the curse of God lies heavy on you. Why? That is not for me to say, but be brave! Do your work in your lowly sphere, praying the good Lord that into heaven above, where all is love, you may, one day, be born—white!"

I do not laugh. I am quite straight-faced as I ask soberly:

"But what on earth is whiteness that one should so desire it?" Then always, somehow, some way, silently but clearly, I am given to understand that whiteness is the ownership of the earth forever and ever, Amen!

Now what is the effect on a man or a nation when it comes passionately to believe such an extraordinary dictum as this? That nations are coming to believe it is manifest daily. Wave on wave, each with increasing virulence, is dashing this new religion of whiteness on the shores of our time. Its first effects are funny: the strut of the Southerner, the arrogance of the Englishman amuck, the whoop of the hoodlum who vicariously leads your mob. Next it appears dampening generous enthusiasm in what we once counted glorious; to free the slave is discovered to be tolerable only in so far as it freed his master! Do we sense somnolent writhings in black Africa or angry groans in India or triumphant banzais in Japan? "To your tents, O Israel!" These nations are not white!

After the more comic manifestations and the chilling of generous enthusiasm come subtler, darker deeds. Everything considered, the title to the universe claimed by White Folk is faulty. It ought, at least, to look plausible. How easy, then, by emphasis and omission to make children believe that every great soul the world ever saw was a white man's soul; that every great thought

the world ever knew was a white man's thought; that every great
deed the world ever did was a white man's deed; that every great
dream the world ever sang was a white man's dream. In fine,
that if from the world were dropped everything that could not
fairly be attributed to White Folk, the world would, if anything,
be even greater, truer, better than now. And if all this be a lie,
is it not a lie in a great cause?

Here it is that the comedy verges to tragedy. The first minor
note is struck, all unconsciously, by those worthy souls in whom
consciousness of high descent brings burning desire to spread
the gift abroad,—the obligation of nobility to the ignoble. Such
sense of duty assumes two things: a real possession of the heritage and its frank appreciation by the humble-born. So long,
then, as humble black folk, voluble with thanks, receive barrels
of old clothes from lordly and generous whites, there is much
mental peace and moral satisfaction. But when the black man
begins to dispute the white man's title to certain alleged bequests
of the Fathers in wage and position, authority and training; and
when his attitude toward charity is sullen anger rather than
humble jollity; when he insists on his human right to swagger
and swear and waste,—then the spell is suddenly broken and
the philanthropist is ready to believe that Negroes are impudent,
that the South is right, and that Japan wants to fight America.

After this the descent to Hell is easy. On the pale, white faces
which the great billows whirl upward to my tower I see again
and again, often and still more often, a writing of human hatred, a deep and passionate hatred, vast by the very vagueness
of its expressions. Down through the green waters, on the bottom of the world, where men move to and fro, I have seen a
man—an educated gentleman—grow livid with anger because
a little, silent, black woman was sitting by herself in a Pullman
car. He was a white man. I have seen a great, grown man curse
a little child, who had wandered into the wrong waiting-room,
searching for its mother: "Here, you damned black—" He was
white. In Central Park I have seen the upper lip of a quiet, peaceful man curl back in a tigerish snarl of rage because black folk
rode by in a motor car. He was a white man. We have seen, you

and I, city after city drunk and furious with ungovernable lust of blood; mad with murder, destroying, killing, and cursing; torturing human victims because somebody accused of crime happened to be of the same color as the mob's innocent victims and because that color was not white! We have seen,—Merciful God! in these wild days and in the name of Civilization, Justice, and Motherhood,—what have we not seen, right here in America, of orgy, cruelty, barbarism, and murder done to men and women of Negro descent.

Up through the foam of green and weltering waters wells this great mass of hatred, in wilder, fiercer violence, until I look down and know that today to the millions of my people no misfortune could happen,—of death and pestilence, failure and defeat—that would not make the hearts of millions of their fellows beat with fierce, vindictive joy! Do you doubt it? Ask your own soul what it would say if the next census were to report that half of black America was dead and the other half dying.

Unfortunate? Unfortunate. But where is the misfortune? Mine? Am I, in my blackness, the sole sufferer? I suffer. And yet, somehow, above the suffering, above the shackled anger that beats the bars, above the hurt that crazes there surges in me a vast pity,—pity for a people imprisoned and enthralled, hampered and made miserable for such a cause, for such a phantasy!

Conceive this nation, of all human peoples, engaged in a crusade to make the "World Safe for Democracy"! Can you imagine the United States protesting against Turkish atrocities in Armenia, while the Turks are silent about mobs in Chicago and St. Louis; what is Louvain compared with Memphis, Waco, Washington, Dyersburg, and Estill Springs? In short, what is the black man but America's Belgium, and how could America condemn in Germany that which she commits, just as brutally, within her own borders?

A true and worthy ideal frees and uplifts a people; a false ideal imprisons and lowers. Say to men, earnestly and repeatedly: "Honesty is best, knowledge is power; do unto others as you would be done by." Say this and act it and the nation must move toward it, if not to it. But say to a people: "The one virtue is to be white," and the people rush to the inevitable conclusion, "Kill the 'nigger'!"

Is not this the record of present America? Is not this its headlong progress? Are we not coming more and more, day by day, to making the statement "I am white," the one fundamental tenet of our practical morality? Only when this basic, iron rule is involved is our defense of right nation-wide and prompt. Murder may swagger, theft may rule and prostitution may flourish and the nation gives but spasmodic, intermittent and lukewarm attention. But let the murderer be black or the thief brown or the violator of womanhood have a drop of Negro blood, and the righteousness of the indignation sweeps the world. Nor would this fact make the indignation less justifiable did not we all know that it was blackness that was condemned and not crime.

In the awful cataclysm of World War, where from beating, slandering, and murdering us the white world turned temporarily aside to kill each other, we of the Darker Peoples looked on in mild amaze.

Among some of us, I doubt not, this sudden descent of Europe into hell brought unbounded surprise; to others, over wide area, it brought the *Schaden Freude* of the bitterly hurt; but most of us, I judge, looked on silently and sorrowfully, in sober thought, seeing sadly the prophecy of our own souls.

Here is a civilization that has boasted much. Neither Roman nor Arab, Greek nor Egyptian, Persian nor Mongol ever took himself and his own perfectness with such disconcerting seriousness as the modern white man. We whose shame, humiliation, and deep insult his aggrandizement so often involved were never deceived. We looked at him clearly, with world-old eyes, and saw simply a human thing, weak and pitiable and cruel, even as we are and were.

These super-men and world-mastering demi-gods listened, however, to no low tongues of ours, even when we pointed silently to their feet of clay. Perhaps we, as folk of simpler soul and more primitive type, have been most struck in the welter of recent years by the utter failure of white religion. We have curled our lips in something like contempt as we have witnessed glib apology and weary explanation. Nothing of the sort deceived us. A nation's religion is its life, and as such white Christianity is a miserable failure.

Nor would we be unfair in this criticism: We know that we, too, have failed, as you have, and have rejected many a Buddha, even as you have denied Christ; but we acknowledge our human frailty, while you, claiming super-humanity, scoff endlessly at our shortcomings.

The number of white individuals who are practising with even reasonable approximation the democracy and unselfishness of Jesus Christ is so small and unimportant as to be fit subject for jest in Sunday supplements and in *Punch, Life, Le Rire*, and *Fliegende Blätter*. In her foreign mission work the extraordinary self-deception of white religion is epitomized: solemnly the white world sends five million dollars' worth of missionary propaganda to Africa each year and in the same twelve months adds twenty-five million dollars' worth of the vilest gin manufactured. Peace to the augurs of Rome!

We may, however, grant without argument that religious ideals have always far outrun their very human devotees. Let us, then, turn to more mundane matters of honor and fairness. The world today is trade. The world has turned shopkeeper; history is economic history; living is earning a living. Is it necessary to ask how much of high emprise and honorable conduct has been found here? Something, to be sure. The establishment of world credit systems is built on splendid and realizable faith in fellowmen. But it is, after all, so low and elementary a step that sometimes it looks merely like honor among thieves, for the revelations of highway robbery and low cheating in the business world and in all its great modern centers have raised in the hearts of all true men in our day an exceeding great cry for revolution in our basic methods and conceptions of industry and commerce.

We do not, for a moment, forget the robbery of other times and races when trade was a most uncertain gamble; but was there not a certain honesty and frankness in the evil that argued a saner morality? There are more merchants today, surer deliveries, and wider well-being, but are there not, also, bigger thieves, deeper injustice, and more calloused selfishness in well-being? Be that as it may,—certainly the nicer sense of honor that has risen ever and again in groups of forward-thinking men has been curiously and broadly blunted. Consider our chiefest industry,—fighting. Laboriously the Middle Ages built its rules of fairness—equal armament, equal notice, equal conditions. What do we see today? Machine-guns against assegais; conquest sugared with religion; mutilation and rape masquerading as culture,—all this, with vast applause at the superiority of white over black soldiers!

War is horrible! This the dark world knows to its awful cost. But has it just become horrible, in these last days, when under essentially equal conditions, equal armament, and equal waste of wealth white men are fighting white men, with surgeons and nurses hovering near?

Think of the wars through which we have lived in the last decade: in German Africa, in British Nigeria, in French and Spanish Morocco, in China, in Persia, in the Balkans, in Tripoli, in Mexico, and in a dozen lesser places—were not these horrible, too? Mind you, there were for most of these wars no Red Cross funds.

Behold little Belgium and her pitiable plight, but has the world forgotten Congo? What Belgium now suffers is not half, not even a tenth, of what she has done to black Congo since Stanley's great dream of 1880. Down the dark forests of inmost Africa sailed this modern Sir Galahad, in the name of "the noble-minded men of several nations," to introduce commerce and civilization. What came of it? "Rubber and murder, slavery in its worst form," wrote Glave in 1895.

Harris declares that King Leopold's régime meant the death of twelve million natives, "but what we who were behind the scenes felt most keenly was the fact that the real catastrophe in the Congo was desolation and murder in the larger sense. The invasion of family life, the ruthless destruction of every social barrier, the shattering of every tribal law, the introduction of criminal practices which struck the chiefs of the people dumb with horror—in a word, a veritable avalanche of filth and immorality overwhelmed the Congo tribes."

Yet the fields of Belgium laughed, the cities were gay, art and science flourished; the groans that helped to nourish this civilization fell on deaf ears because the world round about was doing the same sort of thing elsewhere on its own account.

As we saw the dead dimly through rifts of battlesmoke and heard faintly the cursings and accusations of blood brothers, we darker men said: This is not Europe gone mad; this is not aberration nor insanity; this *is* Europe; this seeming Terrible is the real soul of white culture—back of all culture,—stripped and visible today. This is where the world has arrived,—these dark and awful depths and not the shining and ineffable heights of which it boasted. Here is whither the might and energy of modern humanity has really gone.

But may not the world cry back at us and ask: "What better thing have you to show? What have you done or would do better than this if you had today the world rule? Paint with all riot of hateful colors the thin skin of European culture,—is it not better than any culture that arose in Africa or Asia?"

It is. Of this there is no doubt and never has been; but why is it better? Is it better because Europeans are better, nobler, greater, and more gifted than other folk? It is not. Europe has never produced and never will in our day bring forth a single human soul who cannot be matched and over-matched in every line of human endeavor by Asia and Africa. Run the gamut, if you will, and let us have the Europeans who in sober truth over-match Nefertari, Mohammed, Rameses and Askia, Confucius, Buddha, and Jesus Christ. If we could scan the calendar of thousands of lesser men, in like comparison, the result would be the same; but we cannot do this because of the deliberately educated ignorance of white schools by which they remember Napoleon and forget Sonni Ali.

The greatness of Europe has lain in the width of the stage on which she has played her part, the strength of the foundations on which she has builded, and a natural, human ability no whit greater (if as great) than that of other days and races. In other words, the deeper reasons for the triumph of European civilization lie quite outside and beyond Europe,—back in the universal struggles of all mankind.

Why, then, is Europe great? Because of the foundations which the mighty past have furnished her to build upon: the iron trade of ancient, black Africa, the religion and empire-building of yellow Asia, the art and science of the "dago" Mediterranean shore, east, south, and west, as well as north. And where she has builded securely upon this great past and learned from it she has gone forward to greater and more splendid human triumph; but where she has ignored this past and forgotten and sneered at it, she has shown the cloven hoof of poor, crucified humanity,—she has played, like other empires gone, the world fool!

If, then, European triumphs in culture have been greater, so, too, may her failures have been greater. How great a failure and a failure in what does the World War betoken? Was it national jealousy of the sort of the seventeenth century? But Europe has done more to break down national barriers than any preceding culture. Was it fear of the balance of power in Europe? Hardly, save in the half-Asiatic problems of the Balkans. What, then, does Hauptmann mean when he says: "Our jealous enemies forged an iron ring about our breasts and we knew our breasts had to expand,—that we had to split asunder this ring or else we had to cease breathing. But Germany will not cease to breathe and so it came to pass that the iron ring was forced apart."

Whither is this expansion? What is that breath of life, thought to be so indispensable to a great European nation? Manifestly it is expansion overseas; it is colonial aggrandizement which explains, and alone adequately explains, the World War. How many of us today fully realize the current theory of colonial expansion, of the relation of Europe which is white, to the world which is black and brown and yellow? Bluntly put, that theory is this: It is the duty of white Europe to divide up the darker world and administer it for Europe's good.

This Europe has largely done. The European world is using black and brown men for all the uses which men know. Slowly but surely white culture is evolving the theory that "darkies" are born beasts of burden for white folk. It were silly to think otherwise, cries the cultured world, with stronger and shriller accord. The supporting arguments grow and twist themselves in the mouths of merchant, scientist, soldier, traveller, writer, and missionary: Darker peoples are dark in mind as well as in body; of dark, uncertain, and imperfect descent; of frailer, cheaper stuff; they are cowards in the face of mausers and maxims; they have no feelings, aspirations, and loves; they are fools, illogical idiots,—"half-devil and half-child."

Such as they are civilization must, naturally, raise them, but soberly and in limited ways. They are not simply dark white men. They are not "men" in the sense that Europeans are men. To the very limited extent of their shallow capacities lift them to be useful to whites, to raise cotton, gather rubber, fetch ivory, dig diamonds,—and let them be paid what men think they are worth—white men who know them to be well-nigh worthless.

Such degrading of men by men is as old as mankind and the invention of no one race or people. Ever have men striven to conceive of their victims as different from the victors, endlessly different, in soul and blood, strength and cunning, race and lineage. It has been left, however, to Europe and to modern days to discover the eternal world-wide mark of meanness,—color!

Such is the silent revolution that has gripped modern European culture in the later nineteenth and twentieth centuries. Its zenith came in Boxer times: White supremacy was all but world-wide, Africa was dead, India conquered, Japan isolated, and China prostrate, while white America whetted her sword for mongrel Mexico and mulatto South America, lynching her own Negroes the while. Temporary halt in this program was made by little Japan and the white world immediately sensed the peril of such "yellow" presumption! What sort of a world would this be if yellow men must be treated "white"? Immediately the eventual overthrow of Japan became a subject of deep thought and intrigue, from St. Petersburg to San Francisco, from the Key of Heaven to the Little Brother of the Poor.

The using of men for the benefit of masters is no new invention of modern Europe. It is quite as old as the world. But Europe proposed to apply it on a scale and with an elaborateness of detail of which no former world ever dreamed. The imperial width of the thing,—the heaven-defying audacity—makes its modern newness.

The scheme of Europe was no sudden invention, but a way out of long-pressing difficulties. It is plain to modern white civilization that the subjection of the white working classes cannot much longer be maintained. Education, political power, and increased knowledge of the technique and meaning of the industrial process are destined to make a more and more equitable distribution of wealth in the near future. The day of the very rich is drawing to a close, so far as individual white nations are concerned. But there is a loophole. There is a chance for exploitation on an immense scale for inordinate profit, not simply to the very rich, but to the middle class and to the laborers. This chance lies in the exploitation of darker peoples. It is here that the golden hand beckons. Here are no labor unions or votes or questioning onlookers or inconvenient consciences. These men may be used down to the very bone, and shot and maimed in "punitive" expeditions when they revolt. In these dark lands "industrial development" may repeat in exaggerated form every horror of the industrial history of Europe, from slavery and rape to disease and maiming, with only one test of success,—dividends!

This theory of human culture and its aims has worked itself through warp and woof of our daily thought with a thoroughness that few realize. Everything great, good, efficient, fair, and honorable is "white"; everything mean, bad, blundering, cheating, and dishonorable is "yellow"; a bad taste is "brown"; and the devil is "black." The changes of this theme are continually rung in picture and story, in newspaper heading and moving-picture, in sermon and school-book, until, of course, the King can do no wrong,—a White Man is always right and a Black Man has no rights which a white man is bound to respect.

There must come the necessary despisings and hatreds of these savage half-men, this unclean *canaille* of the world—these dogs of men. All through the world this gospel is preaching. It has its literature, it has its secret propaganda and above all—it pays!

There's the rub,—it pays. Rubber, ivory, and palm-oil; tea, coffee, and cocoa; bananas, oranges, and other fruit; cotton, gold, and copper—they, and a hundred other things which dark and sweating bodies hand up to the white world from pits of slime, pay and pay well, but of all that the world gets the black world gets only the pittance that the white world throws it disdainfully.

Small wonder, then, that in the practical world of things-that-be there is jealousy and strife for the possession of the labor of dark millions, for the right to bleed and exploit the colonies of the world where this golden stream may be had, not always for the asking, but surely for the whipping and shooting. It was this competition for the labor of yellow, brown, and black folks that was the cause of the World War. Other causes have been glibly given and other contributing causes there doubtless were, but they were subsidiary and subordinate to this vast quest of the dark world's wealth and toil.

Colonies, we call them, these places where "niggers" are cheap and the earth is rich; they are those outlands where like a swarm of hungry locusts white masters may settle to be served as kings, wield the lash of slave-drivers, rape girls and wives, grow as rich as Croesus and send homeward a golden stream. They belt the earth, these places, but they cluster in the tropics, with its darkened peoples: in Hong Kong and Anam, in Borneo and Rhodesia, in Sierra Leone and Nigeria, in Panama and Havana—these are the El Dorados toward which the world powers stretch itching palms.

Germany, at last one and united and secure on land, looked across the seas and seeing England with sources of wealth insuring a luxury and power which Germany could not hope to rival by the slower processes of exploiting her own peasants and workingmen, especially with these workers half in revolt, immediately built her navy and entered into a desperate competition for possession of colonies of darker peoples. To South America, to China, to Africa, to Asia Minor, she turned like a hound quivering on the leash, impatient, suspicious, irritable, with blood-shot eyes and dripping fangs, ready for the awful word. England and France crouched watchfully over their bones, growling and wary, but gnawing industriously, while the blood of the dark world whetted their greedy appetites. In the background, shut out from the highway to the seven seas, sat Russia and Austria, snarling and snapping at each other and at the last Mediterranean gate to the El Dorado, where the Sick Man enjoyed bad health, and where millions of serfs in the Balkans, Russia, and Asia offered a feast to greed well-nigh as great as Africa.

The fateful day came. It had to come. The cause of war is preparation for war; and of all that Europe has done in a century there is nothing that has equaled in energy, thought, and time her preparation for wholesale murder. The only adequate cause of this preparation was conquest and conquest, not in Europe, but primarily among the darker peoples of Asia and Africa; conquest, not for assimilation and uplift, but for commerce and degradation. For this, and this mainly, did Europe gird herself at frightful cost for war.

The red day dawned when the tinder was lighted in the Balkans and Austro-Hungary seized a bit which brought her a step nearer to the world's highway; she seized one bit and poised herself for another. Then came that curious chorus of challenges, those leaping suspicions, raking all causes for distrust and rivalry and hatred, but saying little of the real and greatest cause.

Each nation felt its deep interests involved. But how? Not, surely, in the death of Ferdinand the Warlike; not, surely, in the old, half-forgotten *revanche* for Alsace-Lorraine; not even in the neutrality of Belgium. No! But in the possession of land overseas, in the right to colonies, the chance to levy endless tribute on the darker world,—on coolies in China, on starving peasants in India, on black savages in Africa, on dying South Sea Islanders, on Indians of the Amazon—all this and nothing more.

Even the broken reed on which we had rested high hopes of eternal peace,—the guild of the laborers—the front of that very important movement for human justice on which we had builded most, even this flew like a straw before the breath of king and kaiser. Indeed, the flying had been foreshadowed when in

Germany and America "international" Socialists had all but read
yellow and black men out of the kingdom of industrial justice.
Subtly had they been bribed, but effectively: Were they not lordly
whites and should they not share in the spoils of rape? High wages
in the United States and England might be the skilfully manipu-
lated result of slavery in Africa and of peonage in Asia.

With the dog-in-the-manger theory of trade, with the determination to reap inordinate profits and to exploit the weakest
to the utmost there came a new imperialism,—the rage for one's
own nation to own the earth or, at least, a large enough portion
of it to insure as big profits as the next nation. Where sections
could not be owned by one dominant nation there came a policy of "open door," but the "door" was open to "white people
only." As to the darkest and weakest of peoples there was but
one unanimity in Europe,—that which Hen Demberg of the
German Colonial Office called the agreement with England to
maintain white "prestige" in Africa,—the doctrine of the divine
right of white people to steal.

Thus the world market most wildly and desperately sought
today is the market where labor is cheapest and most helpless
and profit is most abundant. This labor is kept cheap and helpless because the white world despises "darkies." If one has the
temerity to suggest that these workingmen may walk the way
of white workingmen and climb by votes and self-assertion and
education to the rank of men, he is howled out of court. They
cannot do it and if they could, they shall not, for they are the
enemies of the white race and the whites shall rule forever and
forever and everywhere. Thus the hatred and despising of
human beings from whom Europe wishes to extort her luxuries
has led to such jealousy and bickering between European nations that they have fallen afoul of each other and have fought
like crazed beasts. Such is the fruit of human hatred.

But what of the darker world that watches? Most men belong
to this world. With Negro and Negroid, East Indian, Chinese,
and Japanese they form two-thirds of the population of the
world. A belief in humanity is a belief in colored men. If the
uplift of mankind must be done by men, then the destinies of
this world will rest ultimately in the hands of darker nations.

What, then, is this dark world thinking? It is thinking that as wild and awful as this shameful war was, *it is nothing to compare with that fight for freedom which black and brown and yellow men must and will make unless their oppression and humiliation and insult at the hands of the White World cease. The Dark World is going to submit to its present treatment just as long as it must and not one moment longer.*

Let me say this again and emphasize it and leave no room for mistaken meaning: the World War was primarily the jealous and avaricious struggle for the largest share in exploiting darker races. As such it is and must be but the prelude to the armed and indignant protest of these despised and raped peoples. Today Japan is hammering on the door of justice, China is raising her half-manacled hands to knock next, India is writhing for the freedom to knock, Egypt is sullenly muttering, the Negroes of South and West Africa, of the West Indies, and of the United States are just awakening to their shameful slavery. Is, then, this war the end of wars? Can it be the end, so long as sits enthroned, even in the souls of those who cry peace, the despising and robbing of darker peoples? If Europe hugs this delusion, then this is not the end of world war,—it is but the beginning!

We see Europe's greatest sin precisely where we found Africa's and Asia's,—in human hatred, the despising of men; with this difference, however: Europe has the awful lesson of the past before her, has the splendid results of widened areas of tolerance, sympathy, and love among men, and she faces a greater, an infinitely greater, world of men than any preceding civilization ever faced.

It is curious to see America, the United States, looking on herself, first, as a sort of natural peacemaker, then as a moral protagonist in this terrible time. No nation is less fitted for this role. For two or more centuries America has marched proudly in the van of human hatred,—making bonfires of human flesh and laughing at them hideously, and making the insulting of millions more than a matter of dislike,—rather a great religion, a world war-cry: up white, down black; to your tents, O white folk, and world war with black and parti-colored mongrel beasts!

Instead of standing as a great example of the success of democracy and the possibility of human brotherhood America has taken her place as an awful example of its pitfalls and failures, so far as black and brown and yellow peoples are concerned. And this, too, in spite of the fact that there has been no actual failure; the Indian is not dying out, the Japanese and Chinese have not menaced the land, and the experiment of Negro suffrage has resulted in the uplift of twelve million people at a rate probably unparalleled in history. But what of this? America, Land of Democracy, wanted to believe in the failure of democracy so far as darker peoples were concerned. Absolutely without excuse she established a caste system, rushed into preparation for war, and conquered tropical colonies. She stands today shoulder to shoulder with Europe in Europe's worst sin against civilization. She aspires to sit among the great nations who arbitrate the fate of "lesser breeds without the law" and she is at times heartily ashamed even of the large number of "new" white people whom her democracy has admitted to place and power. Against this surging forward of Irish and German, of Russian Jew, Slav and "dago" her social bars have not availed, but against Negroes she can and does take her unflinching and immovable stand, backed by this new public policy of Europe. She trains her immigrants to this despising of "niggers" from the day of their landing, and they carry and send the news back to the submerged classes in the fatherlands.

All this I see and hear up in my tower, above the thunder of the seven seas. From my narrowed windows I stare into the night that looms beneath the cloud-swept stars. Eastward and westward storms are breaking,—great, ugly whirlwinds of hatred and blood and cruelty. I will not believe them inevitable. I will not believe that all that was must be, that all the shameful drama of the past must be done again today before the sunlight sweeps the silver seas.

If I cry amid this roar of elemental forces, must my cry be in vain, because it is but a cry,—a small and human cry amid Promethean gloom?

Back beyond the world and swept by these wild, white faces

of the awful dead, why will this Soul of White Folk,—this modern Prometheus,—hang bound by his own binding, tethered by a fable of the past? I hear his mighty cry reverberating through the world, "I am white!" Well and good, O Prometheus, divine thief! Is not the world wide enough for two colors, for many little shinings of the sun? Why, then, devour your own vitals if I answer even as proudly, "I am black!"

Notes

THE SOULS OF BLACK FOLK

I. Of Our Spiritual Strivings

5 "O, water . . . crying to me": Arthur Symons's poem "The Crying of Water" (September 18, 1900).

5 [prefatory spiritual]: "Nobody Knows the Trouble I've Seen." Du Bois unravels the mysteries of the Sorrow Songs (except for Chapters III, V, VIII, and IX, the identities of which remain enigmatic) in Chapter XIV. Chapter II's prefatory spiritual is "My Lord, What a Mourning!"; Chapter IV, "My Way's Cloudy"; Chapter VI, "March On"; Chapter VII, "Bright Sparkles"; Chapter X, "Steal Away Home"; Chapter XI, "I Hope My Mother Will Be There"; Chapter XII, "Swing Low, Sweet Chariot"; Chapter XIII, "You May Bury Me in the East"; and Chapter XIV, "Wrestlin' Jacob."

6 Mechanicsville: The battle of Mechanicsville (in Virginia), which took place on June 26, 1862; otherwise known as the battle of Beaver Dam Creek and part of the Seven Days' Battles. Lee's Confederate troops routed McClellan's Union troops, but ultimately the Confederacy sustained more losses.

6 Housatonic: New England river, flowing from the Berkshires (Massachusetts) to Long Island Sound.

9 "Shout . . . your liberty!": One of the many freedom spirituals.

9 "Take any shape . . . tremble!": From *Macbeth*, III, iv, 102–3.

9 Fifteenth Amendment: Ratified March 30, 1870; granted black suffrage (in theory) and enabled Congress to enforce this amendment.

11 **Toussaint:** Toussaint L'Ouverture, leader of the black forces in Haiti after the uprising against the white French government in August 1791. Napoleon, viewing Toussaint as an obstacle to French power in the New World, devised a scheme to trick him into going willingly to France in 1800, but even so, the French were unable to subdue the island.

II. Of the Dawn of Freedom

14 **"Careless seems . . . above His own":** From James Russell Lowell's "The Present Crisis," dated December 1844, eighth stanza.

14 **[spiritual]:** "My Lord, What a Mourning!"

15 **Freedmen's Bureau:** An organization created by Congress in March 1865 to ensure that recently emancipated blacks in the South would be able to practice their civil rights and to help them in their transition from slaves to freemen (in the realm of shelter, food, education, work, and medicine). The bureau stayed in existence until 1872. Primarily it was a failure because it lacked federal commitment, sufficient funds, and dedicated personnel. Compare note for page 37 on the Revolution of 1876 and the end of Reconstruction.

15 **Ben Butler:** Union General Benjamin F. Butler (1818–1893) was known for his controversial military policy, which declared that fugitive slaves were contraband of war and thus could not be returned to the masters, but rather were made to work for federal forces. In 1862, he gathered a whole regiment of free blacks in Louisiana. He also established one of three military savings banks for free blacks and black soldiers of the Civil War in Norfolk, Virginia.

15 **Fremont:** John Charles (1813–1880), Union major general, explorer, and politician. He was known especially for his controversial emancipation proclamation (August 30, 1861), which stated basically (before Lincoln's proclamation did) that slaves were "freedmen."

15 **Halleck:** Henry W. (1815–1872), Union major general who succeeded Frémont in command of St. Louis, later became Union chief of staff (March 1864). General Halleck adopted the policy of returning runaway slaves to their masters in the West.

16   **Pierce:** Edward Lillie (1829–1897), a Northern abolitionist from Boston, who helped freedmen adjust to their new condition and who wrote the *Memoir and Letters of Charles Sumner.*

16   **Fortress Monroe:** Early in the Civil War, blacks sought refuge within Union lines, near Fort Monroe, Virginia. The earliest school for freedmen was established there in September 1861.

16   **Sherman:** William Tecumseh (1820–1891), Union Civil War general who led the march from Atlanta to the sea (1864) (see note for page 16). Thousands of slaves joined Sherman's ranks on his march.

16   **Hilton Head:** One of the Sea Islands, south of Port Royal Sound, South Carolina. Fort Walker, a Confederate fortification, was situated on the island, which was captured by Captain Samuel F. Du Pont on November 7, 1861.

16   **Port Royal experiment:** Port Royal, South Carolina, came under control of the Union troops in 1861. James M. McKim organized a committee in Philadelphia to allow former slaves the supervision of the cotton plantations. The experiment in free labor fared well, but at the end of the Civil War, the land was returned to the former slave-owners.

17   *Amistad:* Spanish slave ship taken over (August 1839) in a mutiny off the Cuban coast by Cinque and fifty-two other slaves. Spain demanded the return of the slaves, but the Supreme Court, convinced by the argument of John Quincy Adams, ruled that they should be returned to Africa.

17–18 **General Dix . . . Colonel Eaton . . . General Saxton:** Sympathetic Union army officers who presided over freedmen's affairs in the occupied South. Dix issued a proclamation protecting slave property and helped freedmen with their new living arrangements. Eaton was appointed by Grant as superintendent to contrabands for the Mississippi Valley in November 1862. Saxton, an abolitionist, had jurisdiction over the South Carolina Sea Islands and supervised the settlement of 40,000 freedmen on land, thereby following Sherman's order.

18   **Sherman's raid:** General Sherman had moved into Atlanta by September 1864 and had civilians evacuated, after which, in his famous "march to the sea," he cleared a zone from Atlanta to the Atlantic.

18 **"Field-order Number Fifteen":** This was an order issued January 16, 1865, by General Sherman, which proclaimed that the Sea Islands and the plantation areas within thirty miles of rivers, from Charlestown down to Jacksonville, were to be settled by freedmen.

19 **General Howard:** Union major general Oliver Otis Howard (1830–1909) was appointed commissioner of the Freedmen's Bureau on May 12, 1865, and remained commissioner until the end of the bureau in 1872. Although known for his poor administrative sense, he did devote much energy to the establishment of schools for blacks. Howard University, Washington, D.C., was named for him to recognize his work as a commissioner, and he served as its president from 1869 to 1873.

19 **Charles Sumner:** Sumner (1811–1874) was an abolitionist and a U.S. senator. His two-day oration, "The Crime against Kansas," produced such an uproar that the southern congressman Preston Brooks beat him with his cane while Sumner was at his Senate desk, so badly that the injuries plagued him for three years thereafter. An ardent supporter of enfranchisement of blacks, he joined in the impeachment process of Johnson, who had vetoed the Civil Rights Bill.

22 **quest of Saint Louis:** In 1248 Louis IX of France led the Sixth Crusade to the Holy Land. King Louis was canonized in 1297.

27 **Edmund Ware, Samuel Armstrong, and Erastus Cravath:** Edmund Asa Ware (1837–1885), educator and clergyman, was sent by the American Missionary Association to become the superintendent of the Atlanta school district. In 1867 he was appointed superintendent of education for Georgia by General Oliver Howard of the Freedmen's Bureau. Ware helped to establish Atlanta University (chartered in 1867), which opened its doors to freedmen. Ware was the first president of Atlanta University.

Samuel Chapman Armstrong (1839–1893), an educator born to missionary parents, was a Union captain and major in the Civil War and later became the commissioned colonel of the Ninth Regiment, United States black troops. He was appointed an agent of the Freedmen's Bureau and took control of a settlement of blacks in Hampton, Virginia, in 1866. In 1868 he received funding from the American Missionary Association and from individual benefactors to establish the Hampton Normal and Industrial Institute. His original aim was to found an industrial school for black teachers.

Erastus Milo Cravath (1833–1900), a clergyman and educator, became sympathetic to the abolitionist cause early in life, with his father being an active participant in the Underground Railroad. After the Civil War, Cravath devoted the rest of his life to educating the freedmen. He helped to establish and supervise many southern schools for blacks, among them Atlanta University and Fisk University (Nashville, Tennessee), which he hoped would give blacks a liberal education needed for leadership positions. He was elected president of Fisk University (1875) and helped to arrange the Jubilee Singers' tour of Europe.

28 **Fisk, Atlanta, Howard, and Hampton:** Black colleges established in the South. Fisk University was founded in 1866 in Nashville, Tennessee; Atlanta University in 1865; Howard University in 1867 in Washington, D.C.; and Hampton Institute in 1868 in Hampton, Virginia. Although Howard University was established without special admission for blacks, they quickly constituted the majority of the student population.

III. Of Mr. Booker T. Washington
and Others

34 **"From birth . . . unmanned!":** From Byron's "Childe Harold's Pilgrimage," Canto II, stanza LXXIV, line 710. "Hereditary Bondsmen! . . . the blow?" "Childe Harold's Pilgrimage," Canto II, stanza LXXVI, lines 720–21.

34 **Booker T. Washington:** Black educator, writer, and spokesman (1856–1915) who assumed the role of the acknowledged leader of the black cause after the death of Frederick Douglass in 1895.

35 **Tuskegee:** Tuskegee Institute, a black college established as a normal school in 1881 in Tuskegee, Alabama. Booker T. Washington was its founder and first principal.

35 **"Atlanta Compromise":** An address that Booker T. Washington delivered at the Cotton States Exposition in Atlanta, Georgia, on September 18, 1895, advocating economic improvement for

blacks but not political or social equality. The whole of the speech is printed in Chapter 14 of his autobiography, *Up from Slavery*.

35 **Jefferson Davis:** President of the Confederacy.

38 **Maroons:** Small guerrilla bands of runaway slaves formed during the course of the eighteenth century. These fugitive slaves in the West Indies, called Maroons, settled in inaccessible areas (in forests, near swamps, on mountaintops), and were feared by whites for their raids on nearby plantations or settlements and for their incitement of slaves to rebel against the masters. By 1730, conditions had gotten so out of hand in Jamaica under the leadership of the runaway slave Cudjo that the British were forced to send out two additional regiments to protect their territory. In the mid-1700s, fugitive slaves had found incomparable leadership in the ex-slave Macandal, an African who believed he was the black Messiah who would force the whites off the island and establish a black community. He also protested the whites' seizing of the island from the Indians. Macandal's plot to overthrow the government was discovered, and he was executed.

38 **Danish blacks:** The fugitive slaves of the Danish islands (today known as the Virgin Islands), who, like the Maroons, grouped together in the eighteenth century to rebel against white authority.

38 **Cato of Stono:** In 1739 Cato of Stono, a slave, led an insurrection of one hundred slaves in Stono, South Carolina. Their plan to escape to the Spanish colony of Florida was unsuccessful.

38 **Phyllis:** Phillis Wheatley (ca. 1753–1784), brought to Boston as a slave in 1761, became known for her ability to write poetry, and her book, *Poems on Various Subjects, Religious and Moral*, was the first volume of verse published by an Afro-American writer (1773).

38 **Attucks:** Crispus Attucks (1723–1770), who escaped slavery at seventeen from Massachusetts, was a black patriot, the first person to die in the Boston Massacre, preceding the Revolutionary War.

38 **Salem and Poor:** Peter Salem (ca. 1750–1816) was a slave who was granted his freedom when he became a soldier in the American colonial forces. He is best known for his participation in the Battle of Bunker Hill (June 17, 1775), and tradition has it that he killed the first English soldier in battle. He served in the

Continental Army during the remainder of the war but died in the poorhouse.

Salem Poor (1747–?) was a freeman who also fought in the American colonial forces (and also participated in the Battle of Bunker Hill). He was known for his patriotic zeal and acts of courage.

38 **Banneker and Derham:** Born in Maryland in 1731, Benjamin Banneker (d. 1806) became a well-known mathematician and scientist. His annual almanac for farmers (1792–1802) was the first scientific book written and published by an Afro-American.

James C. Derham (ca. 1762–?) was born into slavery in 1762 in Philadelphia. His owners were physicians who taught him the art of medicine. He bought his freedom from them in 1783 and embarked on a successful medical career in New Orleans, Louisiana, where he set up his own practice and treated blacks and whites alike.

38 **Cuffes:** Paul Cuffe (1759–1817), son of an African father and an American Indian mother, born in Boston, where he became a merchant and seaman. Master of his own ship, he fostered trade with African nations and favored emigration of black colonists back to Africa; also, together with his brother, he petitioned for suffrage for Indians and blacks.

38 **Haytian revolt:** See note for page 11.

38 **Gabriel . . . Vesey . . . Nat Turner:** Leaders of slave insurrections, in 1800, 1822, and 1831, respectively.

Gabriel Prosser, a Richmond, Virginia, slave who attempted in 1800 to lead one thousand slaves in rebellion against Richmond. His intent was to establish a black state in Virginia. A turbulent storm and a betrayal by two slave informants led to the plan's failure. The leaders were captured, tried, and executed.

Denmark Vesey, an ex-slave and seaman, initiated a slave rebellion in South Carolina in 1822. Vesey and thirty-four of his co-conspirators were executed.

Nat Turner (1800–1831) was a preacher and rebel who was born into slavery in Southampton County, Virginia. In August 1831 he organized and led the most successful slave revolt in North America. His revolutionary band's rampage through the countryside terrified whites and showed them the fallacy of the myth of the docile slave. Turner was found guilty and executed.

39 **Walker's wild appeal:** David Walker (1785–1830) was born in North Carolina of a free mother and a slave father. He was educated in Boston. His Appeal called on slaves to rebel against their masters.

39 **Forten and Purvis . . . Shad . . . Du Bois . . . Barbadoes:** James Forten (1766–1842), a wealthy and successful black sailmaker, was an abolitionist throughout life. Together with Reverend Richard Allen, he circulated a petition in 1800 calling for Congress to end slavery. In the War of 1812, he helped organize a black volunteer force for the defense of Philadelphia. He formed an alliance with William Lloyd Garrison and other abolitionists in the 1820s. In 1833 Forten helped create the American Antislavery Society. His daughter, Charlotte, wrote *The Diary of Charlotte Forten.*

Robert Purvis (1810–1898) was born of mixed parentage. He became an abolitionist leader in Philadelphia and helped found the American Anti-Slavery Society.

Mary Ann Shad (Shadd) (1823–1893) was born in Delaware but settled in Canada for twelve years, where she edited *Provincial Freemen,* a fugitive slave newspaper.

Alexander Du Bois was W. E. B. Du Bois's grandfather.

James G. Barbadoes (1796–1841) was an abolitionist who helped establish the American Anti-Slavery Society. He tried to colonize a black settlement in Jamaica, but the experiment was unsuccessful. He and two of his children died of fever in the attempt.

39 **Remond, Nell, Wells-Brown, and Douglass:** Charles Lenox Remond (1810–1874), a journalist and member of the Massachusetts Anti-Slavery Society, helped raise money and support for the abolitionist movement in England.

William C. Nell (1816–1874), a historian and journalist active in the Underground Railroad. Early in his life, he refused to apply for admission to the bar because he could not support a Constitution that deprived black slaves of their rights. Later he participated in the movement to desegregate schools in Massachusetts. In 1851, he worked as an assistant to Frederick Douglass, and also published his own pamphlet, "Services of Colored Americans in the Wars of 1776 and 1812."

William Wells Brown (1814–1884), a former slave who became an author and lecturer; known for his slave narrative, *Narrative of William W. Brown, a Fugitive Slave,* and for other works on slavery, among them a novel, *Clotel, or the President's Daughter: A Narrative of Slave Life in the United States,* and for histories, the most notable of which is *The Black Man: His Antecedents, His Genius, and His Achievements.*

Frederick Douglass (ca. 1817–1895), escaped slave, writer, publisher, and abolitionist orator, closely allied early on with the abolitionists William Lloyd Garrison and Wendell Phillips. He published and edited the *North Star,* an abolitionist newspaper. His most famous work is *Narrative of the Life and Times of Frederick Douglass* (1845), of which the expanded versions are *My Bondage and My Freedom* (1855) and *The Life and Times of Frederick Douglass* (1881). He remained a crusader for rights and reform for blacks and women throughout his life.

39 **John Brown's raid:** In October 1859, John Brown, a white man, set out to capture the U.S. Arsenal at Harpers Ferry, Virginia, with the help of a small group of followers, including five blacks. Brown's goal was to liberate and arm the blacks in the vicinity and to move southward, eventually forming a black army of liberation and freeing blacks. The revolt, though unsuccessful, became a rallying point during the Civil War, and John Brown's name was legend.

39 **Elliot, Bruce, and Langston:** Robert Brown Elliott (1842–1884), educated in Boston and in London; editor of the *Leader,* in Charleston, South Carolina, an early southern paper published by blacks; held various state and federal offices thereafter; resigned later in life from the U.S. House of Representatives in an attempt to reform corrupt political practices in South Carolina, where he practiced law until his death.

Blanche K. Bruce (1841–1898), a runaway slave, educator, and government official. In 1861, he escaped to Hannibal, Missouri, where he started a school for blacks; became a wealthy Mississippi planter; became the first black to serve as senator from Mississippi (1875–1881); and worked in government positions thereafter.

John Mercer Langston (1829–1897), lawyer, educator, and government official. A former slave in Virginia, he graduated from Oberlin College in 1849. He was Ohio's first black lawyer,

Virginia's first black congressman, and the first president of Virginia State College; a founder and dean of the Law Department of Howard University; and a grand-uncle of the poet Langston Hughes.

39 **Alexander Crummell:** Episcopalian minister; antislavery spokesman; see note for page 162.

39 **Bishop Daniel Payne:** Payne (1811–1893) was an educator and bishop of the African Methodist Episcopal Church; promoted literary societies and lyceums for his church membership and helped establish Wilberforce University (Ohio) in 1863, over which he presided for sixteen years; wrote numerous works on his church and black people.

39 **Revolution of 1876:** This refers to the disputed presidential election of 1876, which led to the end of Reconstruction (the northern Republican Hayes was allowed to move into the White House, with the proviso that he have the remaining troops removed from the South, thus allowing the white supremacist southern Democrats to regain their power and destroy black political power) and to the "Compromise of 1877," which favored economic growth in the South over rights of southern blacks.

40 **Price:** Joseph C. Price (1854–1893), son of a slave father and free mother who became a minister in the African Methodist Episcopal Zion Church. A powerful speaker, he helped raise funds for black education, and as a foremost educator in North Carolina, he advocated the liberal arts over vocational, industrial training for blacks.

42 **Toussaint the Savior, through Gabriel, Vesey, and Turner:** See notes for pages 11 and 38.

42 **the Grimkes, Kelly Miller, J. W. E. Bowen:** Archibald H. Grimké (1849–1930) and his brother Francis J. Grimké (1850–1937) were both civil rights activists. They were nephews of Sarah Grimké, the abolitionist. Archibald became a lawyer and writer, served as president of the American Negro Academy, and became a prominent leader in the NAACP. Francis studied theology and became a clergyman and author and a trustee of Howard University. He was active in the American Negro Academy and in government affairs in Washington, D.C.

Kelly Miller (1863–1939) was a sociologist and educator. His mother was a slave, his father a soldier in the Confederate Army.

He began his career as a college professor of mathematics at Howard University in 1890; he was dean of Howard University from 1907 to 1918. He wrote many works on the race question and on black history, and added sociology to the curriculum of Howard University.

John Wesley Edward Bowen (1855–1933) was an educator and Methodist clergyman. He earned a Ph.D. from Boston University in 1887, the second black in America to achieve this. He served as a pastor of various churches in New Jersey, Maryland, and in Washington, D.C. He taught at various colleges, including Gammon Theological Seminary, the first black to do so. He also edited *The Voice of the Negro* and worked throughout his life for the complete equality of black ministers within the Methodist church.

45 **Governor Aycock . . . Senator Morgan . . . Mr. Thomas Nelson Page . . . Senator Ben Tillman:** Charles Aycock (1859–1912), the governor of North Carolina from 1901 to 1905, advocated educational reform in his state for both blacks and whites.

John Tyler Morgan (1824–1907), a senator from Alabama from 1876 to 1907; advocate of white supremacy.

Thomas Nelson Page (1853–1922), a novelist who romanticized the Old South with its plantation system.

Benjamin Ryan Tillman (1847–1918), an orator, a spokesman for southern extremists, a proponent of white supremacy. He was governor of South Carolina (1890–1894) and a senator from the same state (1894–1918). In each of these offices he advocated violent suppression of blacks.

IV. Of the Meaning of Progress

48 **"Willst Du . . . weiche Seele!":** From Friedrich Schiller's *Die Jungfrau von Orleans* ("The Maid of Orleans"), IV, i; "If You want to announce Your power, / Choose the ones who are without sin / In Your eternal House; / Send forth Your spirits, / the immortal ones, the pure ones, / Who are beyond feeling and tears! / Don't choose the sensitive maiden, / Not the shepherdess with her gentle soul!"

48 **[spiritual]:** "My Way's Cloudy."

58 **Jim Crow car:** The segregated train car for blacks.

V. Of the Wings of Atalanta

59   "O black boy of Atlanta! . . . The black and white together": From John Greenleaf Whittier's "Howard at Atlanta," sixth stanza.

60   **Alleghanies:** Allegheny mountain range that traverses Maryland, Pennsylvania, Virginia, and West Virginia.

60   **Lachesis:** One of the three Fates, Lachesis carries the globe and decides the length of the thread of life.

60   **Mercury:** The messenger of the gods. Mercury's realm is communication and speech.

60   **Bœotia:** Greek province, the home of Atalanta.

60   **Atalanta:** Beautiful maiden and famous huntress of Greek mythology who took part in races and contests and destroyed those she conquered. She promised to marry anyone who could outrun her, but those who failed to meet her challenge were put to death. Finally she was conquered by Hippomenes, who tactically dropped three golden apples as he ran, which she stopped to pick up.

60   **Hippomenes:** Winner of the race with Atalanta, he gained her hand in marriage.

61   **Bourse:** The stock exchange or meeting place for business.

61   **Third Estate:** Formerly (especially under feudalism) consisted of commoners (the bourgeoisie), while the First Estate was the clergy, and the Second Estate was the nobility.

61   **Pluto:** God of the underworld.

61   **Ceres:** Demeter, the goddess of agriculture and one of the Twelve Great Olympians. Her daughter Persephone was abducted by Pluto.

61   **Apollo:** Sun god, as well as the god of fine arts and medicine; one of the Twelve Olympians.

61   **Venus:** Aphrodite, the goddess of love; one of the Twelve Olympians.

63   **Mammonism:** The worship and greedy pursuit of riches.

64   **Dido . . . tale of Troy:** Dido founded and became the queen of Carthage. She fell in love with Aeneas, who was on his way back to Italy after the Trojan War. After his departure, she put a curse on the Trojans and committed suicide with her sword.

64   *trivium* and *quadrivium*: In the Middle Ages, the academic disciplines were divided into the trivium and quadrivium. The former consisted of the lower branch of the seven liberal arts, or the three arts known as grammar, logic, and rhetoric. The latter

consisted of the four arts known as arithmetic, music, geometry, and astronomy.

64 **Leipsic:** Leipzig, a major cultural, educational, and commercial center in what is now East Germany. In Du Bois's time, the third largest German university was in Leipzig.

64 **Parnassus:** One of the highest mountains in Greece, named after Parnassus, Poseidon's son. The mountain was sacred to Apollo, to Dionysus, and to the Muses; Delphi is located on one of its slopes.

65 **"Entbehren sollst du, sollst entbehren":** From Goethe's *Faust*, "In the Study," line 1549, meaning "You need to forbear, forbear you must!" At this juncture Faust is thinking about the many limitations of life and wishing for death.

65 **Fisk and Howard and Atlanta:** See note for page 28.

65 **from Academus to Cambridge:** Academus was the school founded in Athens by Plato in 387 B.C., which embodied the idea of a liberal arts education. It is the ancestor of the Western university system. Cambridge is a prestigious English university.

66 **Apples of Hesperides:** The Hesperides were the daughters of Atlas and Hesperis and guardians of the golden apples.

66 **Bœotian lovers:** Hippomenes and Atalanta, see note for page 60.

66 **William and Mary, Trinity, Georgia, Texas, Tulane, Vanderbilt:** Prestigious Southern universities.

VI. Of the Training of Black Men

69 **"Why, if the Soul . . . crippled to abide?":** Stanza 44 of "The Rubáiyát of Omar Khayyám," translated by Edward FitzGerald, taken from FitzGerald's fifth revision.

69 **[spiritual]:** "March On."

69 **Jamestown:** First successful English settlement in what is now the U.S. (in Virginia), 1607, of which James Smith became the first leader.

70 ***tertium quid:*** Something that is undefined but connected in some way to two things that are known or definite.

71 **Dr. Johnson:** Samuel Johnson (1709–1784), English lexicographer, essayist, poet, and man of letters, he was one of the most famous literary figures of his day.

75   **Hampton:** Hampton Institute, Virginia, was founded in 1868 by Samuel Armstrong, who had commanded black troops during the Civil War. Booker T. Washington was one of the institute's most eminent graduates.

75   **Spelman Seminary:** The first U.S. college for Afro-American women; founded in 1881 by two New England women, Sophia Packard and Harriet Giles; grew out of the Atlanta Baptist Female Seminary and moved to its present site in 1883. In 1884 the name was changed to Spelman Seminary.

77   **Wilberforce and Lincoln, Biddle, Shaw:** Wilberforce University (Wilberforce, Ohio) was founded in 1856 by the African Methodist Episcopal Church and named for the famous English abolitionist William Wilberforce, who led the campaign against the slave trade in England. (The slave trade was abolished there in 1807, and slavery was completely abolished in 1833.)

Lincoln University (Oxford, Pennsylvania) was founded in 1854 by Reverend John Miller Dickey (affiliated with the American Colonization Society) and Sarah Emlen Cresson (his wife); founded to promote scientific, classical, and theological learning; first institution of higher learning for blacks.

Biddle University (Charlotte, North Carolina) was founded in 1867 by the Presbyterian Church; originally founded to educate black men in the fields of religion and education. Mary Biddle, affiliated with the Presbyterian Church, donated funds, and the university was originally called the Biddle Memorial Institute after her deceased husband; renamed Johnson C. Smith University in 1921.

Shaw University (Raleigh, North Carolina) was established in 1865 by Baptists; in its earlier days, it was known for its medical school, one of the first for blacks.

78   **Commissioner Harris:** William Torrey Harris, U.S. commissioner of education (1889–1906). Harris Teachers College (St. Louis, Missouri), founded in 1857, was named after Harris, who was superintendent of the St. Louis school system (1867–1880).

81   **Talented Tenth:** Du Bois and other black intellectuals posited that 10 percent of the black population (the "talented tenth") should be leaders of the group.

83 **Rhine-gold:** In Germanic mythology, the hoard of gold watched over by Rhine maidens and later owned by the Nibelungen and Siegfried. Also spelled Rheingold.

84 **Balzac and Dumas:** Honoré de Balzac was a nineteenth-century French novelist of the Realist tradition. Alexandre Dumas was a nineteenth-century French novelist of romances and histories.

84 **Aurelius:** Marcus (121–180), Roman emperor from 161–180 and Stoic philosopher.

84 **Pisgah:** The mountain range east of Jordan from which Moses viewed the Promised Land.

84 **Philistine:** Member of a warlike race in ancient Philistia (southwest Palestine).

84 **Amalekite:** Member of a pillaging nomadic tribe in the line of Esau and hostile to the Israelites.

VII. Of the Black Belt

85 **"I am black . . . have I not kept":** From The Song of Solomon 1:5–6.

85 **[spiritual]:** "Bright Sparkles."

86 **Hernando de Soto:** Between 1539 and 1542 this Spanish explorer and conquistador searched without success for gold in the southwestern part of the U.S. but discovered instead the Mississippi River.

86 **Cherokees:** A great tribe of the Iroquoian Indians, formerly dwelling in Georgia and in North Carolina.

86 **Sam Hose:** Black farmhand accused of murdering his employer in April 1899 in a quarrel over wages. He escaped, but while he was being hunted down, an additional charge of rape was brought against him. Once captured, he accepted the murder charge but denied the rape charge even under duress. He was brutally murdered (lynched and burned alive) as a mob of two thousand people looked on.

86 **Oglethorpe:** James Oglethorpe, the founder and first governor of Georgia.

86 **prayers of Whitefield:** George Whitefield (1714–1770), an English evangelist who supported the freeholders in Georgia who petitioned

the English government to remove the restrictions on importing slaves. Whitefield, though he did promote kind treatment of slaves, did not believe that slavery should be abolished because of evidence in the Bible erroneously believed to sanction slavery.

86 **Darien . . . Delegal riots . . . Scotch Highlanders . . . Moravians of Ebenezer:** In Darien, Georgia, on August 23, 1899, an uprising took place, known as the Delegal riots, in which hundreds of blacks, hearing rumors of an impending lynching, gathered together to safeguard the intended victim's welfare. Twenty-one members of the crowd were later accused of insurrection and sent to prison camps.

Scotch Highlanders had settled in this area of Georgia at the end of the eighteenth century when the clan system of the Highlands ended, marking a massive wave of immigration to North America.

Moravians founded two settlements, Ebenezer (1734) and New Ebenezer (1736), near Savannah, Georgia.

86 **Haytian Terror of Toussaint:** See note for page 11.

86 **statute of 1808:** On March 2, 1807, Congress passed an act prohibiting the importation of slaves into U.S. territory after January 1, 1808.

87 **Creek Indians:** A grouping of Muskogean tribes, formerly dwelling in parts of Georgia, Alabama, and Florida.

87 **Indian Massacre at Fort Mims:** At Fort Mims, Alabama, Creek Indians massacred settlers under their chief, William Weatherford, on August 30, 1813.

88 **panic of 1837:** Under Jackson, economic conditions worsened, and in May 1837, New York banks stopped paying in specie, thus beginning the panic. Other banks in major northern cities failed soon afterward. The effects of the panic continued for the next seven years in the western and southern states.

88 **Rhine-pfalz, or Naples, or Cracow:** Rhein-Pfalz, a province in the German Rhineland; Naples, a city in Italy; Kraków, a city in Poland.

94 **Osceola, the Indian-Negro chieftain:** Osceola (ca. 1800–1838) was a Seminole Indian leader born in Georgia. In April 1835 he began organizing his people for what later was known as the Second Seminole War. The black allies of the Seminoles, fugitive slaves of the South, were part of his warrior group, who set out to destroy white oppression.

VIII. Of the Quest of the Golden Fleece

103 **"But the Brute . . . empty skies":** William Vaughn Moody's poem "The Brute."

104 **Jason and his Argonauts:** Jason and his fifty-five companions sailing on the ship *Argo* in quest of the Golden Fleece were known as Argonauts.

113 **its Spanish war interludes and Philippine matinees:** This refers to events in the Spanish-American War (1898), which was fought primarily in Cuba, Puerto Rico, and the Philippines.

119 **rack-rent:** An annual rent that is as high, or almost as high, as the appraised value of the property.

121 **panic of 1893:** Financial crisis in the U.S. whose influence was first felt with the bankruptcy of the Philadelphia and Reading railroads on February 20, 1893. The situation worsened that year with 74 railroads falling into receivership, 600 banks closing, and 15,000 commercial houses collapsing. On June 27, 1893, the New York stock market crashed and precipitated a four-year depression.

IX. Of the Sons of Master and Man

123 **"Life treads on life . . . grave apart":** Elizabeth Barrett Browning's "A Vision of Poets," first stanza of conclusion, lines 820–22.

125 *tertium quid*: See note for page 70.

140 **Phillis Wheatley and Sam Hose:** See notes for pages 38 and 86.

141 **"That mind and soul . . . But vaster":** Tennyson's "In Memoriam," Prologue, lines 27–28.

X. Of the Faith of the Fathers

142 **"Dim face of Beauty . . . To a little sand":** From Fiona Macleod's (pen name for William Sharp) "Dim Face of Beauty," first and third (last) stanzas.

142 **[spiritual]:** "Steal Away Home."

142–143 **Berkshire . . . Suffolk:** Counties in Massachusetts and in England, respectively.

144 **Delphi:** Shrine of Apollo, known for its oracles; located on the slopes of Mount Parnassus.

144 **Endor:** At the behest of King Saul, the Witch of Endor summoned the ghost of the prophet Samuel, who foretold the victory of the Philistines and Saul's death (I Samuel 28:3–25).

145 **Jubilee songs:** Spirituals sung by the Jubilee Singers (see note for page 188).

145 **Bethel of Philadelphia:** Bethel Church, the first separate black Methodist Episcopal church in America, was founded by Richard Allen in 1787.

147 **polyandry:** The state of having two or more husbands at one time.

148 **African Methodist Church . . . Zion Church . . . Colored Methodist:** Churches that split from the mainstream Methodist church to provide more equality and participation for blacks. Black Methodists withdrew from the Methodist Episcopal church to create three independent groups: the African Methodist Episcopal church, or AME (1816); the African Methodist Episcopal Zionist church, or AMEZ (1821); and the Christian Methodist Episcopal church, or CME (1870).

148 **Obi worship:** Witchcraft (commonly known as voodoo) taken to the West Indies by African slaves. Obi is the West African goddess of evil.

149 **"Children, we shall . . . appear!":** From the spiritual bearing the same name.

150 **"O Freedom . . . be free":** From the spiritual entitled "Oh, Freedom."

153 **Denmark Vesey and Nat Turner:** See note for page 38.

154 *Dum vivimus, vivamus:* Latin, meaning "While we live, let us live."

XI. Of the Passing of the First-Born

155 **"O sister . . . when I forget":** From Algernon C. Swinburne's "Itylus," last stanza.

155 **[spiritual]:** "I Hope My Mother Will Be There."

XII. Of Alexander Crummell

161 **"Then from the Dawn . . . his wars":** Tennyson's "Passing of Arthur," lines 457–61.

161 **[spiritual]:** "Swing Low, Sweet Chariot."

162 **Alexander Crummell:** Black clergyman (1819–1898) whose early efforts to become a minister were thwarted. He was accepted as a candidate for Holy Orders in 1839 but denied admission to the General Theological Seminary of the Episcopal church because of his color. Eventually he was received in the diocese of Massachusetts, then studied in Queen's College, Cambridge, England, and became a missionary in Africa (where he was rector of his own parish and professor of psychological science in Liberia). Later in his life he returned to the U.S., where he became rector of St. Luke's Church, Washington, D.C., and founded the American Negro Academy in Washington, D.C., in 1897.

162 **Missouri Compromise:** A measure officially approved by Congress on March 3, 1820, to admit Maine as a free state and Missouri as a slave state and to exclude slavery from the Louisiana Purchase north of the parallel thirty-six, thirty. This measure was nullified by the *Dred Scott* Decision of 1857.

162 **amid the echoes of Manila and El Caney:** This refers to battles of the Spanish-American War (1898) in the Philippines and in Cuba.

163 **Oneida County:** Home to the Oneida Institute, a manual arts school in Whitesboro, New York, attended by Alexander Crummell in 1836.

167 **Fox's "Lives of the Martyrs":** *Actes and Monuments*, popularly known as the Book of Martyrs, by the martyrologist John Foxe (1516–1587), which recounts the history of the Christian church, with special emphasis on the martyrs.

167 **"The Whole Duty of Man":** Published in 1658, this devotional work is an analysis of man's duties to God and to his fellowmen; authorship is unknown, but most likely it was someone well versed in theology.

167 **". . . bear the whips . . . of the unworthy takes":** *Hamlet*, III, i, 70–74.

168 **Wilberforce:** Crummell's contemporary, Samuel Wilberforce (1805–1873), an Anglican prelate and bishop of Oxford (1845) and of Winchester (1869). Wilberforce won the support of the Tractarians, but later diverged from the Tractarian movement. He was the author of the *History of the Protestant Episcopal Church in America* (1844). His father, William Wilberforce (1759–1833), was the more famous of the two—he was an English philanthropist and abolitionist (see note for page 77). William Wilberforce, with the support of others, put a stop to the slave trade in England (1807), and in 1823, helped establish the Anti-Slavery Society, which called for the extinction of all slavery.

168 **Stanley:** Presumably Arthur Penrhyn (1815–1881), English author and clergyman; he was installed as dean of Westminster in 1864. He is known for his many volumes of ecclesiastical history and for his leniency towards the Tractarians and other nonconformists within the church.

168 **Thirwell:** Presumably Connop Thirlwall (1797–1875), an eminent English historian and prelate; he received his M.A. in Cambridge in 1821 and was made bishop of St. David's in 1840; he worked on histories of Rome and Greece.

168 **Ingles:** Presumably John Inglis, born to the Anglican Bishop of Nova Scotia, Charles Inglis (a missionary and the first colonial bishop outside the British Isles). John Inglis was elected to the Council of Clergymen in 1825, became the third bishop of Nova Scotia, and died in London in 1850.

168 **Froude:** Presumably James Anthony Froude (1818–1894), English historian and biographer; religion was a dominating factor in both his life and work; his monumental twelve-volume *History of England from the Fall of Wolsey to the Defeat of the Spanish Armada* was controversial because he viewed the English Reformation from a subjective Protestant perspective.

168 **Macaulay:** Thomas Babington (1800–1859), English statesman and author, son of Zachary Macaulay (1768–1838), known for his antislavery agitation and his part in establishing the Anti-Slavery Society (1823). Thomas Macaulay wrote literary essays as well as histories, the greatest of the latter being the five-volume *The History of England from the Accession of James the Second*

(somewhat biased because of his Whig and Protestant leanings). Macaulay was also politically active: as a Whig orator and member of Parliament, he fought in 1830–1832 for equal rights for Jews, and as a member of the Supreme Council of India (1834–1838), he attempted to reform colonial policy; back at home, he held various positions in Parliament from 1839–1857.

168 **Brodie:** Presumably Sir Benjamin Collins Brodie (1783–1862), a famous English physiologist and surgeon who opposed homeopathy. In 1810 he was elected a Fellow of the Royal Society; his son (1817–1880) of the same name was a chemist.

168 **Wilberforce and Stanley, Thirwell and Ingles, and even Froude and Macaulay; Sir Benjamin Brodie bade him:** These prominent Englishmen, whether they were intellectuals, authors, or religious leaders, were sympathetic to Crummell's plight and welcomed him to England.

XIII. Of the Coming of John

171 **"What bring they 'neath the midnight . . . The river floweth on":** Elizabeth Barrett Browning's "A Romance of the Ganges," stanza 2, lines 10–18.

171 **[spiritual]:** "You May Bury Me in the East."

177 **the music of Lohengrin's swan:** In Richard Wagner's opera *Lohengrin,* the knight Lohengrin travels on a river in a boat drawn by a white swan to defend the Duchess Elsa, falsely accused of murdering her brother, Godfrey. In the end, the swan is transformed into her brother, who had been enchanted by the sorceress Ortrud.

178 **manifest destiny:** A nineteenth-century U.S. idea that the country's destiny is to control and dominate the Western Hemisphere.

186 **"Freudig geführt, ziehet dahin":** From Richard Wagner's "Brautlied," or "Wedding Song," in *Lohengrin,* III, i; Du Bois changed "treulich geführt," or led faithfully, to "freudig geführt" (led happily); the line in its entirety is "Treulich geführt, ziehet dahin / Wo euch der Segen der Liebe bewahr," or "Led faithfully, move on / To where the blessings of love may keep and protect you."

XIV. The Sorrow Songs

187 **"I walk through the churchyard . . . down":** From the spiritual "Lay This Body Down."

187 **[spiritual]:** "Wrestlin' Jacob."

188 **Jubilee Hall:** A building at Fisk University built with funds raised by the Fisk Jubilee Singers.

188 **Port Royal experiment:** See note for page 16.

188 **Hilton Head:** See note for page 16.

188 **Thomas Wentworth Higginson:** Higginson (1823–1911), the white commander of a regiment of black troops in the Civil War, wrote of his experience in *Army Life in a Black Regiment* (1870). This included the first serious study of spirituals and black folk music.

188 **Miss McKim:** Daughter of James M. McKim (see note for page 16), Lucy McKim Garrison (1842–1877) collected slave songs in the Sea Islands off South Carolina during the Civil War and helped edit *Slave Songs of the United States* (1867).

188 **Fisk Jubilee Singers:** In October 1871 a small group of teachers and students, recently emancipated from slavery, formed a musical group to keep Fisk University from bankruptcy; this band of musicians called themselves the "Fisk Jubilee Singers" and made tours of the Midwest and the East and even went to Europe in 1873. Their efforts made Fisk University famous and the fund-raising kept the university financially alive; in the process they popularized the spiritual and made the world aware of blacks' contribution to music.

189 **Chancellorsville:** A locality in Virginia; battle of, May 2–3, 1861, in which the Union army was defeated.

189 **Gettysburg:** A town in southern Pennsylvania; battle of, July 1–3, 1863. After victories at Fredericksburg and Chancellorsville, Lee's Confederate troops were in high spirits. The unplanned battle at Gettysburg came as an unwelcome surprise to the Confederacy, which sustained heavy losses (even greater than those of the Union troops) during the three-day battle; Lee was forced to retreat. Not only is Gettysburg the scene of a major Union victory; it is also the site of Lincoln's famous Gettysburg Address, November 19, 1863, at a national cemetery dedication ceremony.

189 **George L. White:** Treasurer of the early Fisk University, he loved the spiritual, and realized that his floundering institution could be saved by concerts given by talented student singers; his efforts led to the organization of the Fisk Jubilee Singers.

189 **Oberlin:** A college in Ohio that opened its doors to blacks from the day of its establishment in 1833.

189 **Henry Ward Beecher:** Beecher (1813–1887) was one of the most prominent and influential American clergymen during the nineteenth century, as well as an advocate of abolition and women's suffrage. The brother of Harriet Beecher Stowe, he was the pastor of Plymouth Church, Brooklyn, New York, for nearly forty years, where he was an eloquent speaker and commentator on current issues and social reform.

190 **"You may bury . . . in that morning":** The spiritual "You May Bury Me in the East."

193 **"My Lord calls . . . in my soul":** "Steal Away."

193 **"Dere's no rain . . . to go home":** "There's No Rain to Wet You."

193 **"Oh Lord, keep me . . .":** "Keep Me from Sinking Down."

193 **"My soul wants . . .":** "My soul wants something that's new."

194 **"Yonder's my ole mudder . . .":** "O'er the Crossing."

194 **"Poor Rosy, poor gal . . .":** "Poor Rosy."

194 **"Jetz Geh i' an's brunele, trink' aber net":** German folk song, translation: "Now I'm going to the well, but I'm not going to drink from it."

194 **"Dust, dust and ashes . . . home":** "Dust and Ashes."

195 **"There's a little wheel . . .":** "There's a little wheel a-turnin."

195 **Thomas Wentworth Higginson:** See note for page 188.

195 **"Oh, the stars in the elements are falling . . .":** Variation of "My Lord, What a Morning" (also spelled "Mourning" in some versions; the latter spelling is Du Bois's preference).

195 **"Michael, haul the boat ashore . . .":** "Michael, Row me Boat Ashore."

197 **"Let us cheer the weary traveller . . .":** This spiritual bears the same title.